Hannu Kemppanen/Marja Jänis/Alexandra Belikova (eds.)
Domestication and Foreignization in Translation Studies

Hartwig Kalverkämper/Larisa Schippel (Hg.)
TRANSÜD.
Arbeiten zur Theorie und Praxis des Übersetzens und Dolmetschens
Band 46

Hannu Kemppanen/Marja Jänis/Alexandra Belikova (eds.)

Domestication and Foreignization in Translation Studies

Verlag für wissenschaftliche Literatur

Umschlagabbildung: Brücke zu den Utrainseln in Joensuu, Finnland, © Pekka Kujamäki

ISBN 978-3-86596-403-8
ISSN 1438-2636

© Frank & Timme GmbH Verlag für wissenschaftliche Literatur
Berlin 2012. Alle Rechte vorbehalten.

Das Werk einschließlich aller Teile ist urheberrechtlich geschützt. Jede Verwertung außerhalb der engen Grenzen des Urheberrechtsgesetzes ist ohne Zustimmung des Verlags unzulässig und strafbar. Das gilt insbesondere für Vervielfältigungen, Übersetzungen, Mikroverfilmungen und die Einspeicherung und Verarbeitung in elektronischen Systemen.

Herstellung durch das atelier eilenberger, Taucha bei Leipzig.
Printed in Germany.
Gedruckt auf säurefreiem, alterungsbeständigem Papier.

www.frank-timme.de

Content

Foreword 7

THEORETICAL ASPECTS

KAISA KOSKINEN *(Joensuu, Finland)*
Domestication, Foreignization and the Modulation of Affect 13

KINGA KLAUDY *(Budapest, Hungary)*
Linguistic and Cultural Asymmetry in Translation
from and into Minor Languages 33

HANNU KEMPPANEN *(Joensuu, Finland)*
The Role of the Concepts *Domestication* and *Foreignisation*
in Russian Translation Studies 49

JUKKA MÄKISALO *(Joensuu, Finland)*
Meta-theoretical Analysis of the Empirical Use of the Concepts
Domestication/Foreignisation 63

TOWARDS OPERATIONALIZATION

PER AMBROSIANI *(Umeå, Sweden)*
Domestication and *Foreignization* in Russian Translations
of *Alice's Adventures in Wonderland* 79

ALEXANDRA BELIKOVA *(Joensuu, Finland)*
Money flows into windows and doors or *Money flows like a river?*
Identifying Translation Strategies by the Yardstick
of Metaphorical Creativity 101

ESA PENTTILÄ & PIRKKO MUIKKU-WERNER *(Joensuu & Tampere, Finland)*
Domestication and *Foreignization* in Figurative Idiom Translation ... 121

PIET VAN POUCKE *(Ghent, Belgium)*
Measuring *Foreignization* in Literary Translation:
An attempt to Operationalize the Concept of *Foreignization* ... 139

ELENA RASSOKHINA *(Umeå, Sweden)*
"... thou, my Rose, ...": Translating the Direct Address
of Shakespeare's Sonnet into Russian ... 159

IDEOLOGICAL ASPECTS

ALEXANDRA BORISENKO *(Moscow, Russia)*
Fear of *Foreignization*: "Soviet School" in Russian Literary Translation ... 177

MARJA JÄNIS & TAMARA STARSHOVA *(Joensuu, Finland & Petrozavodsk, Russia)*
Cultural and Political Contexts of Translating into Finnish
in Soviet/Russian Karelia ... 189

CHAPMAN CHEN *(Joensuu, Finland)*
Domestication and *Foreignization* in Hong Kong Translation
of Western Theatre ... 209

Author index ... 231

Foreword

The present volume is a collection of articles based on papers presented at the conference *Domestication and Foreignization in Translation Studies*, 29.9.–1.10.2011 in Joensuu, Finland. It was organized by a joint research project of the Department of Foreign Languages and Translation Studies of the University of Eastern Finland and the Faculty of Finnish and Baltic Languages and Cultures of the Petrozavodsk University in Russia. Funded by the Finnish Academy of Science and the Russian Humanitarian Fund, the project is called *From Russian into Finnish and vice versa. Translation in a multicultural environment*.

The conference was devoted to the much-debated traditions of dichotomizing ways of describing translations. The articles of the present volume have been classified into three sections: Section 1 is titled *Theoretical aspects* and it includes articles dealing with defining the concepts of domestication and foreignization and their applicability in translation studies. The articles in Section 2, *Towards operationalization*, describe concrete research undertaken by applying the concepts of domestication and foreignization and discussing their limits and possibilities for research purposes. Section 3, *Ideological aspects*, presents cases where translation is strongly linked with social, political and cultural factors.

Domestication and foreignization are two concepts that have been widely adopted in discussions on translation, the obvious reason being that they can be applied to many of the traditional and fundamental ways of conceiving the essential aspects of translation: the relationship between the source and target text, the translator's choices, reader response, and conflicting cultures. Lawrence Venuti introduced these concepts in his writings of the late 1990's, but they originate from ideas expressed by scholars of German Romanticism. Venuti shared his predecessors' preference of favoring such translating strategies that move readers towards writers, rather than writers towards readers.

The reason why the concepts of domestication and foreignization have been widely applied in translations studies, although often without precise definitions, could be that these words are easy to comprehend (though they are also easily misunderstood), and they arouse positive affects, since they are related to familiar ways of conceiving our position in our own environment and in relation to foreign environments. The first article on theoretical aspects in Section 1 by **Kaisa Koskinen** links the central concepts of domestication and foreignization with the modulation of affect. According to her, affects are present in both strategies, since domesticating strategies can be used for arousing interest by linking the new to the already familiar, but foreignizing also has a lot of potential for affect, arousing interest in something new and different. In her article she discusses the affective aspects of translation strategies and demonstrates, with the help of some case studies, how the chosen translation strategy and affects aroused by it in a translated text have no direct interdependence. She concludes that adding an affective layer to our discussions of translational phenomena could shed light on some textual features, observed for example in corpora of translations.

The asymmetry hypothesis has been suggested by **Kinga Klaudy** in her recent contributions to translation studies. It is based on analyzing translational operations as dichotomies, such as explicitation and implicitation, and she suggests that domestication and foreignization could be added to these analyses. In her article on linguistic and cultural asymmetry, the second article in Section 1, Klaudy applies this dichotomy to translation from and into minor languages and asks, whether domestication could be seen as a sign of asymmetry in translation on the cultural level in the same way as explicitation on the linguistic level, since explicitation and domestication seem to be more frequent strategies than implicitation and foreignization.

Translating from and into Russian as well as Russian translation studies were a central theme in the joint research project organizing the conference. For his article, which is the third in Section 1, **Hannu Kemppanen** made a thorough analysis of the dichotomies used in Russian translation studies, many of which are akin to the concepts of domestication and foreignization. Kemppanen draws his material from multiple sources: monographs on translation studies, conference proceedings, articles in the translation journal *Mosty* (*Bridges*) and those published in the Internet. He concludes that the concepts of domestication and foreignization are rarely used by Russian translation scholars. Instead, the concept of translation strategies is discussed by using other terms, such as *free* and *literal translation*.

The fourth article of Section 1 presents **Jukka Mäkisalo**'s observation that domestication and foreignization are essentially metaphors, which explains difficulties in applying them to empirical research in translation studies. He presents a meta-theoretical analysis of the empirical use of the concepts. His analysis shows how they are attached to divergent issues on translation and how researchers disagree whether they form a dichotomy, a spectrum, or a continuum. He mentions the later reworking of the concepts by Venuti (2000) that refer to the ethnocentric reduction of the foreign text as opposed to the ethnodeviant pressure on values to register the linguistic and cultural difference of the foreign text. Mäkisalo observes that Venuti does not, however, operationalize values as recognizable objects. Mäkisalo also discusses the unmarkedness of domestication, which seems to explain the asymmetry of the dichotomy, when discussing results of concrete research, and reminds us that the concepts of domestication and foreignization have almost never been applied to non-fiction, but only to novels, poetry, drama and children's books.

Although operationalizing the concepts of domestication and foreignization can be considered controversial, they have nevertheless been applied in concrete research. This can be seen in the articles presented in Section 2, *Towards operationalization*. **Per Ambrosiani** has applied the concepts of domestication and foreignization to translations of *Alice's Adventures in Wonderland*. He presents a short excerpt of the original text and its translations into several target languages. Ambrosiani would rather view the results of his investigation by applying an opposition between marked "foreignization" and unmarked "domestication", and would limit the use of the concepts "foreignization" and "domestication" in this case as labels for translation techniques. He also reminds us that the choice of the source text means that his conclusions will be primarily relevant for the field of literary translation, particularly for the translation of children's literature.

The second article in Section 2 concerns translating metaphors. **Alexandra Belikova** presents a new way of defining metaphorical creativity using an algorithm-based methodology, which, according to the author, is presumably free from subjective intuition-based criteria. Belikova claims that although metaphors have been one of the central issues in translation studies, defining the consequences of applying different strategies in translating metaphors has suffered from the vagueness of describing these strategies. She applies her new methodology to the analysis of Russian translations of Finnish media texts. Belikova is doubtful whether the level of metaphorical creativity in the translated texts can be discussed in relation to the concepts of domestication and foreignization. However, reducing the metaphorical creativity in translation can be considered as indirect evidence of domesticating strategies having been implemented when translating media discourse texts from Finnish into Russian.

The subject of the third article in Section 2, by **Pirkko Muikku-Werner** and **Esa Penttilä,** is idiom translation. The recommended translation strategy in bi- and multilingual dictionaries is substitution, but the authors remind us that this is not necessarily the case in real life, where idioms are translated with various strategies. These strategies are placed on a continuum and roughly classified as domesticating and foreignizing. The consequences of applying these strategies are discussed with reference to examples. The domesticating strategy seems to be prevalent, but the authors suggest that adopting a more foreignizing translating strategy could sometimes better communicate the additional properties figurative idioms carry.

Piet van Poucke has worked out a method for measuring foreignization in literary translation, and he presents it in the fourth article of Section 2. His is a quantitative model of assessing translations on a foreignization-domestication scale, and it is based on existing taxonomies of translation *shifts*, following Catford's (1965) and van Leuwen-Zwart's (1989, 1990) definitions. Translation shifts in texts are classified within the framework of Venutian dichotomy as moderate or strong foreignization or domestication. Van Poucke makes use of the concept of *transeme* in presenting a model of the quantitative results of a microstructural analysis of a translated text, and applies his method in comparing two Dutch translations and one English translation of Dostoyevsky's *Besy*.

Shakespeare's *Sonet 109* has been translated into Russian many times. In the fifth article of Section 2, **Elena Rassokhina** demonstrates the problems that have arisen in rendering the direct address *Thou, my Rose* in these translations, since the addressee is a young male, but the noun *roza* in Russian belongs to the feminine word class, and the idea of addressing a male with this word is both linguistically and culturally difficult to accept in Russian culture. Rassokhina has studied all available Russian translations of the sonnet, and classified the ways of rendering 'rose' in translation. According to the results, domestication has been the most pervasive translation strategy throughout the whole history of translating this direct address of the sonnet into Russian, even though there have been variations in the approaches applied by translators.

The articles in Section 3 deal with ideological aspects. In the first article of this section **Alexandra Borisenko** claims that in the Soviet School of Translation foreignization has been feared. The dichotomies used in Soviet translation studies are *literal translation* as opposed to *realistic translation*, and these terms involve strong ideological connotation. The discussion about the conflicting translation methods goes back to the 1920–1930's, and it was more political rather than literary or academic. Borisenko describes the mainstream strategies used in translating world literature in the first decades of Soviet rule as domesticating, since translations were aimed at a mass reader audience. Other translators, especially those of the publishing house *Academia,* aimed at accuracy and would accompany translations with elaborated commentary, footnotes, forewords etc. Accuracy was later called *bukvalizm* and it became a dangerous label. Borisenko refers to several cases demonstrating how foreignizing techniques were undesirable in the Soviet Union, since everything "strange" in a literary text was considered ideologically hostile. At the same time Borisenko points at a certain discrepancy between theory and praxis in the Soviet School of Translation, since in practice foreign elements were rendered as such in many translations. This can be explained by the fact that literary translation allowed a look into the magic world behind the iron curtain. Foreign literature was precious because it was different – thus, foreignizing techniques, emphasizing this difference, were actually employed widely.

The second article in the Section 3, by **Marja Jänis** and **Tamara Starshova,** deals with translating into minority languages, one of the subthemes of the conference *Domestication and Foreignization in Translation Studies.* They refer to Lawrence Venuti's (1998) observation that specifying the minor situation in translation studies requires reconstructing the cultural and political contexts along with analyzing language and textuality. In this article the former aspect, the political and social context, is the main point of interest. It presents a case study of translating into Finnish as a minority language in Russian/Soviet Karelia. The rise and fall of the Finnish language as the literary language of the Finnish and Karelian minority and as the target language in translation are described alongside political upheavals and by analyzing what was translated at different times, how and by whom.

In the last article in Section 3 **Chapman Chen** questions the applicability of Venutian concepts to translation of Western theatre in Hong Kong. He maintains that Hong Kong as an internal colony may domesticate dramas and theatre practices of other countries in order to question the culture and language of the internal colonizer, in this case Mainland China. Chen gives several examples of domesticating Western plays by adaptation to local settings and by linguistic means such as code-switching. He suggests that in the case of Hong Kong theatre domestication can be called subversive, and presents his critical evaluation of the applicability of Venutian concepts to this case.

The articles in this publication were selected through an anonymous peer review procedure. We express our deepest gratitude to our peers, Finnish and foreign, for their valuable contribution to this project.

Joensuu, May 15, 2012

Hannu Kemppanen   Marja Jänis   Alexandra Belikova

Domestication, Foreignization and the Modulation of Affect

Kaisa Koskinen
University of Eastern Finland, Joensuu

Abstract

This article offers a critical overview of Venuti's concepts of domestication and foreignization, arguing that instead of, or at least in addition to, viewing those two strategies as inhabiting opposing poles on the axis of cultural distance, they should be seen from the point of view of emotional affinity. The concept of affect is used to highlight the affective aspects of translated communication, and I argue for a heightened awareness of the role of affects in various research paradigms in translation studies. In the context of Venuti's legacy, the notion of affect also implies a need to return to literary theories, in particular those dealing with aesthetic effect, to understand better the role of affects in writing, translating and reading, and the possibilities of modulating these affects at all stages of the process.

1 Introduction

Domestication and foreignization are often seen as two opposing poles of an axis where one set of translation strategies replaces all unfamiliar elements with domestic variants to help the reader approach the text with ease and familiarity, while the other one follows the original text very closely, ruthlessly ignoring all potential difficulties of comprehension or barriers of reception. In this paper, I will focus on a number of issues that slightly unsettle this received understanding of these two concepts.

The key notion here is affect. I argue that regardless of the actual translation strategies, we experience the translations as either affectively positive or negative depending on our own (natural) tendencies and predilections, our previous life experiences, and how our acculturation and socialization have predisposed us towards particular aesthetic solutions. In other words, emotional distance need not have anything to do with cultural distance, and strategies labelled domesticating and foreignizing may be received in unexpected ways depending on the reader's affective stance to these strategies, to the text itself and to the reading context. Neuroscience posits that affect is closely intertwined with cognition:

> [F]ew if any perceptions of any object or event, actually present or recalled from memory, are ever neutral in emotional terms. Through either innate design or by learning, we react to most, perhaps all, objects with emotions, however weak, and subsequent feelings, however feeble. (Damasio 2004: 93)

It is thus easy to argue that affects and affect modulation also play a role in all writing, reading and translating (see also Davou 2007). This much is fairly well known. What is more challenging for neuroscience and for translation studies is to pinpoint exactly how and why they function as they do, and – as I will argue in this paper – a challenge for translators to try to modulate those affects with the help of particular translation strategies.

2 Foreignization, the Venutian way

In the late 1990s, translation studies witnessed a boom of discussions dividing translations along the axis of domesticating versus foreignizing. The most prominent figure, and the one most often quoted in this context, was without doubt Lawrence Venuti (e.g. 1995, 1998), the American literary translator and professor of literature; yet similar ideas were put forward at the same time and indeed even earlier by francophone scholars such as Antoine Berman. These contributions took the scene of translation studies by storm and were to a large extent a return to German Romanticism, a movement which saw scholars such as Goethe, Schleiermacher and Humboldt express their views on their preferred translation strategies, preferring to take the reader to the writer (foreignizing translation) rather than the writer to the reader (domesticating) (for an overview see e.g. Lefevere 1977; Snell-Hornby 2006).

Since that time, domestication and foreignization have become convenient catchwords for describing and defining translation strategies. In a fairly simplified manner, the former is often equated with reader-orientedness and the latter with staying close to the source text (e.g., Eco 2003). However, if we take a closer look at what Venuti actually said in his books (1995; 1998), things become more complex. First, in Finland at least, the understanding of domestication seems to be at least partially due to a (mis)translation. Domesticating is translated as 'kotouttaa', roughly meaning bringing something home. (At the same time, the same word was taken to mean the process of adapting immigrants, i.e. integrating them, to the Finnish system and culture). In many ways, this is an excellent translation. But if one looks at Venuti's works, where the operative word repeated again and again is 'fluency', one begins to wonder if a more apt translation in the specifically Venutian context might be 'kesyttää', taming, as in domesticated animals. A domesticated, or tamed, translation does not unsettle or challenge the reader in any way. In that sense it is indeed reader-oriented. But fluency means more than just using home-brewed variants and deleting unfamiliar references to the source culture; it also means not being challenging or provocative, not renewing the literary tradition. Domesticating, in this sense, is taking the easy way out, not taking risks.[1]

Foreignizing, then, is even more complex. It is a well-known fact that Venuti does not provide any ready-made tool kit for foreignizing strategies. Nevertheless, it is still quite possible to infer some guidelines and pragmatic strategies from his examples and anecdotes.[2] Significantly, and this is where Venuti parts company with Romantics like Schleiermacher, foreignizing is also essentially a domestically-based strategy. That is, the target culture and target language are the repositories of foreignizing methods, and the manner in which one renders the foreign origin visible is confined to those possibilities accessible in the target system. In a fundamental way, this target-orientedness makes any clear distinction between the two methods collapse: foreignizing, similar to all translation, is at heart domesticating (Venuti 1998: 5). Further, foreignizing can only be applied to those elements that are considered foreign in the target culture (Laaksonen 2010: 29). That is, a translation that preserves all the foreign elements of the source text cannot be considered foreignizing if these elements are not foreign for the target culture readers. There is thus no straightforward way of measuring the degree of foreignness between a culture pair. Similarly, identifying domesticating as the

---

1   Recently the term 'localization' has been used increasingly in lieu of domestication. This clarifies some potential misuderstandings, but at the same it creates new ones with respect to localization processes that go beyond the textual level.

2   In the following I will rely on both my own earlier work (Koskinen 2000) and a recent MA thesis (Laaksonen 2010) where Venuti's writings were scrutinized to distill the strategies he proposes. For a similar interpretation of Venuti, see also Boase-Beier (2006): 67–69.

dominant translation strategy in some research data, as is sometimes reported in the literature (see, e.g, Zare-Behtash / Firoozkoohi 2009 for one such example), is somewhat uninformative from the Venutian perspective since this dominance is what defines domestication in the first place: it is by definition a repetition of what we are used to. If we follow this argument one step further, this also means that these two categories are not historically stable: what was once considered foreignizing may later be construed as domesticating.

On the other hand, from another central perspective, the distinction holds: any translation method that unsettles fluency of reception and disturbs the reader can be considered foreignizing. Unfamiliar lexical items, complex structures disturbing easy readability, violated conventions, anachronisms, anything that makes the reader pause can be classified as foreignizing. An important, and often overlooked, aspect of Venutian foreignization is that these items do not necessarily need to have a direct stimulus in the source text or culture to function successfully in their foreignizing task (see Venuti 1995: 290–292). Venuti's concept of foreignizing is indeed in many ways similar to *ostranenie*, or defamiliarization, an intentional alienation effect used as an artistic device (Koskinen 2000: 52). Indeed, alienation is a term frequently used in Venuti's (1998) work. According to Venuti (1998: 11; italics added):

> Good translation is minoritizing: it releases the remainder by cultivating a heterogeneous discourse, opening up the standard dialect and literary canons to what is *foreign to themselves*, to the substandard and the marginal.

It is also significant that while the translation studies community was absorbing these two concepts with enthusiasm, Venuti himself chose a new term. As the quotation above illustrates, Venuti in his 1998 book no longer talked about foreignizing, but about *minoritizing* and *resistant* translation.[3] This new term emphasizes even more clearly the role of the Venutian translator in resisting the dominant cultural model. This ethico-aesthetic task is, importantly, called for by the *domestic* cultural context, and it serves the domestic needs (as seen by Venuti/the translator).

---

3   Another central concept in Venuti (1998) is the *remainder*. It has its own affective properties (one might actually redefine it as excess of affect), but, for the sake of clarity of argument, the present discussion is delimited to the more commonly known concepts of foreignization and domestication.

In short, domesticating and foreignizing in Venuti's texts do not constitute a binary opposition; they do not sit easily at the two ends of an axis where one can without residue place different translations. Rather, Venuti argues that all translating is domesticating, including foreignizing strategies that are called for and defined by the domestic context. (Similarly, one could argue that all translation is essentially foreignizing, the law of interference being the least contested candidate for a translation universal this far). Furthermore, a particular strategy, when applied in different contexts, can be seen as either domesticating or foreignizing (e.g., dialects) (Laaksonen 2010: 30).

It would be too much a simplification, thus, to argue that domesticating strategies bring the text to the reader, or that foreignizing translations make the reader cross the distance. This Schleiermacherian image has perhaps unhappily left us with a spatial conceptualization of these translation strategies: one close at hand and the other farther away. This imagery of a *physical* distance, with either the reader or the writer being asked to bridge that distance, may obscure the fact that we are actually dealing with degrees of *emotional* affinity more than with degrees of cultural affinity. In an interesting manner, foreignization aims to create an intentional rupture in the readers' *affective* community and alignment with the art work (see Ahmed 2010: 37; see also Venuti 1998: 126 on identification). Instead of the concepts of domesticating and foreignizing it might be more accurate to talk about affinity versus estrangement, familiarity versus strangeness, or naturalness versus unnaturalness, or, in very simple terms, liking versus not liking, that is, affection versus aversion. Spatiality may indeed be an apt source of metaphors: we are *touched* and *moved* by things that we like, some of them are even *close* to our heart, and those that we do not like make us turn away or we push them back or aside. In short, rather than – or in addition to – cultural or geographic distance, we are dealing with *affect*. Now exactly what *is* this affect, and (how) can it affect translation studies?

3 On Affect

Back in 1991, Douglas Robinson, a practising translator and translation theorist, introduced his notion of the somatics of translation.[4] This was not quite taken up in translation studies, but it largely captures the same arena I am trying to cover with the concept of affect. Somatics, Robinson (1991: x) argues, is explicitly physicalist; it means "the visceral processes and the limbic system, particularly the 'emotional'":

> [They are] the ways in which our body "signals" to us what we know and how we should act on it, through muscle memory and anxiety responses like constrictions of the chest or throat, clammy palms, tight shoulders, trembly legs, and so on. In everyday terms we "know in our gut" what we have to do and say.

This "gut feeling" has in many fields been labelled 'affect'. Affect is a baffling concept, in part because it is actively applied and defined in many disciplines, ranging from psychology and philosophy to cultural theory, where they are already talking about an affective turn (following and replacing the linguistic turn that took place in the social sciences about the same time that translation studies was experiencing its cultural turn)[5] (Clough / Halley 2007). Philosophical discussions of affect can be traced back to Spinoza (1632–1677). More recent core names include Lawrence Grossberg in cultural studies, and Silvan Tomkins' work from the 1960s in psychology is also often mentioned. (None of these is a required reference, though, and they do not necessarily meet eye to eye.)[6]

Regardless of the disciplinary framework, in most definitions, affect relates to the subconscious bodily reactions to stimuli. It is used to denote "visceral forces beneath, alongside, or generally *other than* conscious knowing, vital forces insisting

---

[4] In several later publications, Robinson has continued developing his somatic approach, also with direct links to foreignization discussions (see, e.g., Robinson 2011).

[5] To be explicit, I am *not* proposing an affective turn in translation studies, but employing this concept and benefitting from the intense theoretical discussions and empirical findings in other fields could indeed be useful.

[6] I do not have the expertise nor the space here to explore the different research traditions of affect. The reader is advised to see Fonagy *et al.* (2004: Chapter 2) on the philosophical, psychological and neuroscientific history of affect, and Gregg / Seigforth [eds.] 2010 on the cultural studies paradigm.

beyond emotion" (Seigworth and Gregg 2010: 1). Affect thus manifests in physiological symptoms, and because of these "telltale" signs, affect can be detected and measured by facial expressions, heartbeat, sweating, breathing, dilation of pupils and so forth (note the similarity with the quote from Robinson 1991 above):

> Affect gives you away: the telltale heart; my clammy hands; the note of anger in your voice; the sparkle of glee in their eyes. You may protest your innocence, but we both know, don't we, that who you *really* are, or *what* you really are, is going to be found in the pumping of your blood, the quantity and quality of your perspiration, the breathless anticipation in your throat, the way you can't stop yourself from grinning, the glassy sheen of your eyes. Affect is the cuckoo in the nest; the fifth columnist out to undermine you; your personal polygraph machine. (Highmore 2010: 118)

This physiological view of affect also indicates causality: an outside stimulus makes our body react in a particular way. However, affect is also a contextual and interactive phenomenon, and our affects, as well as the emotions they are related to, are also shaped by our individual behavioural traits and our social experiences (which also relates to the fact that we can learn to modulate our affect; I will return to this later in section 5). Some theories capture the dual character of affect by referring to two levels or two types, one immediate and unconscious and the other more subject to control and regulation (Fonagy *et al.* 2004: 75, 78). Throughout our acculturation to our society we encounter particular events and associate particular affects to them, and we internalize some notions of desirable and non-desirable affects. (In Robinson's vocabulary this is called ideosomatic programming). That is the reason why "causality" may also be anticipatory or retrospective (Ahmed 2010: 40). That is, we expect to experience certain affects in certain situations, or once we become aware of an affect we retrospectively link it to a particular stimulus.

Once affect becomes conscious, we experience it as an emotion: fear, desire, joy, sadness, hope and so on.[7] This consciousness involves cultural and ideological overtones. According to Lawrence Grossberg (2010: 316), "emotion is the articulation of affect and ideology". Psychologically, our innate affects can be seen to function as amplifiers (see Tomkins 1995). That is, affect calls us to pay attention and motivates us. Strange things *feel* strange because they have been

---

[7] Different fields employ different vocabularies. See, for example, Demasio (2004: 133 and *passim*.) for a neurological approach where 'emotions' give rise to 'feelings', and these two combined are called 'affects'.

amplified by affect, and pleasant things *feel* pleasant because they have been amplified by affect (see Nathanson / Pfrommer 1996). According to Tomkins, there are nine amplifiers increasing the likelihood that information thus amplified will be interpreted. These non-specific amplifiers are: interest-excitement and enjoyment-joy on the positive side, fear-terror, distress-anguish, anger-rage, dissmell (his neologism), disgust and shame-humiliation on the negative side plus surprise-startle which is too brief and fleeting to be either positive or negative but has a resetting function. (Actually, however, one could argue that surprise is a more positive function than startle.) (Tomkins 1995: 68ff.; see also Gibbs 2010)

Applying the preceding to the field of translation would mean that arousing interest or enjoyment would function as a positive amplifier, making us take notice of the triggering source, i.e. the interesting or enjoyable translation, whereas texts arousing distress, disgust or shame (for example, by being too difficult to comprehend or including taboo items) would trigger a negative effect. Surprise-startle would have an amplifying effect in alerting us, without predetermining whether this amplification would in the end be negative or positive. Affect is, in other words, an intensifier of the reading experience. Transposing perspectives, *not* having any affect would leave the readers nonplussed and uninterested in the qualities of the text, and they would not feel an emotional connection to it one way or the other, perhaps not even have any motivation to continue reading. It follows that translators might be well advised to strive for *affectability*, the capacity to affect.[8] Domesticating strategies can be used for arousing interest by linking the new to the already familiar, and by relying on aesthetic solutions that are familiar and thus not likely to cause negative affect. Conversely, with its in-built aim of unfamiliarity, foreignizing also has a lot of potential for affect (either positive or negative), and although it has greater risk of arousing negative affect, it is less likely to leave the reader entirely unaffected. The most central affect from the point of view of

---

8 In fact, a number of recent research results indicate quite the opposite. Within corpus studies it has been repeatedly argued that *translations* tend to be simplified and levelled out (Baker 1996), and it has also been proposed that this may be due to *translators* being risk-averse in their choices of strategies (Pym 2008). From the point of view of affect, one might argue that this risk-aversion may indeed be the riskiest of choices, because not arousing any affect at all might be the most unwanted response of all.

foreignizing is undoubtedly surprise-startle; rather than constantly unsettling fluency, the strategy aims at creating momentary experiences of the unexpected.

Now my thesis is as follows: regardless of the translation strategies, and without necessarily pre-valorizing either domesticating of foreignizing strategies, we experience the translations as either affectively positive (familiar, pleasant, aesthetically pleasing) or negative (strange, confusing, aesthetically unpleasant or uninteresting), depending on what our own tendencies are, what kinds of previous experiences we have had, and how our acculturation has predisposed us towards particular aesthetic solutions. In other words, emotional distance need not have anything to do with cultural distance: if I am predisposed to favour foreignizing translations (as all the great scholars seem to advise us to be), I feel close to those kinds of translations, and I orient myself towards those kinds of aesthetic solutions, and vice versa.

4 Case studies on affect

One could argue that experiencing translated texts as affectively positive or negative is not directly related to either domesticating or foreignizing strategies. In the following, this potential incongruence between the translation strategies and their effects is illustrated by some examples taken from my own research projects. These projects were not originally designed to shed light on the question of domestication, foreignization or affect; rather, these issues have emerged as relevant through repeated reappearance in unrelated data sets.

4.1 EU translation

My first case concerns translating EU documents into Finnish. When Finland joined the European Union in the mid-1990s, quite an extensive translation process got underway, as always does prior to and after accession. During this process, all relevant EU legislation was translated into Finnish. In this process, an extremely 'Finnicizing' (or domesticating, if you like) strategy for translating the *lexical items* was selected. (At the same time, this strategy did not apply to syntax or genre-specific features). In practice, the strategy dictated that if there was a native Finnish equivalent to any term or word, it was to be used rather than any loan-word, regardless of the normalized usage of the loan word or the potential obscurity of the ur-Finnish equivalent. As a result, report was not to be called 'raportti' but 'kertomus' ("story"), and co-ordination was not to be 'koordinointi' but 'yhteensovittaminen' ("adjusting together"), and so on. (Later, this principle was relaxed, but for the first few years this was the institutionalized translation strategy for all genres).

For the readers, however, these extremely Finnicized translations and other decisions born of this Finnicizing policy, although adequate as such, appeared unnatural and strange – that is, foreignizing. (Just in case that change was unclear, to set it off, I removed one comma and inserted a dash before that is, foreignizing). In other words, the attempted *domesticating* strategy was experienced ironically as *alienating* and *foreignizing*. There were heated discussions, letters to the editor, and an official report on the quality of Finnish EU translations (Karvonen *et al.* 1996). In other words, the strategy that was adopted to safeguard the purity of the Finnish language under the pressure of Brussels was turned on its head, and ended up estranging Finnish readers emotionally from texts originating in the EU. Thus, even these extremely domesticating measures could not salvage their reception: these new genres of texts, with their foreign-sounding structures and flagrantly foreign origins were not Finnish. Rather than solving the foreseen problems of reception, the domesticating strategies actually added to their alienating effect.

We can also assume that this negative affect may have been amplified by a pre-existing negative or even fearful attitude towards the EU institutions. The national referendum vote had passed by a narrow margin (with 56.9 % in favour of accession), and these strange-sounding and awkward-looking translations offered an opportunity to mock the very institutions that almost half the population had not voted for in the first place. A pre-existing (negative) affect thus functioned as an amplifier in the reception of the translations. Conversely, we can also suppose that 56.9 % of voters were positively attuned at the outset. However, public support for translations was limited. Support for the EU was, and is, often linked with internationalization in general, and a typical reaction from the pro-EU activists and officials dealing with the EU affairs was to claim that Finnish translations were not read and not that relevant because the officials preferred to use the original.

(On the opinions of Finnish officials see also Piehl 2000). Originality is, of course, a relative matter in the EU context, and often the respondents were actually referring to the *English* version that might well have been another translation (back in the 1990s, French had a much more dominant status as a drafting language than it has now). The desire to achieve (the illusion of a) direct contact with the original text probably relates to a more general human desire for authenticity, a pleasure we evidently derive from knowing the origins and history of things we own and observe (see Bloom 2010). Translation always unsettles that pleasure, and this may paradoxically be one reason behind both those strategies that aim at hiding the translatedness of the text ("domesticating") and at exhibiting an affinity to the source text ("foreignizing").

4.2 Retranslation

Another case where I have had to rethink the role of these two translation strategies concerns the history of literary retranslations in Finland, a project I have been working on together with my colleague Outi Paloposki from the University of Turku. One of the early key texts on retranslation is the article "La retraduction comme espace de la traduction" by Antoine Berman (1990), where he formulates what has later become known as the Retranslation Hypothesis. According to Berman, first translations tend to be assimilationist (or, domesticating), and this creates a need for a retranslation that stays closer to the original (i.e. that would be more foreignizing).[9] Although the hypothesis itself has been questioned a number of times (see e.g. Paloposki / Koskinen 2004), retranslations can be studied from the point of view of these two translation tendencies. It is only that the situation is more complex than the hypothesis would have us assume.

One source of complexity is indeed affect. Our observations repeatedly indicate the central role of affect memory in the reception of retranslated texts. Professional critics and lay readers alike seem to approach retranslation not only analytically but also emotionally, and this emotional approach seems to be to a large extent

---

9 It is evident that while Berman's dualism fits in rather nicely with many contemporary discussions on domesticating and foreignizing in translation studies, allowing me to equate assimilation with domestication and closeness with foreignization, these concepts do not match Venuti's usage without significant residue.

ideosomatically programmed (Paloposki / Koskinen 2009). Affect memory, an emotionally expressed feeling that recurs when recalling a significant experience, may indeed have an effect in all reception, but it is particularly dominant in some genres. Children's classics are one such example: a new translation may well be "better" or more accurate or "closer" to the original, but many adult readers prefer a version that repeats their childhood experiences. That is the reason why a new translation is often in many ways bound by earlier versions; the names of the characters and places, memorable events and sayings and so on are not easily changed. A repetition or return to the past outweighs questions of domestication and foreignization in such cases. Or rather, the childhood version *is* the domesticated version for the readers, regardless of the textual characteristics of the two translations. This affect memory, and the dual audiences always affecting children's literature – in this case parents and grandparents wishing to transmit their own childhood experiences to the next generation(s) intact – may also partially explain our finding that children's books seem to be revised rather than retranslated more often than adult literature (Koskinen / Paloposki 2005).

This same phenomenon is particularly visible in genres related to cultural rituals.[10] According to Robinson (1991: 224) the Bible is an excellent example because of its "ideosomatic effect of elevating complacent familiarity to the level of universal law". We do not so much respond to the content but to our own affect memory of the contexts where they have been previously recited:

> There is, in fact, a kind of bodily reassurance in a translation like the KJV [King James Version]: "The Lord is my shepherd, I shall not want" may sound to Eugene Nida like a lack of desire for God --- but of course for the Christian who memorized those words in childhood the "normal" somatic response, the response to the words if heard on the street, is massively overridden by the somatics of security. When I say these words, my world feels stable and safe. (Robinson 1991: 225)

Similar attitudes can be found with regard to Finnish retranslations of the Bible. For example, some readers still prefer the familiar 1938 translation of the Bible to the most recent, fluent and domesticated Finnish version from 1992, not so much in spite of, but precisely *because* of its more foreignizing style that lends the text a

---

10   Because of the affective power of music, songs that enjoy a central cultural status are particularly sensitive to affectivity.

more elevated and ceremonial aura *and* because this more foreignized version (itself a retranslation) of the text is more familiar to them than the newer retranslation. There are passages that we have learnt by heart such as "Ja tapahtui niinä päivinä...," the opening words of Luke 2 – in the 1938 version – which have traditionally been read out in school Christmas celebrations and at other events, as well as in many homes on Christmas Eve. Because of their ritual role, passages like this resonate emotionally in ways that other versions may be unable to echo. The technically more foreignizing earlier retranslation is thus, for these readers, more domesticating than the overtly more accessible new version. In spite of its fluent and "domesticated" translation strategy, the new version remains foreign to readers who had already responded emotionally, creating a bond with the previous version.

4.3 Linguistic Landscape

My final example is taken from my most recent research project on translatedness in the linguistic landscape of the suburb of Hervanta, Tampere, and it is based on my own affective experience during that fieldwork (see also Koskinen, in press). The case in question is a shop of Russian produce, named *Meidän kauppa*, 'our shop'. All signage is translated between Finnish and Russian, and the sign has the Finnish name and the Russian 'nash magasin' side by side (see Picture 1).

On a purely textual level, this translation strategy is best described as a literal one, with no obvious domesticating or foreignizing traits. But for a reader (like myself) who is not part of the 'us' in-group, which I infer to be the Russian-speaking minority living in Hervanta, the *effect* of this neutral translation strategy is foreignizing: because of the inclusive possessive pronoun 'meidän' (our), you are both invited to come along, and simultaneously you realize that not understanding half of the messages, you are not. The bold statement of 'our shop' is also a declaration of space. This is *our place*! Most likely, Russian inhabitants of Hervanta will also react affectively, but their reading of the signage is likely to tend towards more domesticating interpretations.

Picture 1. "Our shop" in Hervanta, Tampere. © Lauri Hietala

4.4 Affect and translation strategies

These three examples indicate that it is not necessarily a definable translation strategy as such that makes us feel either safe and familiar or alienated. Rather, our response is a combination of the textual stimulus, our specific reading context, personal and cultural background as well as disposition and state of mind. A negative predisposition either to the text itself, its author or the context of reception may affect our interpretation, making us perhaps subconsciously look for reasons or excuses to distance ourselves from the text. In that case a foreignizing strategy might make us complain about the text being too foreign, whereas a domesticating strategy might make us suspicious, feeling that the text is trying too hard to please us.

Our affective stance is fundamentally contextual and historical, and it depends on our previous experiences and affect memory: a foreignizing translation that is very familiar to us is in fact a domesticating translation *for us*, in which case a more domesticating translation of that same text would be foreignizing *for us*. This also applies to translations without any obvious domesticating or foreignizing tendency on the textual level; depending on the reader's personal position vis-à-vis the translation and its context, the effect can bend in either direction. The author of the translation can also modulate the readers' affective engagement – and this is precisely what the two translation strategies can be used for. They can be seen as "affective scripts", designed to maximize positive affect and to minimize negative affect (cf. Gibbs 2010: 196).

5 Modulating affect

Primary affects are, according to the above definition, non-conscious. But cultural, ideological and personal conceptions of acceptability, preference and desired effects make us (attempt to) control and regulate both whether and to what an extent we allow particular affects to surface in our own cognition and behaviour and what kinds of affects we try to induce in others. Affect regulation is in fact a central aspect of child development, socialization and acculturation (see Fonagy *et al.* 2004: 92–96). It is thus not particularly surprising that affects and their modulation can also be seen to occupy a central role in the production and reception of texts.

The idea of a writer modulating the affective properties of the text is not new. One can for example refer to the entire rhetorical tradition, or to the notion of interpersonality in Halliday's functional linguistics. Political discourse is a prime example of the modulation of affect, propaganda and agitation being extreme cases of processes that are used by all writers to different degrees and more or less consciously (see Koskinen 2010b for a discussion of the role of affect in EU communication). Another approach that offers a comprehensive framework for analyzing the affective strategies used by writers is Appraisal theory (Martin / White 2005).

The vocal modulating agent that we are concerned with in this paper is the translator. To cause a positive affect, or at least, to avoid negative affect the translator can employ different translation strategies. Prior to writing the target text, translators are readers. As human beings, translators also have their own affective reactions to the text and context, and these can have significant effects on the outcome (Tirkkonen-Condit / Laukkanen 1996), leading to the necessity that translators learn to modulate their own affects. This is the most typical understanding of modulating affect in psychological literature: as we grow up we learn to control our impulses and chaotic affects, and do not allow ourselves to be swayed by our emotions. Robinson (1991) focuses on another aspect of affect, that is, affect as a resource for the translator. Somatically oriented translators can use their own affective responses to the source text and to their different potential translation solutions as a support tool, basing their decisions on their gut reactions. Clearly, translation studies has revealed numerous examples of excessive modulating committed by translators: to shelter their readers from negative affects, translators have employed naturalization, omissions, and in extreme cases also various forms of censorship. Extreme domestication can be seen as another example of this kind of affective scripting.

6 Conclusions

Writers – translators included – may use all the strategies they can to modulate the readers' affects, but at the end of the day the readers have the final say. They can be swayed by the text, or they can resist the affective modulations imposed on them by the writer. For theorists, the role of affect at all stages of production and reception, with all the involved complexities and situationalities, offers challenges that are not yet sufficiently resolved in translation studies literature. The challenge is most directly one for cognitive approaches. If we accept the conclusion reached by Anna Gibbs (referring to Tomkins), that "there can be no 'pure cognition', no cognition uncontaminated by the richness of sensate experience, including affective experience" (Gibbs 2010: 200), we also need to infer that there can be no cognitive translation studies without a strong emphasis on affect. The necessity to pay attention to affect in process studies has long been recognised. Tirkkonen-Condit and Laukkanen argued as early as 1996 that "affect deserves particular attention in empirical translation research". The recent rise of affect theory in cultural studies highlights the necessity to take affect into account in culturally oriented translation research, as well.

Currently, there is no general theory of affect (although there is something called affect theory both in cultural studies and in psychology), and it is thus perhaps not too surprising that there is no shared understanding of it within translation studies.

Affects are muddy, vague, hard to measure (as soon as an affect is verbalized, for example, it is no longer an affect), and they are a shifting and changeable phenomenon rather than an absolute, on/off single switch, a process rather than a fixed position. The same can be said of affect theory: it, too, is muddy, vague and changeable, both methodologically and conceptually. But I still have my gut feeling that the notion of affect can lend us new and valuable viewpoints into translating and into the reception of translations. I think we need to add an affective layer to our descriptions of translational phenomena, functioning as a set of explanatory mechanisms that can, for example, shed light on various textual features found in translated corpora. (On explaining by mechanisms see Koskinen 2010a.) Methodologically, this affective layer could be produced via various research paradigms. One option would be to take the natural scientific route, operating with tools such as the EEG, tomography and pupillometrics (pupil size is known to respond to positive and negative affects), bringing the questions of affect in contact with recent process studies (see O'Brien 2011: 5–6 and *passim.*). Another option might entail a return to verbalizations like think aloud protocols, not only those elicited from the translators but also from the readers of translations, which might open an indirect view to the underlying affects (this is the approach of Tirkkonen-Condit / Laukkanen 1996). A third route will involve a return to literary and cultural theories, that is, a renewed engagement of translation studies with theories of aesthetics, and a continued engagement with cognitive stylistics (see Boase-Beier 2006). This third one is most directly related to Venuti's heritage, and it is also a return to the origins of his theoretical models in the tradition of literary scholarship. Whichever route one selects, an increased understanding of the role of affect in translating will enhance our knowledge of what translation is about.

References

Ahmed, Sara (2010): "Happy Objects." In: Gregg, Melissa / Seigworth, Gregory J. [eds.] (2010): *The Affect Theory Reader*, Durham and London: Duke University Press. 29–51.
Baker, Mona (1996): "Corpus-based translation studies: The challenges that lie ahead." In: Somers, Harold [ed.] (1996): *Terminology, LSP and translation: Studies in language engineering in honour of Juan C. Sager*. Amsterdam/Philadelphia: John Benjamins Publishing Company. 175–186.
Berman, Antoine (1990): "La Retraduction comme espace de traduction." In: *Palimpsestes* 13 (4), 1–7.

Bloom, Paul (2010): *How Pleasure Works: The new science of why we like what we like.* New York: Norton.

Boase-Beier, Joan (2006): *Stylistic Approaches to Translation.* Manchester: St. Jerome.

Clough, Patricia / Halley, Jean [eds.] (2007): *The Affective Turn: Theorizing the Social.* Durham and London: Duke University Press.

Davou, Bettina (2007): "Interaction of Emotion and Cognition in the Processing of Textual Material." In: *Meta* 52 (1), 37–47.

Damasio, Antonio (2004): *Looking for Spinoza. Joy, Sorrow and the Feeling Brain.* London: Vintage Books.

Eco, Umberto (2003): *Mouse or Rat? Translation as Negotiation.* London: Weidenfeld & Nicholson.

Fonagy, Peter / Gergely, György / Jurist, Elliot / Target, Mary (2004): *Affect Regulation, Mentalization, and the Development of the Self.* New York: Other Press.

Gibbs, Anna (2010): "After Affect. Sympathy, Synchrony, and Mimetic Communication." In: Gregg, Melissa / Seigworth, Gregory J. [eds.] (2010): *The Affect Theory Reader.* Durham and London, Duke University Press. 186–205.

Gregg, Melissa / Seigworth, Gregory J. [eds.] (2010): *The Affect Theory Reader.* Durham and London: Duke University Press.

Highmore, Ben (2010): "Bitter after Taste: Affect, Food, and Social Aesthetics." In: Gregg, Melissa / Seigworth, Gregory J. [eds.] (2010): *The Affect Theory Reader.* Durham and London: Duke University Press. 118–137.

Karvonen, Pirjo et al. (1996): *Suomi eurooppalaisessa kieliyhteisössä* [Finnish in the European language community]. Unpublished memo, Ministry of Education.

Koskinen, Kaisa (2000): *Beyond Ambivalence. Postmodernity and the Ethics of Translation* (PhD). (=Acta Universitatis Tamperensis 774). Available at: http://acta.uta.fi/pdf/951-44-4941-X.pdf. Visited 20 November 2011.

—— (2010a): "Agency and causality: Towards explaining by mechanisms in Translation Studies." In: Kinnunen, Tuija / Koskinen, Kaisa [eds.] (2010): *Translators' Agency.* Tampere Studies in Language, Translation and Culture, B series (electronic). Available at: http://tampub.uta.fi/tup/978-951-44-8082-9.pdf. Visited 21 November 2011.

—— (2010b): "On EU Communication 2.0. Using Social Media to Attain Affective Citizenship." In: Baker, Mona / Olohan, Maeve / Calzada Perez, María [eds.] (2010): *Text and Context. Essays on Translation and Interpreting in honour of Ian Mason.* Manchester: St. Jerome. 139–156.

—— (in press): "Linguistic Landscape as a Translational Space: The Case of Hervanta, Tampere." In: Ameel, Lieven / Scott, Maggie / Vuolteenaho, Jani [eds.] (in press): *Urban Symbolic Landscapes: Power, Language, Memory.* COLLeGIUM, Studies Across Disciplines in Humanities and Social Sciences. Available at: http://www.helsinki.fi/collegium/e-series/index.htm. Visited 1 March 2012.

Koskinen, Kaisa / Paloposki, Outi (2005): "Mapping retranslation." In: Salmi, Leena / Koskinen, Kaisa [eds.] (2005): *Proceedings of the XVII World Congress.* Tampere: International Federation of Translators. 194–195.

Laaksonen, Jenni (2010): *Venutilaisten strategioiden toimeenpano. Reaalioiden kotouttaminen ja vieraannuttaminen Rosa Liksomin novellikokoelman käännöksissä* [Putting Venutian strategies into practice: domesticating and foreignizing and Rosa Liksom's short stories]. [Unpublished pro gradu thesis]. Tampere: University of Tampere.

Lefevere, André (1977): *Translating literature: The German tradition from Luther to Rosenzweig*. Assen: Van Gorcum.

Martin, J. R. / White, P. R. R. (2005): *The Language of Evaluation. Appraisal in English*. Basingstoke: Palgrave/MacMillan.

Nathanson, D. L. / Pfrommer, J. M. (1996): "Affect theory and psychopharmacology." In: Nathanson, Donald L. [ed.] (1996): *Knowing Feeling*. New York: Norton. 177–190. Available at: http://www.reocities.com/MotorCity/8457/annals1.html. Visited 18 November 2011.

O'Brien, Sharon (2011): 'Introduction'. In: O'Brien, Sharon [ed.] (2011): *Cognitive Explorations in Translation: Eyes, Keys, TAPs. IATIS Yearbook 2010*. London and New York: Continuum. 1–14.

Paloposki, Outi / Koskinen, Kaisa (2004): "Thousand and One Translations. Revisiting Retranslation." In: Hansen, Gyde / Malmkjær, Kirsten [eds.] (2004): *Claims, Changes and Challenges* (selected contributions from the *EST Congress*, Copenhagen 2001). Amsterdam/Philadelphia: John Benjamins Publishing Company. 27–38.

—— (2009): "Pro Age – voiko viisikymppinen käännös olla kaunis?" [Pro Age – can a 50 year old translation be beautiful?] Paper presented in the *KäTu Symposium*, University of Tampere, 25 April, 2009.

Piehl, Aino (2000): "Finska EU-tjänstemäns syn på EU-texter." [EU texts: Finnish officials' viewpoints] In: Lindgren, Birgitta [ed.] (2000): *Bättre språk i EU*. Stockholm: Nordiska språkrådet. 21–29.

Pym, Anthony (2008): "On Toury's laws of how translators translate." In: Pym, Anthony / Schlesinger, Miriam / Simeoni, Daniel [eds.] (2008): *Beyond Descriptive Translation Studies. Investigations in homage to Gideon Toury*. Amsterdam/Philadelphia: John Benjamins Publishing Company. 311–328.

Robinson, Douglas (1991): *The Translator's Turn*. Baltimore and London: Johns Hopkins University Press.

—— (2011): *Translation and the Problem of Sway*. Baltimore and London: Amsterdam/Philadelphia: John Benjamins Publishing Company.

Seigworth, Gregory J. / Gregg, Melissa (2010): "An Inventory of Shimmers." In: Gregg, Melissa / Seigworth, Gregory J. [eds.] (2010): *The Affect Theory Reader*, Durham and London: Duke University Press. 1–25.

Snell-Hornby, Mary (2006): *The Turns of Translation Studies: New Paradigms or Shifting Viewpoints?* Amsterdam/Philadelphia: John Benjamins Publishing Company.

Tirkkonen-Condit, Sonja / Laukkanen, Johanna (1996): "Evaluations a key towards understanding the affective dimension of translational decisions." In: *Meta* 41 (1), 45–59.

Tomkins, Silvan (1995): *Exploring Affect. The selected writings of Silvan S. Tomkins*. Demos, E. Virginia [ed.]. Cambridge: Cambridge University Press.

Venuti, Lawrence (1995): *The Translator's Invisibility. A History of Translation*. London and New York: Routledge.

―――― (1998): *The Scandals of Translation. Towards an Ethics of Difference*. London and New York: Routledge.

Zare-Behtash, Esmail / Firoozkoohi, Sepideh (2009): "A Diachronic Study of Domestication and Foreignization Strategies of Culture-Specific Items in English-Persian Translations of Six of Hemingway's Works." In: *World Applied Sciences Journal* 7 (12), 1576–1582. Available at: http://idosi.org/wasj/wasj7(12)/19.pdf. Visited 18 November 2011.

Linguistic and Cultural Asymmetry in Translation from and into Minor Languages

Kinga Klaudy

ELTE University, Budapest, Hungary

Abstract

The aim of the paper is to extend the asymmetry hypothesis (AH) to include cultural asymmetry between translation from a major into a minor language and vice versa, and to relate the AH to the domestication/foreignization dichotomy (Venuti 2005). In this paper the "minor" language is Hungarian in comparison with Russian and English as "major" languages. The asymmetry hypothesis (Klaudy 2001, 2009) assumes that explicitation and implicitation are not symmetric strategies, as translators, if they have a choice, tend to use operations involving explicitation rather than operations involving implicitation. The paper concludes that domestication and foreignization are also asymmetric operations; while translators prefer explicitation on the linguistic level, on the cultural level translators seem to prefer domestication.

1 The asymmetry hypothesis

The asymmetry hypothesis was formulated in Klaudy (2001), further developed in Klaudy (2009), and tested against data in Klaudy and Károly (2004, 2005, 2007) and in Becher (2010). The hypothesis claims that in bidirectional translation analysis explicitation and implicitation are not always symmetric operations, as translators, when they have a choice, prefer operations involving explicitation (concretization of meaning, division of meaning, addition of meaning, grammatical concretization, grammatical addition, upgrading of noun phrases and participial phrases into clauses), and often fail to perform operations involving implicitation (generalization of meaning, contraction of meanings, omission of meaning, grammatical generalization, grammatical omission, downgrading of clauses into noun phrases or participial phrases).

The concept of interlanguage asymmetry was introduced into translation research by the Russian scholar Gak:

> In translation confrontation takes place between units of two different languages. These units can be of two types in their relationship to each other. (1) Isomorphous units have identical meaning or are characterized by identical positions in the corresponding language systems. […] Allomorpous units do not correspond to systemic equivalents in the other language. (Gak 1993: 33)

According to Gak, isomorphous units in interlanguage are in a symmetric relationship, while allomorphous units are in an asymmetric relationship. Since Gak relates the concept of symmetry and asymmetry to language systems, his approach can be called static. In adapting the asymmetry hypothesis for translation, Klaudy (2009) takes a dynamic approach, relating the concept of symmetry and asymmetry to transfer operations.

According to Klaudy (2009) **operational symmetry** occurs when explicitation in one direction is paralleled by implicitation in the opposite direction. For example, specification of personal pronouns in the Hungarian–Russian direction parallels, or at least may be expected to parallel, generalization of personal pronouns in the Russian–Hungarian direction.

(1) Hungarian ST – Russian TT (specification of personal pronouns):

> Fügét is vett, mazsolát is vett. Mélyhűtött őszibarackot és málnát is vett. Be volt rúgva. (Örkény 1968: 59)
> **Он** купил фиги. И изюм. И свежемороженные персики, и малину. **Он опьянел** от покупок. (Voronkina 2008: 286)

(2) Russian ST – Hungarian TT (generalization of personal pronouns):

> Весь вечер **он** (...) **думал** об одном, как бы одну увидеть **её**, но **она избегала его**. (Tolstoy 1977: 68)
> Egész este (...) egyre csak leste az alkalmat, hogy négyszemközt találkozhasson vele, de ő elkerülte. (Szőllősy 1962: 71)

On the other hand, **operational asymmetry** occurs when explicitation in one direction is **not** paralleled by implicitation in the opposite direction. For example, upgrading of phrases into clauses in the English–Hungarian direction is not paralleled by downgrading of clauses into phrases in the Hungarian–English direction.

2 Two methods of investigating operational asymmetry

Operational asymmetry can be investigated by two-way comparisons of translated texts. Bidirectional comparison can be independent or not-independent. Independent bidirectional comparison is based on translations from L1 into L2 and from L2 into L1 produced independently from each other. Klaudy (2007), for example, investigated Hungarian translations of Russian authors (Tolstoy, Chekhov, Dostoyevsky, Bulgakov, Trifonov) and Russian translations of Hungarian authors (Jókai, Mikszáth, Móricz, Déry, Sarkady) and found that translators specify reporting verbs in translating from Russian into Hungarian, but fail to generalise reporting verbs in translating from Hungarian into Russian. The same results were obtained by Klaudy and Károly (2005) in a study of reporting verbs in Orwell's *1984* translated from English into Hungarian and in Kosztolányi's *Anna Édes* translated form Hungarian into English (Szirtes 1991).

The other method of investigating the AH is non-independent bidirectional comparison (back-translation), when we investigate translations from L1 into L2 and back-translations of the same text from L2 into L1. Klaudy (1996), for example, investigated additions in a speech by Árpád Göncz, former President of Hungary translated into English and back-translated into Hungarian. She found that items inserted in the Hungarian–English translation were retained in the English–Hungarian back-translation "even in cases where they could or should have been omitted" (Klaudy 1996: 110).

Transfer operations can be divided into language specific and non language-specific operations. Language specific operations can be obligatory in both directions, obligatory in only one direction or optional in both directions. AH research is interested in the two latter types because in these cases translators have a choice and, since choices are not entirely subjective, linguistic explanations can be offered for them.

3 Linguistic asymmetry – previous research

3.1 Asymmetry between specification and generalization of reporting verbs

Specification of reporting verbs is a standard transfer operation in Russian–Hungarian (RU–HU) and English–Hungarian (EN–HU) translation. Generalization of reporting verbs is a standard transfer operation in the Hungarian–English (HU–EN) and Hungarian–Russian (HU–RU) direction. Both operations are optional. Studies by Klaudy (2007) and Klaudy and Károly (2005) claim that while translators do perform specifications in the RU–HU and the EN–HU direction, they fail to perform generalizations in the opposite direction. The reason for the specification of reporting verbs in the EN–HU and the RU–HU direction lies in the differences between literary traditions: while Russian and English authors prefer to use the central verb of the semantic field of reporting, i.e. *skazat'* and *say* respectively, Hungarian authors opt for more peripheral verbs, and use a large variety of more specific verbs for reporting. Table 1 compares reporting verbs in literary works by Russian and Hungarian authors. As we can see from the Table, 100 Russian reporting verbs include 16 types in Tolstoy's, 21 types in Dostoyevsky's and 24 types in Chekhov's works. The reporting verbs used by Hungarian authors show a greater variety; in a sample of 100 verbs, there are 36 types in Jókai's, 53 in Mikszáth's, and 35 in Móricz's works.

Table 1. Variability of reporting verbs in original RU and HU works.

	Token	Type	Type/token
Tolstoy	100	16	0.16
Dostoyevsky	100	21	0.21
Chekhov	100	24	0.24
Jókai	100	36	0.36
Mikszáth	100	53	0.53
Móricz	100	35	0.35

The translation of reporting verbs was analyzed for specification or generalization in 800 sentences. 400 sentences were drawn from original texts: (1) *Anna Karenina* by Tolstoy, (2) *1984* by Orwell, (3) *Szent Péter esernyője* by Mikszáth (1957a), and (4) *Édes Anna* by Kosztolányi. The other 400 sentences were drawn from their translations.

Table 2. Specification of reporting verbs in RU–HU translation.

Russian original Tolstoy, L. N. *Anna Karenina*	Frequency of verbs	Hungarian translation Translated by Klára Szőllősy	Frequency of verbs
1. сказать	55	1. mond 'say'	37
2. проговорить	10	2. kérdez 'ask'	11
3. отвечать	6	3. felel 'answer'	10
4. спросить	6	4. szól 'utter'	5
5. думать	5	5. válaszol 'answer'	5
6. прибавить	4	6. hozzátesz 'add'	4
7. говорить	2	7. gondol 'think'	4
8. повторить	2	8. ismétel 'repeat'	3
9. послышаться	2	9. kezd 'begin'	3
10. продолжать	2	10. folytat 'continue'	3
11–17. = verbs occuring once	6	11. sóhajt 'sigh'	2
		12. kiált 'shout'	2
		13– 23. = verbs occuring once	11
Total	100	Total	100

Table 3. Specification of reporting verbs in EN–HU translation.

English original Orwell, G. *Nineteen Eighty-Four*	Frequency of verbs	Hungarian translation Translated by Szíjgyártó László (1989)	Frequency of verbs
1. say	79	1. felel 'answer'	18
2. whisper	4	2. kérdez 'ask '	14
3. murmur	3	3. megállapít 'remark'	10
4. add	2	4. kijelent 'state'	10
5. yell	2	5. mond 'say'	4
6. begin	2	6. kezd 'begin'	4
7. agree	2	7. megjegyez 'comment'	4
8–14. = verbs occuring once	7	8. megszólal 'say/utter'	3
		9. kiált 'shout'	3
		10. mormol 'murmur'	3

		11. suttog 'whisper'	3
		12. közöl 'tell'	2
		13. hozzátesz 'add'	2
		14. folytat 'continue'	2
		15–32. = verbs occuring once	18
Total		100	Total	100

As Table 2 shows, the 100 reporting verbs (token) of the Russian source text consist of 17 different reporting verbs (type), while the 100 reporting verbs (token) of the Hungarian target text contains 23 different reporting verbs (type). As Table 3 shows, the English source text consists of 14 different reporting verbs (type), while the 100 reporting verbs (token) of the Hungarian target text contain 32 different reporting verbs (type). The increasing type/token ratios (0.17<0.23. and 0.14<0.32) indicate that the Hungarian translators used more specific verbs than the author of the source text, i.e. resorted to the explicitation of the meaning implied in the Russian and English original.

As authors of original English texts prefer to use the central verbs of the semantic field of verbs of saying, the number of different verbs should have been decreased in the English translation of the Hungarian novel. This, however, did not happen.

Table 4. Unperformed generalization of reporting verbs in the HU–EN direction.

	Total No. of verbs	No. of different verbs	Type/token
Édes Anna (HU)	100	56	0.56
Anna Édes (EN)	100	56	0.56
Szent Péter… (HU)	100	27	0.27
St. Peter's… (EN)	100	24	0.24

As we can see from Table 4, the diversity of Hungarian reporting verbs is preserved in the English translation: the translator did not generalise reporting verbs to bring them into line with English literary tradition. The type-token ratio in *Anna Édes*, the English translation of Kosztolányi's work, remains just as high as in the ST (0.56).

St. Peter's Umbrella, the English translation of Mikszáth's *Szent Péter esernyője*, shows a minimal decrease, from 0.27 to 0.24.

The data presented above lend support for the asymmetry hypothesis: semantic specification of reporting verbs (explicitation) was performed in translating from Russian and English into Hungarian, but semantic generalization was not performed in the opposite direction.

3.2 Asymmetry between addition and omission of extra categories

In another attempt to verify the AH, grammatical additions and omissions were studied by Klaudy and Károly (2004). These standard transfer operations are motivated by systemic differences between languages, and thus they appear to be obligatory in both directions. Grammatical addition is a standard transfer operation whereby grammatical (functional) elements that are not present in the SL text must be inserted into the TL text. Grammatical omission is a standard transfer operation whereby certain grammatical (functional) elements present in the SL text, being redundant in the TL, do not appear in the TL text. The systemic reason behind these operations is the phenomenon of so called missing categories: certain grammatical categories (gender, number, case, article, prepositions, postpositions, verbal prefixes, separable verbal prefixes, definite conjugation) may exist in one language, but not in the other. If we translate into a TL language that has one of these "extra" categories compared to the SL, additions will appear. Conversely, in translating into a TL in which, compared to the SL, a category is missing, omissions will occur. Addition and omission of articles, for example, are symmetric operations in RU–HU and HU–RU translation, since there is no article in Russian. Another reason for grammatical addition and omission may be that, although a particular grammatical category does exist in both languages (e.g. the personal pronoun in both English and Hungarian), its **functions** are different, and its use is governed by different rules in the two languages. Functional differences can make additions obligatory in one direction, while in the other direction omission is optional. Addition of the indefinite article, pronominal subjects and objects, as well as personal or possessive pronouns is obligatory in HU–EN translation. However, omission of the same categories is optional in EN–HU translation, and our experience in editing translations showed that optional omission was not always practised by translators. To confirm this observation, a small corpus was compiled, consisting of 100 sentences from Orwell's *1984* translated from English into Hungarian and 100 sentences from Mikszáth's *St Peter's Umbrella* translated from Hungarian into English.

Table 5. Unperformed omission of extra categories in the EN–HU direction.

	Obligatory additions HU–EN	Optional omissions EN–HU	Unperformed omissions EN–HU
Subject	50	47	7
Indefinite article	16	10	16
Pronominal subjects and objects	5	7	3
Possessive determiner	25	20	2
Total in 100 sentences	96	84	28

As is shown in Table 5, while the translators did perform addition (explicitation) in the HU–EN direction, they sometimes failed to perform omission (implicitation) in the EN–HU direction. Unperformed omissions of extra categories, e.g. retention of unnecessary indefinite articles in the Hungarian translations are unmistakable signs of SL influence (cf. translationese).

The asymmetry hypothesis was studied by Becher (2011) to elucidate the asymmetric relationship between addition and omission of connectives. His bidirectional parallel corpus consists of German business texts translated into English and English business texts translated into German (ca. 80 000 words). In this corpus he counted (manually) 114 additions of connectives in the EN–DE translation and 48 additions in the DE–EN translation, 32 omissions of connectives in EN–DE translation and 51 omissions in DE–EN translation. He concluded that German texts exhibit more additions and fewer omissions of connectives than the English target texts. Speakers of German tend towards a greater degree of cohesive explicitness than speakers of English. According to these data, explicitations are not counterbalanced by implicitations, i.e. "the quantitative results confirm the Asymmetry Hypothesis for this data set" (Becher 2011: 31).

4 Extending the asymmetry hypothesis to the cultural level

In the second part of this paper the concept of operational asymmetry in translation will be related to the domestication/foreignization dichotomy in the research of translation from and into minor languages. The terms domestication and foreignization were introduced by Venuti (1995). Domestication means translation strategies which result in transparent, natural-sounding, fluent TL style, minimize the strangeness of TT by the removal of SL realia, and require less effort on the part of the receptor. Foreignization means using translation strategies which retain the foreign flavour of the original. Foreignization, which results in a non-fluent style, deliberate breaking of TL conventions and retention of SL realia in the TL text, requires more effort on the part of the receptor.

The question is whether the explicitation/implicitation asymmetry has a connection with domestication/foreignization strategies, and how it is influenced by the minor/major status of the two languages. In this paper the "minor" language is Hungarian in comparison with Russian and English as "major" languages. It can be assumed that domestication characterizes translation from less widely spoken languages into more widely spoken languages, e.g. from Hungarian into Russian or English, and foreignization characterizes translations from more widely spoken languages into less widely spoken languages, e.g. from Russian or English into Hungarian. If domestication in one direction (from minor into major) is paralleled by foreignization in the other direction (from major into minor), the relationship can be regarded as symmetric, if domestication in one direction (from minor into major) is not paralleled by foreignization in the other direction (from major into minor), the relationship can be regarded as asymmetric.

In the following we will compare four languages and cultures: English, Russian, Hungarian and Finnish from three points of view: (1) minor or major status of the languages under study, (2) linguistic relatedness, and (3) cultural closeness. (Further research did not include Finnish language texts.)

4.1 Minor or major languages, closeness of languages and cultures

The minor or major status of a language can be defined from different angles. English is spoken by 341 million speakers. It is spoken as a native language on four continents. Russian is spoken by 167 million speakers and is spoken as a native language on two continents. Hungarian is spoken by 14 million speakers and it is spoken as a native language in Europe only, and Finnish is spoken by 7 million speakers and it is spoken as a native language in Europe only. On the basis of the above we can class English and Russian as more widely spoken languages, while Hungarian and Finnish must be regarded as less widely spoken languages.

As for linguistic relatedness, English and Russian belong to the Indo-European language family. Finnish and Hungarian belong to the family of Uralic languages.

In 1964 Nida proposed a typology of different combinations of linguistic and cultural relatedness. He distinguished three frequent types: (1) closely related languages and close cultures (e.g. Hebrew and Arabic), (2) close cultures and non-related languages (e.g. Swedish and Finnish), (3) distant languages, distant cultures (e.g. English and Zulu), and, a rare case, (4) distant cultures and cognate languages (e.g. Hindi and English). According to Nida's typology, our language pairs can be characterised in the following way:

1. Hungarian and Finnish = Close cultures and related languages
2. English and Russian = Close cultures and related languages
3. English and Hungarian = Close cultures and non related languages
4. Russian and Hungarian = Close cultures and non related languages

Cultural closeness, of course, has to be substantially refined taking into consideration proximity factors and distancing factors such as religion, geography, climate, density of population etc. Among the proximity factors we have to mention first Christianity, which characterizes all the four cultures. As for distancing factors, closeness to the sea and experience in navigation have played an important role in English, Russian and Finnish culture, but not so in Hungarian culture. Long winters have left their imprint on Russian and Finnish culture, but less so on English and Hungarian culture. Russians and Hungarians have had experience of totalitarian regimes in the recent past, while English and Finnish people have not had this experience. Population density in England and Hungary is relatively high, so these nations do not experience the wide open spaces experienced by people living in Russia and Finland.

All these factors heavily influence translators' work, as Nida stated: "[…] differences between cultures cause many more severe complications for the translator than do differences in language structure" (Nida 1964: 161).

4.2 Relationship between cultural differences and cultural asymmetry

Cultural differences are not the same thing as cultural asymmetry. Cultural asymmetry means first of all three things: (1) one-way traffic in the information channels between cultures; (2) one of the cultures is emissive (where 'emissive' means having a power to emit and distribute widely its own cultural achievements), while the other is receptive (where 'receptive' means willingness to internalize other people's cultural achievements and of course does not mean lack of originality and creativity); (3) information flows from more widely spoken languages to less widely spoken languages.

It may be assumed that translation from less widely spoken languages into more widely spoken languages (from Hungarian into Russian or English) involves domestication, and translation from more widely spoken languages into less widely spoken languages (from English and Russian into Hungarian) involves foreignization. The supposed reason for the domestication from minor into major is the following: due to the limited knowledge of the target audience about the source culture, the translator has to make an extra effort to be understood. The supposed reason for foreignization from major into minor is that the main function of translation from more widely spoken languages is to widen the conceptual and cultural horizon of the target audience, and to introduce new ideas and new concepts into the target culture, which necessarily means the introduction of SL concepts and words into the target text.

Let us see some examples of foreignization occurring in translation from a widely spoken language, such as English or Russian into a less widely spoken language, such as Hungarian:

- In the 20th century, before World War II, the use of Russian words in the translation of Russian classics into Hungarian had the function of creating atmosphere;

- In the 20th century, after World War II, the use of Russian words in Hungarian political language characterized the "insider" talk of Hungarian political leaders;
- Since the beginning of the 21st century, the use of English words in journalistic and scientific Hungarian texts has been a consequence of globalization and the development of information technology.

Let us look at examples of domestication occurring in translation from Hungarian as a less widely spoken language into more widely spoken languages like English, German, or Russian. We collected examples for one of the domesticating strategies, namely removal in the target text of SL realia (archaisms, Latinisms, units of measurements etc.).

Removal of SL archaisms in HU–EN, HU–RU translation:

(3) Hungarian ST: Ebéd után **csibukra** gyújtott a várúr ... (Mikszáth 1957b: 15)
(3a) English TT: After lunch the count lit up his **pipe** ... (Sturgess 1982: 17)
(3b) Russian TT: Posle obeda hozjain zakurival **trubku** ... (Leybutin 1962: 18)

In example (3), the connotations of *csibuk* 'pipe', connected with its archaic flavour, are not rendered in the translations.

Removal of SL units of measurement in HU–EN translation:

(4) Hungarian ST: Azt üzente Cseténé, hogy hozzon **egy kiló** kenyeret és **húsz deka** felvágottat. (Örkény 1968: 55)
(4a) English TT: That's why she asked Mrs Csete to tell Kopp to take home a **loaf of** bread and **some** cold cuts. (Sollosy 1994: 50)

In example (4), the connotations of *kiló* 'kilo' and *húsz deka* 'twenty decagrams', the usual units of measurement used in talking about weights of groceries in Hungary, are not rendered in the translations.

Removal of Latinisms in HU–EN, HU–RU translation:

(5) Hungarian ST: A **vitalicumot** félévenként kapták ... (Mikszáth 1957b: 20)
(5a) English TT: This **income** was paid every six months ... (Sturgess 1982: 23)
(5b) Russian TT: **Den'gi** vyplačivalis' baronam každy v god ... (Leybutin 1962: 24)

In example (5), the word *vitalicum* is probably not known by present-day Hungarian readers, but it is recognized as a Latin word used by many educated people in Mikszáth's time. These connotations are lost in the translations.

At the beginning of this chapter (4.2.) we assumed that domestication characterizes translation from less widely spoken languages into more widely spoken languages, e.g. from Hungarian into Russian or English, and foreignization characterizes translations from more widely spoken languages into less widely spoken languages, e.g. from Russian or English into Hungarian. Based on our analysis of approximately 200 book-length translations (mainly of literary works) from English, German, French and Russian into Hungarian, and 200 translations in the opposite direction (Klaudy 2003), we claim that all the above mentioned types of domestications can also be found in the opposite direction, that is, in translations from more widely spoken into less widely spoken languages.

(6) English ST: ... as he had never worked with **Carter Paterson** and was unused to such exertions, ... (Durrell 1963: 62)
(6a) Hungarian TT: ... Soha nem dolgozott a **bútorszállító szakmában**, nem szokott efféle erőmutaványokhoz, ... (Sárközi 1966: 64)

In example (6) The English trade name, which is, the name of the company *Carter Paterson*, was left out from the Hungarian translation and instead we find the general name of the activity carried on by the company: *bútorszállító szakma* 'furniture removal business'.

(7) English ST: He was alone in the great **Belgravia house** with Baines and Mrs Baines. (Greene 1972: 457)
(7a) Hungarian TT: ... így egyedül maradt **a nagy házban** Baines-szel és a feleségével. (Szobotka 1974: 280)

In example (7), the name of *Belgravia*, a reference to the characters' social status, is omitted and replaced by the much weaker innuendo of *nagy ház* 'great house'.

If domestication in one direction (from minor into major) is not paralleled by foreignization in the other direction (from major into minor), the relationship between domestication and foreignization can be regarded as asymmetric. Thus, the asymmetry hypothesis, which claims that translators, given a choice, tend to use operations involving explicitation rather than operations involving implicitations, can be extended from the linguistic level to the cultural level: translators, given the choice, tend to adopt domesticating rather than foreignizing strategies.

The domestication/foreignization dichotomy is probably not applicable to language pairs in their totality, but it is a good starting point for research if we want to investigate the proportion of domesticating and foreignizing strategies in different literary periods, different genres (literary translation, audiovisual translation), in the solution of specific translation problems (translation of film titles, translation of proper names etc.), or in the individual style of translators.

5 Conclusion

The aim of this paper was no more than to think over the relationship between the asymmetry hypothesis and the domestication/foreignization dichotomy. The asymmetry hypothesis extended to the cultural level (which would be worth examining in the future on large bidirectional databases of different language pairs) can be summarized in the following two points: (1) Domestication and foreignization are not symmetric operations: we cannot claim that domestication in one direction (from minor to major) is necessarily complemented by foreignization in the opposite direction (from major to minor); (2) While translators prefer explicitation on the linguistic level, on the cultural level translators seem to prefer domestication.

References

A. Source texts and translations studied

Durrell, Gerald (1963): *My Family and Other Animals*. London: Penguin Books.
Greene, Graham (1972): *Collected Stories*. London: The Bodley Head.
Györgyné, Sárközi (1966): *Családom és egyéb állatfajták* [Durrell, Gerald. *My Family and Other Animals*]. Budapest: Európa. Translated by Sárközi Györgyné.
Kosztolányi, Dezső (1988): *Édes Anna*. Budapest: Szépirodalmi Kiadó.
László, Németh (1988): Tolsztoj, L. N. *Anna Karenina* [Tolstoy, L. N. *Anna Karenina*]. Bukarest: Kriterion. Translated by Németh László.

Leybutin, G. (1962) = Lejbutin, G. (1962): Miksat, Kal'man. *Osada Becterce* [Mikszáth, Kálmán. *Beszterce ostroma*]. Translated by G. Leybutin. Budapešt: Corvina.

Mikszáth, Kálmán (1957a): *Szent Péter esernyője*. Budapest: Akadémiai Kiadó.

—— (1957b): *Beszterce ostroma*. Budapest: Akadémiai Kiadó.

Orwell, George (1954): *Nineteen Eighty-Four*. London: Penguin Books.

Örkény István (1968): *Egyperces novellák*. Budapest: Magvető.

Sárközi, Györgyné (1972): Durrell, Gerald. *Családom és egyéb állatfajták* [Durrell, Gerald. *My Family and Other Animals*]. Budapest: Európa. Translated by Sárközi Györgyné.

Sollosy, Judy (1994): Örkény, István. *One Minute Stories* [Örkény, István. *Egyperces novellák*]. Sydney: Brandl and Schlesinger. Translated by Sollosy Judy.

Sturgess, Dick (1982): *The Siege of Beszterce* [Mikszáth, Kálmán. *Beszterce ostroma*]. Budapest: Corvina. Translated by Dick Sturgess.

Szíjgyártó, László (1989): Orwell, George. *1984* [Orwell, George. *Nineteen Eighty-Four*]. Budapest: Európa Könyvkiadó. Translated by Szíjgyártó László.

Szirtes, George (1991): Kosztolányi, Dezső. *Anna Édes*. Budapest: Corvina. Translated by George Szirtes.

Szobotka, Tibor (1974): Greene, Graham. *Válogatott elbeszélések* [Greene, Graham. *Collected Stories*]. Budapest: Európa. Translated by Szobotka Tibor.

Szőllősy, Klára (1962): Tolsztoj, L. N. *Feltámadás*. Budapest: Európa [Tolstoy, L. N. *Voskresenie*]. Translated by Szőllősy Klára.

Tolstoy, L. N. (1977): *Voskresenie*. Moskva: Sovremennik.

—— (1946): *Anna Karenina*. Leningrad: Lengiz.

Voronkina, T. (2008): Erken', Ištvan. *Rasskazy-minutki* [Örkény, István. *Egyperces novellák*]. Moskva: Vagrius.

Worswick, B. W. (2002): Mikszáth, Kálmán. *St Peter's Umbrella* [Mikszáth, Kálmán. *Szent Péter esernyője*]. Budapest: Corvina. Translated by B. W. Worswick.

B. Secondary sources

Becher, Viktor (2011): "When and why translators add connectives? A corpus based study." In: *Target* 23 (1), 26–47.

Gak, V. (1993): "Interlanguage asymmetry and the prognostication of transformations in translation." In: Zlateva, Palma [ed.] (1993): *Translation as Social Action*. London: Routledge. 32–39.

Klaudy, Kinga (1996): "Back Translation as a Tool for Detecting Explicitation Strategies in Translation." In: Klaudy, Kinga/ Lambert, José/ Sohár, Anikó [eds.] (1996): *Translation Studies in Hungary*. Budapest: Scholastica. 99–114.

—— (2001): "The Asymmetry Hypothesis. Testing the Asymmetric Relationship between Explicitations and Implicitations." Paper presented at the Third International Congress of the

European Society for Translation Studies, *Claims, Changes and Challenges in Translation Studies*, Copenhagen 30 August – 1 September 2001.

—— (2003): *Languages in Translation. Lectures on the Theory, Teaching and Practice of Translation. With Illustrations in English, French, German, Russian and Hungarian.* Budapest: Scholastica.

Klaudy, Kinga / Károly, Krisztina (2004): "Unperformed Omissions in Translation – The Asymmetry Hypothesis Further Developed." A paper presented at the Fourth International Congress of the European Society for Translation Studies *Doubts and Directions in Translation Studies*, Lisboa, 2–4 September 2004.

Klaudy, Kinga / Károly, Krisztina (2005): "Implicitation in Translation: Empirical Evidence for Operational Asymmetry in Translation." In: *Across Languages and Cultures* 6 (1), 13–28.

Klaudy, Kinga / Károly, Krisztina (2007): "The Asymmetry Hypothesis Further Developed: the Asymmetry of Upgrading and Downgrading in Translation." Paper presented at the Fifth International Congress of the European Society for Translation Studies *Why Translation Studies Matters*, Ljubljana, 3–5 September 2007.

Klaudy Kinga (2007): *Nyelv és fordítás* [Language and Translation]. Budapest: Scholastica (in Hungarian).

—— (2009): "The Asymmetry Hypothesis in Translation Research." In: Dimitriu, Rodica / Shlesinger, Miriam [eds.] (2009): *Translators and their readers. In Homage to Eugene A. Nida.* Brussels: Les Editions du Hazard. 283–303.

Nida, Eugene A. (1964): *Toward a science of translating.* Leiden: Brill.

Venuti, Lawrence (1995): *The translators's invisibility. A history of translation.* London & New York: Routledge.

The Role of the Concepts *Domestication* and *Foreignisation* in Russian Translation Studies

Hannu Kemppanen
University of Eastern Finland

Abstract

The starting point of the study comes from observations on the rare use of the terms *domestication* and *foreignisation* in Russian translation studies literature. The study aims, first, at finding out in an analysis of research literature whether there are any grounds for the claim that Venuti's dichotomy has a marginal position in Russian translation studies, and, secondly, at examining whether there are analogous binary oppositions used by Russian scholars instead of *domestication* and *foreignisation*. The material consists of publications on translation theory and the practice of translation. The analysis showed that the concepts *domestication* and *foreignisation* are used infrequently in Russian translation studies literature. They are totally missing in books on translation theory, translation studies text books and conference proceedings. There are rare occurrences of the Venutian concepts in the *Mosty* translation journal and in some scholarly articles published in the Internet. The analysis revealed that the dichotomy of *domestication* and *foreignisation* is replaced in Russian translation studies by the dichotomy of free vs. literal translation.

1 Introduction

The notion of *translation strategies* has been discussed by translators and translation studies scholars for ages. Nevertheless Jääskeläinen (2009: 375–376) states the difficulty of defining 'strategies' in translation studies and other research fields as well (in second language research and cognitive psychology). According to Jääskeläinen "strategies relate to things which happen with the texts, such as domestication and foreignisation (e.g. Venuti 1998) and to things which take place during the translation process." This definition shows that the notion of strategy can be approached by analysing the product – the text – and the process. These two notions are obviously related with each other, so that the process is reflected in the product.

One of the problems connected with defining the term *strategy* is the use of different terms for the same or a close concept: *procedures*, *methods*, *tactics*, even *norms* (Jääskeläinen 2009: 376). One way to clarify the concept is to make a basic difference between strategies which are applied on different levels of translation, i.e. divide them into *global* and *local strategies* (Kearns 2008). The 'global' refers here to an overall strategy that is used by the translator on the level of the whole text, and 'local' to a strategy which is used for solving an individual translation problem in a text. The global strategies have usually been divided by translation studies scholars on the basis of dichotomous categorisations. One of the most used dichotomies during the last 15 years is the juxtaposition of *domestication* and *foreignisation*, introduced by Lawrence Venuti (1995). If we ignore the theoretical nuances in the approaches based on binary oppositions, Venuti's views on translation can be seen as a continuation of the scholarly discussion on free vs. literal translation. According to Galeyeva (2006) the idea of dichotomous distinctions can be traced to the special character of translation with two texts – the source and the target text – involving two languages and cultures.

The present study examines the concept of dichotomous translation strategies from a point of view that has not hitherto been taken: the role of the Venutian concepts *domestication* and *foreignisation* in Russian translation studies. The idea for the study was developed in the framework of a research project entitled *From Russian into Finnish and vice versa. Translation in a multicultural environment,* which concentrated on translation between the mentioned language pair, but aimed at solving more generic research questions as well – at operationalising the Venutian concepts of domestication and foreignisation. The project has introduced several angles to this research question: a corpus-based study on untypical lexical elements as markers of foreignness (Kemppanen 2009), a comparison of the results of a statistical analysis and a reception test (Mäkisalo / Kemppanen 2010), a study on the reception of a translation from the point of review articles (Kemppanen 2011), an analysis of translations of metaphors (Belikova 2012) and domestication vs. foreignisation in terminological work (Pasanen 2012).

The Russian–Finnish language pair orientation of the project requires analysing the use of Venutian concepts not only in the Western research tradition, but in Russian translation studies as well. The Western tradition is examined by Mäkisalo (2011) in a meta-analysis of the concepts *domestication* and *foreignisation* used in scholarly articles on translation studies. The present contribution focuses on translation research published in Russia.

An educated guess based on earlier observations is that Russian translation research cannot be considered as a potential source for ideas on the operationalisation of the concepts *domestication* and *foreignisation*. Accordingly, the aim of this study is, first, at examining if there are any grounds for the claim that Venuti's dichotomy is rarely discussed in Russian translation studies literature. Secondly, the study aims at finding out whether there are analogous binary oppositions used by Russian scholars instead of *domestication* and *foreignisation*. The material of the analysis consists of books on translation theory, textbooks targeted at the practice of translation, as well as scholarly articles issued in conference proceedings, in the translation journal *Mosty (Bridges)* and in Internet publications.

2 The dichotomy of *domestication* and *foreignisation*

American translation scholar Lawrence Venuti introduced the terms *domestication* and *foreignisation* in his works in the 1990s (Venuti 1991, 1992, 1995 and 1998). He argues for foreignising translation and has strongly criticised the American tradition of literary translation for the domination of the domesticating translation strategy. Venuti's idea of defending the foreignising strategy is based on ideas of earlier translators and translation studies scholars, such as Friedrich Schleiermacher (1992 [1813]) and Antoine Berman (2000 [1985]).

The term *domestication* is used in translation studies for a strategy involving a translation practice where elements foreign to the target culture are replaced by more familiar ones. According to Venuti (1992, 1995), domesticating translation is characterised by the dominance of linguistic, ethnic and ideological features of the target culture, as well as by the fluency of the text – naturalness of syntax, unambiguity, modernity of the presentation and linguistic consistency. A typical feature of a domesticating translation is transparency – a tendency to avoid non-idiomatic expressions, archaisms, jargon and repetition. In other words, the translator imitates text features of the target culture.

Foreignisation refers to an opposite strategy of translation. Venuti (1992: 11) defines this concept as a translation practice where elements foreign to the target culture are given a special stress. A foreignising translation is dominated by linguistic, ethnic and ideological features from the source culture, resistance to the norms of fluency and by the unmaskedness of the translator.

Venuti's dichotomy has inspired many scholars in different fields of translation studies. His ideas have been acknowledged especially by researchers who are focused on cultural studies, post-colonial studies and feminist translation studies. Robinson (1997: 98) mentions such scholars as Jill Levine, Lori Chamberlain, Sherry Simon, Samia Mehrez, Richard Jacquemond, Eric Cheynitz and Tejaswini Niranjana. It is clear that Venuti's strong orientation towards the source text and source culture gives an opposite point of view compared to functional, target text and target culture oriented approaches.

Venuti's ideas have, however, met criticism as well. Tymoczko (2000: 34) criticises him for the obscurity of his terms. Venuti uses specific terminology without proper definitions, and changes his terms into new ones in order to avoid precise defining and defending of them. Robinson (1997: 97–112), for his part, remarks that Venuti applies in his texts the same strategies he has evaluated negatively in his research work. According to Robinson, Venuti himself is fluent and elitist, although in the theoretical considerations he stresses the negative nature of these discursive features.

The dichotomous character of the categorisation of translation strategies has not been accepted by all scholars either (Tymoczko 2000; Boyden 2006). Pedersen's (2005) and Kruger's (2007) studies on audiovisual translation and translation of children's literature have shown that choosing a suitable strategy depends on several factors. For example, it is mostly expected that translating children's literature involves the use of a domesticating strategy. However, translating for children in a multicultural environment, such as South Africa, can serve educational purposes if the translator applies foreign elements in order to familiarise the target audience with neighbouring cultures (Kruger 2007).

3 Material and methods

The present study is based on an analysis of translation studies literature written by Russian scholars. The material consists of different types of publications: 1) monographs on translation studies, 2) articles in conference proceedings, 3) articles in the translation journal *Mosty* (*Bridges*) and 4) scholarly articles published in the Internet. The total number of analysed publications comprises 912 items – mainly articles but also including 50 monographs.

The compilation of the research material showed that Russian translation studies literature is dominated by text books – monographs with orientation on the practice of translation. Within this genre the books differ from each other with respect to the proportion of theoretical and practical information. Text books present basic concepts on translation theory, but mostly they deal with practical problems of translation and concentrate on a certain language pair, usually Russian and English. These books provide lots of translation exercises and concrete examples of translation solutions.

In addition to text books with a practical orientation, the research material comprises monographs on translation theory as well. Actually, drawing a line between these two categories of publications is quite difficult. Translation theory books may include chapters which serve practical purposes and they are used in translator training at the universities.

The main part of the material – the articles – can be grouped into three different categories according to their format of publication. The first group consists of articles in proceedings of the conference Feodorov Readings (Fëdorovskie čtenija) held regularly at the Saint-Petersburg State University. The materials in this publication deal mostly with translation theory, but themes on the practice of translation occur as well. The analysis covers 490 articles in seven compilations of proceedings published between 2000 and 2009. The second group of articles comprises contributions of translation scholars and translators in the journal *Mosty*. The total number of articles is 372, and they have been taken from 26 numbers of the journal published between 2004 and 2010. *Mosty* is mainly oriented to translation practices, but it also contains theoretical issues. The third category of articles includes Internet publications. With this group of texts the analysis is restricted to those materials which could be found by using the keywords *domestication* and *foreignisation* via search engines. Only scholarly articles were accepted as research materials. In other words, materials with Venutian concepts were excluded if they represented blogs, chat forums and other social media networks.

The analysis consists of searching for occurrences of the two terms *domestication* and *foreignisation* in Russian translation studies publications. These concepts are examined with a special reference to the context where they are used: do they occur in descriptions of macro-level, global strategies or are they, perhaps, applied for purposes of operationalisation? The latter question is especially interesting from the point of view of the larger framework of the research project mentioned above. In addition, the analysis examines possible comments on the Venutian dichotomy. It could be hypothesised that Venuti's ideas have awakened the same kind of controversy in Russian publications on translation studies as they have done among translation studies scholars in the West.

4 The use of the Venutian dichotomy in Russian translation studies

The analysis showed clearly that Russian translation scholars use the concepts of *domestication* and *foreignisation* very rarely. Still, the picture looks very different in different categories of publications. Books on translation theory and textbooks with a practical orientation totally ignore these terms. The situation is the same with conference proceedings.

Articles published in the translation journal *Mosty* provide only a slightly different view: the terms *domestication* and *foreignisation* are used in five articles in the whole sample. The Venutian concepts are used by Alexandra Borisenko in her two articles (the second number of 2007 and the first number of 2008) and by Viktor Lanchikov in two articles as well (the third number of 2007 and the first number of 2008). The contributions of Borisenko and Lanchikov comprise a scholarly argumentation between two translation theoreticians and translators with very different angles on the Russian translation tradition.

Borisenko (2007, 2008) asserts that Russian translation studies do not take into account the possibility of using the foreignising strategy for certain communicative purposes and that attempts by translators to foreignise are viewed very negatively. Lanchikov (2007) harshly criticises Borisenko's position claiming that she does not know the classics of Russian translation studies. It is obvious that Lanchikov does not like the concept of bringing new ideas from Western translation studies into Russian academic discussion. He makes a comment that one of the most serious mistakes made by Borisenko is the use of sources from the Internet instead of classics published in paper format. The two scholars continued arguing in two more articles on the tradition of Soviet translation studies, and, especially, on the role of the foreignising strategy as one of the approaches to translation.

5 Contrasting *domestication* and *foreignisation* with other dichotomies

The analysis showed that the concepts of *domestication* and *foreignisation* are rarely used in Russian translation studies. This fact does not, however, mean that the question about global translation strategies is not discussed by Russian scholars. The use of translation strategies is examined from point of views differing from Venuti's ideas, but these approaches nevertheless share the idea of a juxtaposition of two opposite strategies.

The material of the present study provides examples where Venuti's dichotomy is contrasted with other binary oppositions. Galeyeva (2006) discusses different dichotomies used in Western translation studies and refers to Hatim and Mason (1997), who introduce several parallel opposite concepts: literal vs. free translation, form vs. content, formal vs. dynamic equivalence, semantic vs. communicative translation, visibility vs. invisibility of the translation. The last mentioned pair of concepts links Galeyeva's (2006) article with the ideas of Venuti (1995), who strongly advocates a foreignising strategy and stresses the active role of the translator in creating a text where his or her translation options become visible.

A list of parallel dichotomies occurs in Voinich's (2010) article, where she provides the following oppositions of translations: free – literal (word-for-word, precise), unfaithful – faithful, artistically full-valued – artistically incomplete, *target-oriented* –

source-oriented, domestication – foreignisation. The italicized terms are given in English in a Russian text. Voinich finishes the list with Russian translations of Venuti's terms: *odomašnivanie* (domestication) and *ostranenie* (foreignisation). This is actually an interesting detail. Usually these terms are written in Russian texts as *domestikacija* and *forenizacija*, as a combination of the English stems and Russian endings.

In addition to contrasting several dichotomies, Russian translation scholars introduce more simple parallels, where Venutian concepts are compared only with one opposition – the traditional dichotomy of free vs. literal translation (Nesterova 2005; Borisenko 2007). Both theorists stress the role of Friedrich Schleiermacher in developing the ideas of foreignising translation. It must be added that Nesterova and Borisenko mention also some Russian scholars who have been defending the use of the foreignising strategy, such as Valery Bryusov, Mikhail Gasparov and Viktor Golyshev. In order to point out Gasparov's role in Russian translation studies, Borisenko even refers to Gasparov as "our Schleiermacher".

Borisenko (2007) criticises very strongly the negative stance of Russian translation studies scholars to foreignising translation. She especially argues against those theorists who claim that there exists one absolutely "right" way of translating. Borisenko also aims her criticism at translation studies scholars who use different cryptonyms for "a good translation", such as *creative* or *realistic translation* (see chapter 6 in the present article). She writes that translation theorists, neglecting the foreignising strategy as one possible approach to translation, lose in certain situations an ideal opportunity to achieve an exact rendering of linguistic and cultural elements of the source text.

6 Compensatory dichotomy: free vs. literal translation

Instead of *domesticating translation*, Russian translation studies literature uses the traditional term *free translation (vol'nyj perevod)*. *Foreignising translation* is replaced by the term *literal translation (bukvalistskij perevod)*.[1] The latter concept is linked with other, synonymous or close terms, meaning 'literal or word-for-word translation':

---

1 The Russian term *bukvalistskij perevod* is translated into English by some scholars with the term *literalist translation* instead of *literal translation* (see e.g. Alexandra Borisenko's article in this volume). The first one stresses the conscious choices of the translator.

bukvalism, bukval'nyj perevod, bukval'nost', doslovnost', doslovnyj perevod'. The great variety in naming the strategy of literal translation gives a hint of the evaluative definitions of this concept.

Russian translation theorists, indeed, show very clearly their stance on the use of global strategies. Nowadays it is typical to refer to evaluative assumptions of the classics of Soviet translation studies in Russian translatology as well. Books of the Soviet classics are published in new editions with minor additions and commentaries. The new edition of Yakov Retsker's (2004) *Teorija perevoda i perevodčeskaja praktika* [Translation theory and the practice of translation], first published in 1974, serves as a good example. The new issue is provided with the following annotation: "You are holding in your hand a new edition of this book with up-to-date commentaries made by professor Dmitry Yermolovich, Yakov Retsker's student, and reflecting the current state of the art in translation studies." As a matter of fact, Yermolovich's commentaries deal only with changes in the language and the selection of dictionaries, not with new tendencies in translation theory and approaches to translation.

In addition to new editions of translation theory classics of the Soviet era, the humble respect for Soviet scholars is clearly represented in the definitions of translation strategies included in *Tolkovyj perevodovedčeskij slovar'* [Explanatory translation studies dictionary] compiled by Lev Nelyubin (2003). This dictionary is the first, and the only one so far in the field of translation studies in Russia. It gives the definitions of terms without referring to any sources. The author of the book describes it in the following way: "the dictionary is by its nature a learner's dictionary with a pragmatic and cognitive orientation", and because of this users of the dictionary have to find the cited definitions in the books listed in the section of references. This organisation of the material in the dictionary makes it very laborious, if it is even possible, to compare different definitions and theoretical approaches behind the definitions. An interesting detail is also the fact that the list of references in the dictionary, consisting of 222 sources, does not include any publication written in some other language than Russian, although according to the preface "the book is aimed at graduate and post graduate students, doctoral candidates, teachers in faculties of translation, linguistics, philology and foreign languages, at those who study the theory, technique, methodology and practice of translation, and at all readers interested in problems of translation."

The discourse in the field of translation studies in Russia is characterised by pondering the question of the invariance of translation, of the existence of an unchangeable, ideal level of the quality of translation. Both free and literal translation represent a deviation from this norm. Nelyubin (2003: 32) provides the following definition of 'free translation': "A translation performed on a level higher than that which is sufficient for rendering the unchangeable content level while obeying the norms of the target language." This definition has originally been given by Leonid Barkhudarov (1969) in his work *Urovni jazykovoj ierarhii i perevod* [The levels of linguistic hierarchy and translation].

The definition above treats free translation as an abnormal approach. Deviation from the norm is, however, stressed much more clearly in the definitions of literal translation. Borisenko (2007: 27–28) claims that the fight against literalism has characterised Russian translation theory. She provides an illustrative example taken from one of the classics of Russian translation studies, the book by Yakov Retsker (2004 [1974]) *Teorija perevoda i perevodčeskaja praktika* [Translation theory and practice of translation], which is included in the research material of this study as a reissue. Retsker has given the sixth chapter of the book a very expressive title: "On the nature and dangers of literal translation". The reader is encouraged to make the "right" conclusions about using the strategy of literal translation already at the beginning of the chapter.

Lev Nelyubin's (2003: 26) translation studies dictionary gives several definitions of *literalism*. All of them are characterised by value-laden descriptions as follows: literal translation is "a translation **mistake**", "creating **incorrectly** understood exactness…", "**slavish copying** of foreign language elements". All of these definitions include the clearly expressed idea of abnormality connected with the use of a literal translation strategy. In addition to the mentioned evaluative descriptions, there occur more neutral characterisations as well. Such a definition can be found, for example, in Irina Alexeyeva's (2004: 78) text book on translation studies, where she examines the approach of literal translation in the framework of translation history. Alexeyeva refers to Schleiermacher, who considered it very important to preserve "the spirit of language" in translation and raised the idea of foreignisation as the main method in transferring specific features of the original.

In addition to the results mentioned above, the analysis revealed that instead of using dichotomous global strategies it is typical for Russian translation studies scholars to discuss the process and the product of translation in terms of seeking "the golden mean". Solving translation problems requires a compromise between literal and free translation. The methods for reaching "the golden mean" are described with different terms according to the theoretical approach of each translation studies scholar. Voinich (2010) lists several terms which have been used in Russian translation studies for describing an ideal translation method or result of the translation process: **adequate translation, realistic translation, full-valued translation, harmonious translation,** and **artistically exact translation.** Borisenko (2007: 31) includes in this list the term **creative translation.** The approaches behind these concepts are linked with each other by the idea of a translation invariance that excludes the possibility of choosing different translation strategies for different communicative purposes.

7 Concluding remarks

The analysis shows that in Russia publications on translation studies are characterised by an infrequent use of the concepts of *domestication* and *foreignisation*. Instead, Russian translation scholars discuss the question of translation strategies by using the dichotomy of free and literal translation. Despite the differences in the theoretical background, the Western and Russian discourse of translation studies shares common features as well. A fluent free translation is more suitable for a wide readership. At the same time Russian translation studies scholars take a critical attitude towards literal translation. Very often it is simply called "incorrect". However, there are defenders of this strategy as well. The difference between the Western and Russian tradition lies mainly in the scholars cited: in Russian texts Schleiermacher, Berman and Venuti mentioned infrequently, and are replaced by Russian authors, such as Bryusov, Gasparov and Golyshev.

In addition to the results mentioned above, the analysis reveals that Russian translation studies typically discuss the question of translation strategies by using concepts referring to "an ideal translation". It is obvious that the existence of an ideal strategy which can be applied constantly for all purposes neglects the possibility of using different strategies for different communicative situations. It can be claimed that the idea of an invariant translation fitted well in the Soviet tradition of translation studies, which clearly served the political purposes of Soviet society, including translation policy. However, it is an interesting fact that the results of the present study suggest that this notion, "the golden mean", described with several different terms by the translation theorists, is still actively discussed in current Russian translation studies. A more thorough analysis of this concept, with special reference to its historical background, would help to understand the specific use of strategy dichotomies in Russian translation theory.

References

Alexeyeva (2004) = Alekseeva, I. S. (2004): *Vvedenie v perevodovedenie. Učebnoe posobie dlja studentov filologičeskih fakul'tetov vysšíh učebnyh zavedenij.* Moskva & Sankt-Peterburg: Academia.

Barkhudarov (1969) = Barhudarov, L. S. (1969): "Urovni jazykovoj ierarhii i perevod." In: *Tetradi perevodčika.* Vyp. 6, 3–11.

Belikova, Alexandra (2012): "Operationaalinen lähestymistapa metaforailmausten konventionaalisuuden arvioinnissa." In: Kemppanen, Hannu / Mäkisalo, Jukka / Delikova, Alexandra [eds.] (2012): *Kotoista ja vierasta mediassa. Venäjästä suomeksi ja suomesta venäjäksi -workshop Joensuussa 7.–8.10.2010.* Joensuu: University of Eastern Finland. 28–43. (= Publications of the University of Eastern Finland. Reports and Studies in Education, Humanities, and Theology. 4).

Berman, Antoine (2000 [1985]): "Translation and the Trials of the Foreign. [La Traducion comme épreuve de l'étranger]." In: Venuti, Lawrence [ed.] (2000 [1985]): *The Translation Studies Reader.* Translated by Lawrence Venuti. London & New York: Routledge. 284–297.

Borisenko, A. L. (2007): "Ne kriči: 'Bukvalizm!'". In: *Mosty* 14 (2), 25–34.

—— (2008): "Eščë raz o bukvalizme." In: *Mosty* 17 (1), 7–14.

Boyden, Michael. (2006): "Language politics, translation, and American literary history." In: *Target. International Journal of Translation Studies* 18 (1), 121–137.

Buzadzhi (2009) = Buzadži, D. E. (2009): "Perevodčik prozračnyj i neprozračnyj." In: *Mosty* 22 (2), 31–38.

Galeyeva, N. (2006) = Galeeva, N. (2006): "Dihotomii v perevodčeskoj dejatelnosti." In: *Kosmopolis*, 1 (15), 126–133. Available at: http://cosmopolis.mgimo.ru/fileserver/15/15-11.pdf.

House, Juliane (1977): *A Model for Translation Quality Assessment.* Tübingen: TBL Verlag Gunter Narr.

Jääskeläinen, Riitta (2009): "Looking for a working definition of 'translation studies'." In: Mees, Inger M. / Alves, Fabio / Göpferich, Susanne [eds.] (2009): *Methodology, Technology and*

Innovation in Translation Process research. A Tribute to Arnt Lykke Jakobsen. Copenhagen: Samfundslitterartur. (= Copenhagen Studies in Language. 38).

Kearns, John (2008): "Strategies." In: Baker, Mona / Saldanha, Gabriela [eds.] (2008): *Routledge Encyclopedia of Translation Studies.* 2nd rev. edn. London and New York: Routledge. 282–285.

Kemppanen, Hannu (2011): Pamphlet or a scholarly work? Book reviews and determining the place of a translation. In: Kujamäki, Pekka / Kolehmainen, Leena / Penttilä, Esa / Kemppanen, Hannu [eds.] (2011): *Beyond Borders – Translations Moving languages, Literatures and Cultures.* 145–162.

Kruger, Haidee (2007): "Towards a paradigm for the study of the translation of children's literature in the South African educational context. Some reflections." *Language Matters. Studies in the Languages of Africa* 38 (2), 275–298.

Lanchikov (2007) = Lančikov, V. K. (2007): "Penthaus iz slonovoj kosti. O stat'e A. L. Borisenko "Ne kriči: 'Bukvalizm!'" In: *Mosty* 15 (3), 15–29.

—— (2008): "Po zakonam voobščistiki." In: *Mosty* 17 (1), 14–19.

Mäkisalo, Jukka / Kemppanen, Hannu (2010): "Frekvenssejä ja reseptiota: Kaksi näkökulmaa kotouttamiseen ja vieraannuttamiseen." In: *MikaEL. Kääntämisen ja tulkkauksen tutkimuksen symposiumin verkkojulkaisu. Electronic proceedings of the KäTu symposium on translation and interpreting studies*, 4. Available at: http://www.sktl.fi/toiminta/seminaarit/mikael-verkkojulkaisu/arkisto-archive/vol-4-2010/.

Mäkisalo, Jukka (2011): "Meta-theoretical analysis of the empirical use of the concepts domestication/foreignization." Paper read in *Domestication and Foreignization in Translation Studies*-conference. University of Easter Finland, Joensuu 29.9.–1.10.2011.

Nelyubin (2003) = Neljubin, L. L. (2003): *Tolkovyj perevodovodčeskij slovar'.* Moskva: Flinta/Nauka.

Nesterova, N. M. (2005): "'Čužoe vmig počustvovat' svoim': dialektika vtoričnosti perevoda." In: *Vestnik VGU, Serija 'Lingvistika i mežkul'turnaja kommunikacija"* 1, 92–97. Available at: http://www.vestnik.vsu.ru/pdf/lingvo/2005/01/nesterova.pdf.

Newmark, Peter (1981): *Approaches to Translation.* Oxford etc.: Pergamon Press.

Nida, Eugen A. (1964): *Toward a Science of Translating. With Special Reference to Principles and Procedures Involved in Bible Translating.* Leiden: E. J. Brill.

Pasanen, Päivi (2012): "Kotouttaminen ja vieraannuttaminen sanastotyössä." In: Kemppanen, Hannu / Mäkisalo, Jukka / Belikova, Alexandra [eds.] (2012): *Kotoista ja vierasta mediassa. Venäjästä suomeksi ja suomesta venäjäksi -workshop Joensuussa 7.–8.10.2010.* Joensuu: University of Eastern Finland. 69–76. (= Publications of the University of Eastern Finland. Reports and Studies in Education, Humanities, and Theology. 4).

Pedersen, Jan (2007): "How is culture rendered in subtitles?" In: Nauer, S. [ed.] (2007): *Challenges of Multidimensional Translation.* Proceedings of the Marie Curie Euroconferences *MuTra: Challenges of Multidimensional Translation* – Saarbrücken 2–6 May 2005. Available at: http://www.euroconferences.info/proceedings/2005_Proceedings/2005_proceedings.html.

Retsker (2004 [1974]) = Recker, Ja. I. (2004 [1974]): *Teorija perevoda i perevodčeskaja praktika.* Moskva: R. Valent.

Robinson, Douglas (1997): *What is Translation? Centrifugal Theories, Critical Interventions.* Kent, Ohio & London, England: The Kent State University Press.

Schleiermacher, Friedrich (1992 [1813]): "On Different Methods of Translating." In: Schulte, R. / Biguenet, J. *Theories of Translation.* Chicago & London. Translated by W. Barscht. 36–54.

Tymoczko, Maria (2000): "Translation and political engagement: activism, social change and the role of translation in geopolitical shifts." In: *The Translator* 6 (1), 23–47.

Venuti, Lawrence (1991): "Genealogies of translation theory: Schleiermacher." In: *TTR* 4 (2), 125–150.

Venuti, Lawrence [ed.] (1992): *Rethinking Translation. Discourse, Subjectivity, Ideology.* London & New York: Routledge.

—— (1995): *The Translator's Invisibility. A History of Translation.* London & New York: Routledge.

—— (1998): *The Scandals of Translation: Towards an Ethics of Difference.* London: Routledge.

Voinich (2009) = Vojnič, I. V. (2009): "Strategii perevoda i *vidimost'/nevidimost'* perevodčika (na materiale russkojazyčnyh perevodov tragedii V. Šekspira 'Julij Cezar'." In: *Vestnik Čeljabinskogo gosudarsvennogo universiteta*, 30 (168). *Filologija. Iskusstvovedenie.* Vyp. 35, 56–63. Available at: http://www.lib.csu.ru/vch/168/vcsu09_30.pdf.

—— (2010) = Vojnič, I. V.: "Zolotaja seredina" kak strategija perevoda: o (ne)vozmožnosti eë dostiženija". In: *Mir nauki, kul'tury, obrazovanija*, 1(20), 41–45. Available at: http://e-lib.gasu.ru/MNKO/archive/2010/1/nko20101.pdf.

Meta-theoretical Analysis of the Empirical Use of the Concepts *Domestication/Foreignisation*

Jukka Mäkisalo
University of Eastern Finland, Joensuu

Abstract

The paper analyses and describes the use of the concepts *domestication* and *foreignisation* as they have been used in empirical academic literature in Translation Studies. For the operationalisation of the concepts, it has been a problem that, originally, they are metaphorical. The material consists of 31 articles written in English studying the phenomena empirically, though not necessarily using the specific names D/F. The overall distribution in the qualitative use of the concepts is divergent. Researchers use dissimilar words for the same phenomena, attach the concepts of D/F to divergent issues in translations, and moreover use the concepts as if they were separate or formed a dichotomy or a continuum. A theoretical framework is suggested where the concepts and their empirical operationalisation will be commensurate.

1 Theoretical background

The most cited sentence from Schleiermacher's works is the following:

> Entweder der Übersezer läßt den Schriftsteller möglichst in Ruhe, und bewegt den Leser ihm entgegen; oder er läßt den Leser möglichst in Ruhe und bewegt den Schriftsteller ihm entgegen (Schleiermacher 1813 [1838]).

Susan Bernofsky (1997: 176) offers the following translation to English:

> Either the translator leaves the writer alone as much as possible and moves the reader toward the writer, or he leaves the reader alone as much as possible and moves the writer toward the reader.

Since Schleiermacher, the former method of translation has been called *foreignisation* and the latter *domestication*.

Regarding the citation from Schleiermacher, Lawrence Venuti (2000: 69) adds that there are only two methods of translation, and he gives an interpretation:

"a domesticating method, an ethnocentric reduction of the foreign text to target-language cultural values, bringing the author back home, and a foreignising method, an ethnodeviant pressure on those values to register the linguistic and cultural difference on the foreign text, sending the reader abroad." Thus, Schleiermacher, speaking also about interpreting, does not think a third choice is possible. In fact, he denies it.

Amidst the several aspects in the structure of the two concepts, one is of utmost importance from the viewpoint of research interest, and that is the fact that the concepts as Schleiermacher defined them are actually literary metaphors. According to St. André (2010), during the long history of translations theorists have used a bewildering range of metaphors to describe translations and translating. However, the long history does not give us the right to use any concept loosely and inaccurately. In general, it is the hard fact in scientific research that what guides theoretical modelling should be supported by empirical study rather than be based on thinking only.

As metaphors, the concepts of domestication and foreignisation do not easily bend to the needs of empirical research. The problem of operationalisation appears to take place at least at two levels. At the theoretical level, one is supposed to find the proper theoretical concepts that define foreignisation and domestication empirically, that is in texts (that are translations). At the empirical level, one is supposed to find methods to recognise features or elements of foreignness and possibly even measure the degree of foreignness in translated texts. Of the two, the problem at the theoretical level is more acute, since the actual foreign and domestic features of translations appear to vary vastly in the research literature, and since and therefore, before measuring anything, it is necessary to know what to measure.

The problems of operationalisation was a central case study of the research project *From Russian to Finnish and vice versa,* conducted in the University of Eastern Finland and funded by the Academy of Finland. The project focused on analysing various linguistic, textual, cultural and ideological shifts that have been conventional and necessary in translations between Finnish and Russian. This is why a qualitative meta-analysis of the concepts *foreign* and *domestic* used in translation studies was needed. What kind of features have researchers been attaching to these concepts in general – textual, lexical, grammatical, referential, political, cultural, ideological and so on – and hence, how have they operationalised the concepts theoretically?

As an example illustrating the problem of operationalisation, we might focus on the definition by Venuti mentioned above. His area of research has been characterised as cultural studies (for criticism, see Munday 2008: 152–154). Venuti defines the *domestic* as "an ethnocentric reduction of the foreign text to target-language cultural values" and the *foreign* to be as "an ethnodeviant pressure on those values to register the linguistic and cultural difference on the foreign text" (Venuti 2000: 69). The central features of both concepts are theoretically attached to the very values of SL or TL culture, and more accurately, to a change of the cultural values of the SL when translating: they are either preserved during translating and the text will be foreign, or they are reduced in order to accommodate TL cultural values instead, and the text will become domestic. In Venuti's work, the second phase of operationalising at the empirical level is based on intuition. He does not operationalise values as empirically (and objectively) recognizable objects in his material. As in linguistic semantics, for instance, when recognising and analysing various meanings of a word, Venuti intuitively identifies the (cultural) values of translated text, through the knowledge and acquaintance of the cultures at hand. An approach like this, based on intuition, is of course perfectly legitimate in cultural studies. On the role of intuition in linguistics, see for instance Itkonen (1983: 79–81). Venuti's theoretical views on the concepts D/F have been challenged by Jeremy Munday (2008: 153–154), who criticizes Venuti for not offering any "specific methodology to apply the analysis of translation", when studing various aspects of D/F.

The central questions in the analysis at hand are the following:

(1) What is the semantic structure of the concepts and their relationship with each other? Are the concepts symmetrical? Do they form a dichtotomy or a continuum? What is the possibility of a third concept between them?
(2) What empirical features have been attached to the concepts? Are they mainly seen as cultural, or attached to cultural values, in a Venutian way? How diverse is the quality of features?

(3) Is it possible to find a mutual base, or a common denominator, for all of the conceptualisations of D/F? Or are the various conceptualisations incommensurate?

2 Bibliographical material and the analysis

A systematic review (or meta-analysis) is a theoretical and methodological (and statistical) review (analysis) of empirical research on the subject, and it tries to compile a synthesis of the empirical results, in order to be able to systematise the description of the phenomenon, that is the concepts, the model or the theory at hand (or to explain the effect of various factors).

Here the analysis is a theoretical and methodological review of the empirical use of the concepts of D/F with two qualitative aims: in order to (1) find out the implicit (meta) knowledge attached to the concepts as used in translation studies and (2) systematise their description.

The search for empirical research of the concepts D/F in translation studies was conducted both by using the electronic database of Finnish university libraries and manually by searching through actual journals and books on the shelves of two academic libraries (at the University of Eastern Finland, Joensuu, and the Copenhagen Business School, Copenhagen). The manual search was necessary in order to detect also those articles that don't use the names *domestication* and *foreignisation* but still, nevertheless, study the phenomenon. The list of the articles is attached at the end of the article in References.

The exact criteria for a study to be acceptable for the analysis was that it had to be
- an empirical
- article
- written in English and
- studying D/F or the phenomenon (without necessarily using the words D/F).

The number of articles in the analysis is 31, and they were published between the years 1995–2010. A bibliographical database was compiled from them, containing all the information required to answer the questions mentioned in the previous chapter. Table 1 presents an example of the information compiled for one article (Kwieciński 1998).

Table 1. An example of using *foreignisation* in an analysis of Polish voice-over translations from American English in Polish television. The term refers to change in values of cultural references, for instance changing *shrimps* from a fast-food reference to an exotic cultural novelty.

| 14 | Kwieciński, Piotr | 1998 | Translation Strategies in a Rapidly Transforming Culture. A Central European Perspective | The Translator 4 (2), 183–206 | foreignisation | continuum | Cultural references | English-Polish | Literal translation (in voice-over): loss in intended meaning (Denny's is a downmarket fast-food restaurant) and changed cultural value (in Poland shrimps are an exotic culinary novelty) |

It is worth mentioning, here, that several articles were not included since the words *domestic, domesticating* or *adaptation* were used in another framework than translation. For instance, in Carvalho (1996) an English play is *domesticated* by *translating* it into English, which means actually that it goes through a literary adaptation for different dramaturgical needs.

3 Results

The following names were used to refer to 'domestication': *domestic(ation), adaptation, intercultural manipulation, naturalisation, familiarisation, manipulation, islamisation*. And the following names were used to refer to 'foreignisation': *foreign(isation), source-oriented translation strategy, preservation, internationalisation*.

What is the semantic structure of the concepts and their relationship? In 13 of the 31 articles only one of the concepts is used in the empirical survey, either *domestication* or *foreignisation*, or some of their variants mentioned above. Thus they view the phenomena in a (traditional) bipolar way, and I take it for granted here that they do not explicitly think that the concepts form a continuum. For instance, when analysing the domestic strategies of the translation of *Alice's Adventures in Wonderland* into Russian, Vid (2008) points out the cultural adaptation of personal names (*Alice* into *Anja*, *Mary-Ann* into *Maša*) and length and monetary units (*mile* into *versta*). In her analysis – and this observation is not to be taken as criticism – foreignisation has no other dimension or level.

Moreover, ten researchers do explicitly think that the concepts form a dichotomy, and that translations are either domestic or foreign. Only 8 of the researchers seem to think that the concepts *domestication* and *foreignisation* form a spectrum. The sixteen-year time scale of the articles, that is 1995–2010, does not have any effect on the definition or usage of the concepts (see Table 2).

Table 2. The time-scale of the articles according to the quality of the opposition.

Quality of the opposition	Number of articles	Years of publication
D without opposition	10	1995–2008
F without opposition	3	1995–2008
Dichotomy	10	1998–2008
Continuum	8	1995–2010

For instance, Lindfors (2001) analyses lexical choices in the Finnish translation of an African novel written in English, where in one sentence *maize* has been domesticated into *maissi*, but *mhunga* and *rukweza* have been maintained as such; she forms a spectrum from loan words to literal dictionary equivalents (actually correspondents) and to wrong dictionary equivalents.

Now the question is whether the various conceptualisations of D/F are commensurate. In other words, what to do with the Schleiermacherian view of D/F as a dichotomy, if researchers split into two explicitly separate groups? Notice also that some researchers state that a translation can be both domesticated and foreign at the same time:

> There is no reason, why translation cannot be both foreignising and domesticating at the same time; in fact, most translations are both. But we could not also question what is foreign and what domestic, if, like adverts, some things are everywhere but also very local? What seems to be the case, in the West at least, is that ideas of what is domestic, that is, familiar, seem to be expanding, allowing us to feel at home in much of the world. (Evans 2008, 93)

It is possible that we may stick with the old Schleiermacher, if we distinguish between the concepts and reality, as we should anyway. This makes it also possible to systematise the description of the concepts. In particular, the spectrum is not describable without other concepts, for instance style, cultural code, or linguistic levels (syntax, lexicon etc.). When we add other concepts to the dichotomy D/F, we may *de facto* form a spectrum of instances of translations. However, the conceptualisation of D/F remains a dichotomy. I also think that the crucial test for the structure of these concepts lies in the use of an individual expression, not at the level of text or a book.

As regards the question what empirical features have been attached to the concepts D/F, see Table 3, which contains all instantiations. The features vary from cultural values and beliefs (e.g. Amin-Zaki 1995; Venuti 2010) – which lie behind the actual translation – and cultural references (e.g. Franco Aixelá 1995; Kwieciński 1998) of the translation to rhythm and metre (e.g. Bernofsky 1997) in lyrical translation or the lay-out of the actual book (e.g. Sinibaldi 2008), and also to the reception of translation (e.g. Sengupta 1995).

Table 3. Empirical features of D/F classified and attached to specific domains in translation as communication.

	Empirical features	
Domain	**Domestication**	**Foreignisation**
values	Assimilation to TL culture and its values; changing moral values or text function	Shift of values between SL and TL culture in literal translations
cultural references	Changing local names, various measures (of length, weight etc), monetary units, food items, historical events and characters, puns and wordplays, cultural beliefs, brands	Preserving local names, various measures (of length, weight etc), monetary units, food items, historical events and characters, puns and wordplays, brands
cultural codes	Reproducing meanings of ST; changing proper names; neutralisation of taboo words; less marked structures; TL colloquial speech	Rendering ST word for word; respecting syntax; literal translation; preserving proper names; literalisation of metaphors; presenting new literary genre
style	Style shifting; non-simplification; normalisation or neutralisation	
language	Loss of phonological and syntactic features of ST; fluency, easy readability; onomatopoeias modified to TL; TL speech patterns	Idiomatic SL discourse
rhythm, metre	TL verse; modernisation of poems	ST metre and rhythm
syntax	Idiomatic TL syntax; grammatical errors of ST corrected or neutralised	Correspondence at grammatical level
reception	Idiomatic TL syntax; grammatical errors of ST corrected or neutralised	

	Empirical features	
Domain	Domestication	Foreignisation
lexicon	Referring concepts on more abstract level; discontinuities of text; archaic TL expressions	Literal translation; loan words; (wrong) dictionary correspondents; neologisms of ST; loss of SL meaning
lay-out	Book covers, lay-out conventions	Translator's footnotes

In Table 4, the domains of the features of Table 3 are classified in accordance with the four groups of conceptual use. We may see that there are no striking qualitative differences between the groups, whether we look at them as two groups (dichotomy / continuum), three (one without the other / dichotomy / continuum) or four. However, there is a difference between the first two: F without D has not been attached to character names or other cultural references, to genre or to style; when these features have been untouched in translation, that is have been left as foreign, they will not be prominent to readers, and that is exactly what the researchers are analysing here – prominent features of translations.

Table 4. The domains of the features of Table 3 classified in accordance with the four groups of conceptual use.

D without F	F without D	Dichotomy	Continuum
Character names	Pragmatic register	Cultural references	Cultural references
Style	Literal translation	Style	Cultural values
Genre change		Metre and rhythm	Style
Colloquial speech		Word choice	Syntax
Cultural references			Textual dimensions
Word choice			Familiarity

After realising that we may add other concepts to the dichotomy D/F and may *de facto* form a spectrum of instances of translations, it is only natural to think also that the spectrum of D/F is not something absolute, but that it is dynamic and also relative in nature – as conceptualisations of literary style usually are.

Finally, I would like to touch on an issue that the article by Paloposki and Koskinen comes up with. They propose that "Unmarkedness is often associated with domestication: translations are indistinguishable from same-language original works." (Paloposki / Koskinen 2004: 29.) The idea of unmarkedness originates from the linguistic school of structuralism at the beginning of the 20th century. In linguistic phonology, phonemes have features that are articulatorily natural to them, for instance stops are typically voiceless like [k], and in special cases they are voiced like [g]. The typical variant is called *unmarked*, because it lacks any special feature like voiced, which is called *marked*.

The idea is derivative to Gideon Toury's theoretical constructions (see, for instance, Toury 1995) on target-language and target-culture oriented paradigm within the so-called descriptive translation studies, where one of the central statements is that the reception of translated texts takes place in the framework of parallel target-language text. Readers tend to figure out, unconsciously, any text – translated or non-translated – on the grounds of their cultural and textual experience; in most cases, their experience is naturally built up from elements of target-language culture.

At this point it should be noted that in Table 4 the options "D without F" and "F without D" are substantially unbalanced; the features attached to the former outnumber the features of the latter. It is hypothesised here that this is because the features of the source-language culture are more prominent to the readers than features of the target-language culture.

The possibility of *foreignisation* being unmarked as a translation strategy has been studied by Mäkisalo / Kemppanen (2010). They conducted an experiment, where subjects (teachers and students in translation studies; n=18) were asked to rank original and translated history texts in Finnish (and from Russian) as D/F on a scale 1–5, and in addition were asked to explicitly name features that they regarded as D/F.

The subjects were able to distinguish between original and translated texts competently. They also named 33 features of foreignisation and 12 of domestication in the texts, which lays the emphasis on foreignisation. Moreover, the qualitative difference of the features between D/F was obvious:

Table 5. The features of D/F explicitly mentioned in questionnaire (Mäkisalo / Kemppanen 2010).

Feature	Domestic	Foreign
Viewpoint of the text	2	10
Syntax		10
Word		4
Phrase structure/collocation	3	4
Word order		2
Fluency (style)	7	1
Other		2
	12	33

The features attached to D were different from those attached to F. The conclusion was that (1) concrete features were attached to D, whereas more abstract or general features were attached to F, and (2) D is regarded as a default, or unmarked, value of a text. Furthermore, it is worth mentioning here that Anthony Pym (1996: 166–171) – when criticising Venuti's quantitative aspects of translation policy – actually identifies *fluency* with *domestication*. In this respect, it would seem that the result of the test is far from irrelevant in exploring the phenomenon.

4 Theoretical conclusions

The metaphorical nature of the Schleiermacherian concepts *domestic(ation)* and *foreign(isation)* has, in the empirical use, had the consequence that they have been operationalised and named in various and diverse ways. Alternatively, domestication has been referred to also as *adaptation, intercultural manipulation, naturalisation, familiarisation, manipulation* and *islamisation*, and foreignisation also as *source-oriented translation strategy, preservation, internationalisation*.

In most of the empirical articles referred to here (23 of 31), the concepts are used as if they formed a dichotomy, and in more than half of them (13 of 23) *domestic(ation)* or *foreign(isation)* is used without the other. In 8 of 31 articles, the concepts form a continuum, or a spectrum, where intermediate states may be found.

On these grounds, it is possible to systematise theoretically the various use of the concepts. We may reasonably propose that the pair of concepts D/F are indeed a dichotomy, since there is not a third qualitative option between them. However, when used empirically, the dichotomy may split into a continuum or a spectrum, where there are intermediate quantitative states between the ends of the continuum, but still, no third concept.

Furthermore, there are some grounds to claim that the dichotomy is asymmetrical, where domestication is unmarked. Features of the source-language culture are more prominent to readers than features of the target-language culture. Yet, this is more like a hypothesis for further studies than a well proven fact.

Finally, after all that was said above about the dichotomy D/F, it is important to mention one exception in the material. Dealing with children's literature, Pascua-Febles (2006) has a slightly different conceptual pair in her analysis, and that is *adaptation–internationalisation*. With the former she refers to adaptations of personal names and changes in style, but with the latter she refers not to the source-language preservation but to the possibility of references to international or global culture or commercial markets. What matters here is the fact that *internationalisation* is not something outside the dichotomy D/F, but, rather, it is qualitatively another kind of end of the same dichotomy, as if there was a dichotomy *adaptation–internationalisation*, where translations are either part of the global culture or adapted to local cultures.

The issue of internationalisation – or globalisation, if you like – requires one further point, which, I think, is of great importance. It was revealed by the survey that the perspective from which translation scholars approach literature is fairly limited. Basically, the searches carried out would have included all kinds of literature, i.e. any genre would have counted as instantiating the phenomenon. However, only fiction was represented: novels, poetry, drama, children's books. In other words, non-fiction was not at all investigated. Studies on the specific genres of, for instance, academic, encyclopaedic, or commercial text would certainly reveal something new on the conceptualisation of D/F. More generally, such studies would shed light on the strategies of translating, especially when thinking of the cultural globalisation, the present world that we live in.

References

A. Articles used as primary sources

Agost Caños, Rosa (1995): "The Colloquial Register and Dubbing." In: Jansen, Peter [ed.] (1995): *Translation and the Manipulation of Discourse*. Selected Papers of the *CERA Research Seminars in Translation Studies 1992–1993*. Leuven: CETRA – The Leuven Research Center for Translation, Communication and Cultures. 183–200.

Amin-Zaki, Amel (1995): "Religious and Cultural Considerations in Translating Shakespeare Into Arabic." In: Dingwaney, Anuradha / Maier, Carol [eds.] (1995): *Between Languages and Cultures. Translation and Cross-cultural texts*. Pittsburgh: University of Pittsburgh Press. 223–244.

Bernofsky, Susan (1997): "Schleiermacher's translation theory and varieties of foreignisation." In: *The Translator* 3 (2), 175–192.

Consiglio, Maria Cristina (2008): "'Montalbano Here': Problems in Translating Multilingual Novels." In: Hyde Parker, Rebecca / García, Karla Guadamarra [eds.] (2008): *Thinking Translation: Perspectives from Within and Without*. Conference Proceedings, Third UEA Postgraduate Translation Symposium. Roca Baton: BrownWalker Press. 47–68.

Davies, Eirlys E. (2003): "A Goblin or a Dirty Nose? The Treatment of Culture-Specific References in Translations of the Harry Potter Books." In: *The Translator* 9 (1), 65–100.

—— (2007): "Shifting voices: A comparison of two novelists' translations of a third." In: *META*, 52 (3), 450–462.

Evans, Jonathan (2008): "When Domestication is an Estranging Effect: Adriana Hunter's Translation of Beigbeder's 99 Francs." In: Parker, Rebecca Hyde / García, Karla Guadamarra [eds.] (2008): *Thinking Translation: Perspectives from Within and Without*. Conference Proceedings, Third UEA Postgraduate Translation Symposium. Roca Baton: BrownWalker Press. 87–94.

Franco Aixelá, Javier (1995): "Specific Cultural Items and their Translation." In: Jansen, Peter [ed.] (1995): *Translation and the Manipulation of Discourse*. Selected Papers of the CERA Research Seminars in Translation Studies 1992–1993. Leuven: CETRA – The Leuven Research Center for Translation, Communication and Cultures. 109–123.

Gonzáles Cascallana, Belén (2006): "Translating Cultural Intertextuality in Children's Literature." In: Van Coillie, Jan / Verschueren, Walter P. [eds.] (2006): *Children's Literature in Translation. Challenges and Strategies*. Manchester UK: St. Jerome. 97–110.

Hagfors, Irma (2003): "The Translation of Culture-Bound Elements into Finnish in the Post-War Period." In: *META*, 48 (1–2), 115–127.

Joosen, Vanessa (2006): "From Breaktimes to Postcards. How Aidan Chambers Goes (Or Does Not Go) to Dutch." In: Van Coillie, Jan / Verschueren, Walter P. [eds.] (2006): *Children's Literature in Translation. Challenges and Strategies*. Manchester UK: St. Jerome. 61–78.

Jänis, Marja (2007): "Ridiculing the Other by foreignizing translations." In: *Translation, interpreting and social activism*. 1st International Forum, Granada, Spain, April 28–30 2002. Available at: http://www.translationactivism.com/articles/Marja_Janis.pdf.

Karamcheti, Indira (1995): "Aimé Césaire's Subjective Gepgraphies: Translating Place and the Difference It Makes." In: Dingwaney, Anuradha / Maier, Carol [eds.] (1995): *Between Languages and Cultures. Translation and Cross-cultural texts*. Pittsburgh: University of Pittsburgh Press. 181–197.

Kwieciński, Piotr (1998): "Translation Strategies in a Rapidly Transforming Culture. A Central European Perspective." In: *The Translator* 4 (2), 183–206.

Leppihalme, Ritva (1998): "Foreignizing strategies in drama translations. The case of the Finnish Oleanna." In: Chesterman, Andrew / Gallardo San Salvador, Natividad / Gambier, Yves [eds.] (1998): *Translation in Context*. Selected Contributions from the EST Congress, Granada 1998. Amsterdam: John Benjamins. 153–162. (= Benjamins Translation Library. 39).

Lindfors, Anna-Marie (2001): "Respect or ridicule: Translation strategies and the images of a foreign culture." In: *The Electronic Journal of the Department of English at the University of Helsinki* 1, 1–6.

Lindqvist, Yvonne (1995): "Spoken Language in Literary Prose – a Translation Problem. A Case Study of The Catcher in the Rye by J. D. Salinger." In: Jansen, Peter [ed.] (1995): *Translation and the Manipulation of Discourse*. Selected Papers of the CERA Research Seminars in Translation Studies 1992–1993. Leuven: CETRA – The Leuven Research Center for Translation, Communication and Cultures. 77–107.

Mazi-Leskovar, Darja (2003): "Domestication and Foreignisation in Translating American Prose for Slovenian Children." In: *META*, 48 (1–2), 250–265.

Oittinen, Riitta (2006): "No Innocent Act. On the Ethics of Translating for Children." In: Van Coillie, Jan / Walter P. Verschueren [eds.] (2006): *Children's Literature in Translation. Challenges and Strategies*. Manchester UK: St. Jerome. 35–45.

Paloposki, Outi / Kaisa Koskinen (2004): "A thousand and one translation. Revisiting retranslation." In: Hansen, Gyde, Malmkjaer, Kristen / Gile, Daniel [eds.] (2004): *Claims, Changes and Challenges in Translation Studies*. Amsterdam: John Benjamins. 27–38. (= Benjamins Translation Library. 50).

Paloposki, Outi / Oittinen, Riitta (1998): "The domesticated foreign." In: Chesterman, Andrew / Gallardo San Salvador, Natividad / Gambier, Yves [eds.] (1998): *Translation in Context*. Selected Contributions from the EST Congress, Granada 1998. Amsterdam: John Benjamins. 373–390. (= Benjamins Translation Library. 39).

Parini, Ilaria (2008): "Domesticating or Foreignizing Texts? Case Study: Niccolo Ammaniti's Ti prendo e ti porto via translated into English." In: Parker, Rebecca Hyde / García, Karla Guadamarra [eds.] (2008): *Thinking Translation: Perspectives from Within and Without*. Conference Proceedings, Third UEA Postgraduate Translation Symposium. Roca Baton: BrownWalker Press. 135–155.

Pascua-Febles, Isabel (2006): "Translating Cultural References. The Language of Young People in Literary Texts." In: Van Coillie, Jan / Walter P. Verschueren [eds.] (2006): *Children's Literature in Translation. Challenges and Strategies*. Manchester UK: St. Jerome. 111–121.

Rossi, Paula (2003): "Translated and Adapted – The Influence of Time on Translation." In: *META*, 48 (1–2), 142–153.

Rudvin, Mette / Orlati, Francesca (2006): "Dual Readership and Hidden Subtexts in Children Literature. The Case of Salman Rushdie's 'Haroun and the Sea of Stories'." In: Van Coillie, Jan / Walter P. Verschueren [eds.] (2006): *Children's Literature in Translation. Challenges and Strategies*. Manchester UK: St. Jerome. 157–184.

Sengupta, Mahasweta (1995): "Translation as Manipulation: The Power of Images and Images of Power." In: Dingwaney, Anuradha / Maier, Carol [eds.] (1995): *Between Languages and Cultures. Translation and Cross-cultural texts*. Pittsburgh: University of Pittsburgh Press. 159–174.

Sinibaldi, Caterina (2008): "Translation and Ideology: From Theory to Practice. Analysis of Two Italian Translations of Alice in Wonderland." In: Parker, Rebecca Hyde / García, Karla Guadamarra [eds.] (2008): *Thinking Translation: Perspectives from Within and Without*. Conference Proceedings, Third UEA Postgraduate Translation Symposium. Roca Baton: BrownWalker Press. 185–194.

Van Coillie, Jan (2006): "Character Names in Translation. A Functional Approach." In: Van Coillie, Jan / Walter P. Verschueren [eds.] (2006): *Children's Literature in Translation. Challenges and Strategies*. Manchester UK: St. Jerome. 123–139.

Venuti, Lawrence (2010 [2000]): "Translation as cultural politics: Régimes of domestication in English." In: Baker, Mona [ed.] (2010 [2000]): *Critical Readings in Translation Studies*. Oxon: Routledge. 65–79.

Vid, Natalia (2008): "Domesticated translation: the case of Nabokov's translation of Alice's Adventures in Wonderland." In: *Nabokov Online Journal*, Vol. II. Available at: http://etc.dal.ca/noj/articles/volume2/08_Vid.pdf.

Øster, Anette (2006): "Hans Christian Andersen's Fairy Tales in Translation." In: Van Coillie, Jan / Walter P. Verschueren [eds.] (2006): *Children's Literature in Translation. Challenges and Strategies*. Manchester UK: St. Jerome. 141–155.

B. Secondary sources

Itkonen, Esa (1983): *Causality in Linguistic Theory. A Critical Inverstigation into the Philosphical and Methodological Foundations of Non-Autonomous Linguistics*. Bloomington: Indiana University Press.

Munday, Jeremy (2008): *Introducing Translation Studies. Theories and Applications*. Second edition. London: Routledge.

Mäkisalo, Jukka / Hannu Kemppanen (2010): "Frekvenssejä ja reseptiota: Kaksi näkökulmaa kotouttamiseen ja vieraannuttamiseen." [Domesticated or foreignized? A corpus and reception analyses compared] In: *MikaEL – The Publications of the Annual Finnish Symposium in Translation and Interpreting Studies*, 4, 1–14. Available at: http://www.sktl.net/mikael/vol4.php.

Schleiermacher, Friedrich (1838 [1813]): "Über die verschiedenen Methoden des Übersetzens." In: *Friedrich Schleiermacher's sämmtliche Werke*. 3. Dritte Abtheilung. Zur Philosophie. Berlin. 207–245. Available at: http://www.bible-researcher.com/schleiermacher.html.

St. André, James (2010): "Translation and Metaphor: Setting the Terms." In: André, James St. [ed.] (2010): *Thinking Through Translation with Metaphors*. Manchester: St. Jerome Publishing. 1–12.

Toury, Gideon (1995): *Descriptive Translation Studies and beyond*. Amsterdam: John Benjamins.

Venuti, Lawrence (2010 [2000]): "Translation as cultural politics: Régimes of domestication in English." In: Baker, Mona [ed.] (2010 [2000]): *Critical Readings in Translation Studies*. Oxon: Routledge. 65–79.

Domestication and *Foreignization* in Russian Translations of *Alice's Adventures in Wonderland*

Per Ambrosiani
Umeå University, Sweden

Abstract

In chapter 2 of Lewis Carroll's *Alice's Adventures in Wonderland* Alice tries to talk to a Mouse, but does not receive an answer: "'Perhaps it doesn't understand English,' thought Alice. 'I dare say it's a French mouse, come over with William the Conqueror.'". Accordingly, Alice addresses the Mouse in French: "Où est ma chatte?". Russian translators of *Alice* have translated this sequence in different ways—for example, in Vladimir Nabokov's translation (1923), which is often considered a typical example of a domesticated translation, the Mouse does not understand Russian. The mouse is probably French and the reason that it is in the same place as Anya (Alice) might be that it has stayed behind (in Russia?) after the retreat of Napoleon (in the 1812 war between France and Russia), and Alice speaks to the Mouse in French: "Ou est ma chatte?". On the basis of an analysis of examples of Russian and other translations, the present contribution will try to problematize the concepts domestication and foreignization, applying them not only to the translation of "domestic" source text elements, but also to source text elements that can be seen as "foreign".

1 Introduction

The aim of the present article is to discuss and to attempt to operationalize the translation studies concepts *foreignization* and *domestication*, which were introduced by Lawrence Venuti in his influential 1995 monograph *The Translator's Invisibility: A History of Translation* (Venuti 1995).[1] A further aim is to try to present a more comprehensive classification than those proposed earlier by broadening the

---

1   Cf. Venuti 1995: 19ff. (for a recent, brief introduction, see Yang 2010). I am grateful to the participants of the conference *Domestication and Foreignization in Translation Studies* for questions and comments that helped me to develop my conference presentation into the present article. I am also grateful to two anonymous reviewers, whose comments have helped me to elaborate parts of the discussion.

discussion to include the translation of not only "domestic", but also "foreign" elements in the source text. However, instead of beginning with the concepts and then trying to find examples that will fit the theory, in my present contribution I will begin with the empirical materials, i.e., a short source text and its translations into several target text languages (of which Russian will be the main one). As I will try to show, some of the analyzed target texts can indeed be easily described with the help of the concepts *foreignization* and *domestication*, but the analysis of other examples will be more problematic. Therefore, I will argue that the very concepts *foreignization* and *domestication* themselves need further elaboration in order for them to be even more useful when describing and analyzing the relationship between different types of source texts and their related, translated target texts. Consequently, my analysis will focus on the source text–target text relationship, whereas less attention will be paid to what may in principle be equally important features: the relationship between different target texts into the same or different languages, the intentions of the authors and translators, the reactions of real or implied readers to the respective source and target texts, etc.[2]

In order to be able to compare a large number of target texts of the same source text, the present analysis concentrates on Lewis Carroll's *Alice's Adventures in Wonderland* (1865) and its translations. The primary focus of the study will be translations into Russian[3], but I have also included examples of translations of *Alice* into Chinese, Czech, Dutch, Finnish, French, German, Italian, Norwegian, Swedish, and Ukrainian in order to further illustrate some of the points in the

---

2   Of course, some of these distinctions are by themselves problematic: the translator is by default a reader of the source text (and sometimes also of earlier target texts, cf. Ambrosiani 2010: 35f. for details relating to the translation history of *Alice* into Russian). Cf. also the preface to Zakhoder's (1972) translation of *Alice*, where the narrator declares that he would have preferred a different title for his translation, but that he did not dare to: "Net, bud' moja volja, ja nazval by knižku, naprimer, tak: "Alënka v Voobrazilii". Ili "Alja v Udivljandii". [...] No stoilo mne zaiknut'sja ob etom svoëm želanii, kak vse načinali na menja strašno kričat', čtoby ja ne smel. I ja ne posmel!" (Zakhoder 2007 [1972]: 5). (here and in the following all Russian examples are transliterated from the Cyrillic into the Latin alphabet)

3   The present analysis includes examples from eleven of more than twenty published translations of *Alice's Adventures in Wonderland* into Russian, cf. Ambrosiani 2010: 34f., 58f., Parker 1994, Rushaylo 1991, Weaver 1964: 60–61, 130–132.

discussion. It is important to state, however, that the analyzed examples are not meant to constitute any statistically representative sample of the total body of translations of *Alice* into these languages[4] – the aim of the present analysis is not to try to distinguish between more and less common solutions to certain translation problems, but rather to present an *inventory of attested solutions*. Naturally, this inventory cannot claim to cover all the solutions made by translators, but by extending the study to include a broader sample of target texts I hope to limit the risk of not having taken into account important translation possibilities that have been used by translators of the *Alice* text.

The choice of source text, of course, means that the conclusions of my analysis will be primarily relevant for the field of literary translation, and particularly for the translation of children's literature. For this type of translation, the relationship between the "text world" and "real world" (cf. Nord 1994: 523) is of particular importance: both the authors/translators and readers of both source and target texts can, in principle, choose between two main options. Either the "text world" is seen as a faithful representation of the "real world", with the same logic, or else the "text world" is seen as a world of its own, without claims to equivalence with the "real world". Thus, for example, references in the *Alice* source text (notwithstanding its location in "Wonderland") to the "text world" 'English' language generally refer to "real world" English, whereas this is not necessarily the case in all the target texts (see further below).[5]

2 The source text

Lewis Carroll's *Alice's Adventures in Wonderland* has been the object of countless studies by scholars within literature, language, culture, and translation studies (see, for example, Horton 2002: 98f. for a short overview of the text's use in translation

---

[4] As far as I am aware, the standard overview by Weaver (1964) has still not been replaced by any similarly comprehensive study. However, more recent data is available for some target languages, cf., for example, Kibbee 2003: 320, who lists twenty-three translations of *Alice* into French, Cammarata (2007, eight Italian translations), Horton (2002: 112, eleven German translations).

[5] For a methodologically important study of fictional language representation see Delabastita 2010.

analysis "[d]espite its somewhat unrepresentative literary status as an exercise in children's nonsense literature"). For reasons of space, the material that will be analyzed in the present study is limited to just one short excerpt from chapter 2 of the source text:

(1) 'Perhaps it doesn't understand English,' thought Alice. 'I dare say it's a French mouse, come over with William the Conqueror.' (For, with all her knowledge of history, Alice had no clear notion of how long ago anything had happened.) So she began again: 'Où est ma chatte?' which was the first sentence in her French lesson-book. (Carroll 2001: 26)

Despite the excerpt's shortness, it includes at least seven or eight "translation units"[6] that are of relevance for the aims of the present study (see Table 1 for a comparison with the text of the Russian translation by Demurova 1991 [1967][7]): 1) the name of the language that the Mouse does not seem to understand (which is also the language that is normally spoken in Alice's world) (English); 2) the name of the main character herself (Alice)[8]; 3) the (foreign) nationality of the Mouse (French); 4) the location of Alice's world[9]; 5) the reason why the (assumed foreign) Mouse is in the same location as Alice; 6) the linguistic form of Alice's words to the Mouse; 7) the (non-existent) translation of this utterance into the source text language; 8) the source of Alice's knowledge of foreign languages (French).

---

6   For the use of the term "translation unit" ("a 'horizontal' segment in the chronological sequence of linguistic elements") see Nord (1997: 69).

7   Cf. Demurova 1991 [1967]: "– Možet, ona po-anglijski ne ponimaet? – podumala Alisa. – Vdrug ona francuženka rodom? Priplyla sjuda vmeste s Vil'gel'mom Zavoevatelem... Chot' Alisa i gordilas' svoim znaniem istorii, ona ne očen' jasno predstavljala sebe, čto kogda proischodilo. I ona opjat' načala: – Où est ma chatte? (Gde moja koška?) V učebnike francuzskogo jazyka eta fraza stojala pervoj."

8   Cf., for example, Nord (2003: 186f.), who discusses the personal names that correspond to <Alice> in translations into German, Spanish, Portuguese, French, and Italian.

9   Notwithstanding the fact that Alice's Wonderland is clearly located in an English cultural setting (cf. Horton 2002: 99), this location is not indicated explicitly in the source text. In several target texts a deictic "here" is added, cf., for example Ceni 2003: 17: "Presumo che sia un topo francese, arrivato *qui* con Guglielmo il Conquistadore" (italics added), Parisot 1979 [1968]: 108: "c'est sans doute une souris française venue *ici* avec Guillaume le Conquérant" (italics added), etc. However, some target texts indicate the location explicitly, cf., for example, Bossi 2007 [1963]: 28: "Sarà un topo francese venuto *in Italia* con Carlo VIII" (italics added).

Table 1. Translation units in the *Alice* excerpt.

Translation unit no.	Source text translation unit	Target text translation unit (Demurova 1991 [1967])
1.	English (language)	po-anglijski
2.	Alice	Alisa
3.	French (mouse)	francuženka 'French female'
4.	– [here]	sjuda 'here'
5.	William the Conqueror	Vil'gel'm Zavoevatel'
6.	'Où est ma chatte?'	Où est ma chatte?
7.	–	(Gde moja koška?) 'where is my cat'
8.	French (lesson-book)	učebnik francuzskogo jazyka 'French language textbook'

Depending on their relationship to the source and target text cultures, the source text translation units can be seen as representing either "domestic" or "foreign" "culturemes".[10] With regard to the aims of the present analysis, the translation units <English> (1), <Alice> (2), and <William the Conqueror> (5)[11] can be classified as "domestic" (D), whereas <French> (3), <'Où est ma chatte'> (6)[12], and <French> (8) can be seen as "foreign" (F).

---

10 Cf. Nord 1997: 34: "A cultureme is a social phenomenon of a culture X that is regarded as relevant by the members of this culture and, when compared with a corresponding social phenomenon in culture Y, is found to be specific to culture X."

11 Thus, <William the Conqueror> is here primarily seen as a character of *domestic* (English) history rather than as a *foreign* invader, cf. Horton (2002: 102), who mentions William the Conqueror together with the Archbishop of Canterbury, medieval rulers, and Shakespeare as examples of "[k]nowledge, concepts, values" in the cultural systems in *Alice in Wonderland*.

12 For the utterance in French, we could distinguish between its denotative "foreign" status and a connotative "domestic" status because French was an important subject in the school curriculum in nineteenth-century England, cf. Evenepoel / Van Poucke 2009: 95; Horton 2002: 99, 106.

3 The translation of the translation unit <English>

Translation unit 1 (<English>) has been translated in several different ways in the different target texts. In most cases the source text reference to the English language (*po-anglijski, l'anglais, l'inglese, anglicky*, etc.) is retained, see examples 2–5:

(2) "Navernoe, ona ne ponimaet po-anglijski, (Shcherbakov 1977: 44)
(3) "Peut-être ne comprend-elle pas l'anglais, (Parisot 1979 [1968]: 108)
(4) "Forse non capisce l'inglese" (Ceni 2003: 17)
(5) Možná že nerozumí anglicky, (Skoumal / Skoumalová 2000 [1961]: 19)

However, in several target texts an explicit reference to any particular language is missing, and <English> has been replaced with less specific expressions such as <our language> (*po-našemu, po-našomu, vårt språk*), <my language> (*la mia lingua, minun kieltäni*), <this language> (*cette langue*), <human language> (*po-človečeski*), etc., see examples 6–13:

(6) "Navernoe, ona ne ponimaet po-našemu," (Zakhoder 2007 [1972])
(7) "Možet, ona ne govorit po-našemu," (Oryol 1988: 25)
(8) "Može, vona ne tjamyt' po-našomu?" (Kornijenka 2001)
(9) Kanske det inte förstår vårt språk. (Runeberg 1921: 22)
(10) "Forse non intende la mia lingua," (Pietrocòla-Rossetti 1872: 24)
(11) – Ehkä se ei ymmärrä minun kieltäni (Kunnas / Manner 1972: 25)
(12) "Peut-être ne comprend-elle pas cette langue," (Bué 1869: 25)
(13) Možet, ona vse-taki po-človečeski ne ponimaet? (Jakhnin 2002 [1991]: 33)

No language at all is mentioned in examples 14–16; the focus is instead on the speaker herself 'perhaps she/it does not understand *me*':

(14) "Možet, ona ne ponimaet menja? (Selivyorstova 2010: 16)
(15) Vielleicht versteht sie mich nicht (Karau 2008)
(16) "Kanskje den ikke forstår meg?" tenkte Alice. (Hopp 1979: 20)

Finally, in a few target texts the source text reference to English has been replaced by a reference to the target language: *po-russki* 'Russian', *Nederlands* 'Dutch', and *l'italiano* 'Italian', see examples 17–19:

(17) Možet byt', ona ne ponimaet po-russki, (Nabokov 1976 [1923]: 18)[13]

---

13 Similar examples can be found in at least four other translations into Russian, cf. Anon. 1879: 21: "Ona, možet byt', ne ponimaet po-russki", Granstrem (1908: 22): "Možet byt',

(18) "Misschien verstaat hij geen Nederlands," (Reedijk / Kossmann 1948)
(19) "Forse non capisce l'italiano" (Bossi 1963: 28)

If we try to classify the target text translation units in examples 2–19 as either "foreign" or "domestic" in the same way as was done for the source text translation units (cf. above, Table 1), it is apparent that the translation units of examples 2–5 (<English>) can be considered "foreign", and the translation units of examples 17–19 "domestic" (<Russian>, <Dutch>, <Italian>, respectively).[14] However, in order to classify the remaining examples 6–16 we need to distinguish between "explicit" and "implicit" characterization of the respective translation units. Thus, examples 2–5 and 17–19 are characterized by their *explicit* reference to the source and target text cultures respectively, whereas the translation units of examples 6–16 (<our language>, <my language>, <me>, etc.) can be seen as *implicitly* "domestic": nothing in these examples indicates anything "foreign", and they therefore implicitly refer to the target text culture. For a schematic overview of the relationship between the "foreign" and "domestic" in the target text examples see Table 2.

Table 2. Target text translation units with explicit and implicit reference to source/target culture

	Explicit reference	Implicit reference
"foreign"	<English>	—
"domestic"	<Russian>, <Dutch>, <Italian>	<our language>, <my language>, <me>, etc.

As Table 2 suggests, the target texts contain no implicitly "foreign" translation units, which indicates that the relationship between the "foreign" and "domestic"

---

ona govorit po-russki", Frenkel (2006 [1923]: 41): "Možet byt', ona ne ponimaet po-russki?", Kononenko (2000): "Možet ona po-russki ne ponimaet?".

14 The characterization of the expression *po-anglijski* 'English' in a Russian target text (cf. example 2) as "foreign" presupposes an implicit acceptance (by the reader) of an equivalence relation between the "text world" and the "real world", cf. above. If, however, the reader can be persuaded to accept that such an equivalence does not exist, and that "English" can function as the medium of communication in a text translated into Russian, *po-anglijski* 'English' could also be characterized as "domestic".

in the target texts is best described as a privative opposition between a *marked* "foreign" and an *unmarked* "domestic" feature characterizing the respective translation units.

In order to characterize the dynamic relationship between the "domestic" source text translation unit <English> and its corresponding explicitly "foreign" and explicitly or implicitly "domestic" target text translation units, we can, following Venuti (1995), use the terms "foreignization" and "domestication".

In its most basic sense, the term "foreignization" is used to describe a situation where a source text linguistic expression that can be classified as "domestic" is translated in such a way that it can be classified as "foreign" in the target text. Thus, in examples 2–5 the source text "domestic" translation unit <English> is translated into the respective target text "foreign" translation units *po-anglijski, l'anglais, l'inglese, anglicky* 'English', which obviously do not refer to the respective target text languages. The source text situation is illustrated by Figure 1, where the "domestic" translation unit is located within the frame of the source text language. The target text situation is illustrated by Figure 2, where the translation unit, with the same reference to "English" as in the source text ("literal translation")[15], is now located outside the frame of the target text language and thus seen as "foreign".

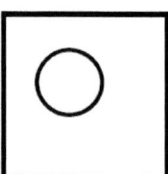

Figure 1. Source text frame with "domestic" translation unit <English>.

---

15   This is described by Schleiermacher in his famous metaphor as moving the reader closer to the author, cf. Pym 1995: 5ff. See also Levý (1969: 84), who discusses the opposition between the "klassizistischen Theorie der adaptierenden Übersetzung" and the "romantischen Theorie der wortgetreuen Übersetzung".

Figure 2. Target text frame with "foreign" translation unit <English>.

The term "domestication", on the other hand, is normally used to describe a situation where a source text "domestic" translation unit, which *could* be translated in such a way that it would be seen as "foreign" in the target text, is instead translated in such a way that it will *not* be seen as "foreign". Alternatively, it is translated in such a way that it can be seen as either explicitly (examples 17–19) or implicitly (examples 6–16) "domestic". The target text situation is illustrated by Figure 3: the result of a possible "foreignizing" translation has been avoided, and the target text translation unit has been relocated into the target text frame in order to be seen as "domestic".

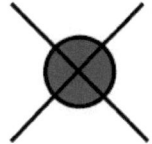 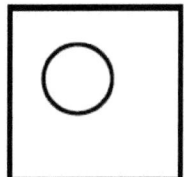

Figure 3. Target text frame with "domesticated" translation unit <Russian>, <our language>, etc.

4 The translation of the translation unit <William the Conqueror>

The analysis of the target text corresponding expressions of the "domestic" source text translation unit <William the Conqueror> (cf. Table 1, translation unit 5) is basically similar to the analysis of the translation unit <English> (cf. above): many target texts, in different target languages, refer to the same historical character as the source text here (Russian *Vil'gel'm Zavoevatel'*, Finnish *Vilhelm Valloittaja*, French *Guillaume le Conquérant*, Czech *Vilém Dobyvatel*, etc.), see examples 20–23:

(20) Priplyla sjuda s vojskami Vil'gel'ma Zavoevatelja! (Zakhoder 2007 [1972])

(21) tullut tänne laivassa Vilhelm Valloittajan matkassa (Kunnas / Manner 1972: 25)
(22) qui est venue ici avec Guillaume le Conquérant." (Papy 2005 [1961]: 58)
(23) přišla sem s Vilémem Dobyvatelem. (Skoumal / Skoumalová 1961: 19)

Likewise examples 2–5 (cf. above, Figure 2), the target text situation can be illustrated as in Figure 4, with the translation unit located outside the frame of the target text language and thus seen as "foreign".

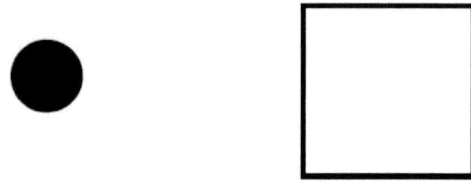

Figure 4. Target text frame with "foreign" translation unit <William the Conqueror>.

However, in a few target texts the source text translation unit <William the Conqueror> is replaced by the French emperor Napoleon, who, in the history of Russia, Italy, and the Netherlands, can perhaps be seen as an equally important historical character as William the Conqueror in the history of England, see examples 24–27[16]:

(24) prišedšaja vmeste s Napoleonom?" (Frenkel 2006 [1923]: 41)
(25) ostavšajasja pri otstuplenii Napoleona." (Nabokov 1976 [1923]: 18)
(26) venuto quì con Napoleone." (Pietrocòla-Rossetti 1872: 24)
(27) die met Napoleon mee is gekomen." (Reedijk / Kossmann 1948)

Just as in examples 17–19, a possible "foreignizing" translation has been avoided in examples 24–27, and the target text translation unit has been relocated into the

---

[16] Cf. also Bossi 2007 [1963]: 28: "venuto in Italia con Carlo VIII", referring to Charles VIII of France, who invaded Italy at the end of the fifteenth century. Kibbee (2003: 312) reports similar examples in French target texts: "ce peut être une souris anglaise débarquée avec le Prince Noir", "je pourrais m'imaginer que c'est une souris allemande qui est arrivée en France à la suite des armées prussiennes", "Ce doit être une souris anglaise, venue ici avec ses compatriotes pendant la guerre de Cent Ans".

target text frame in order to be seen as explicitly "domestic"[17], cf. Figure 5 (similar to Figure 3, above).

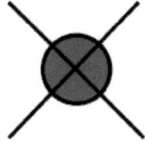 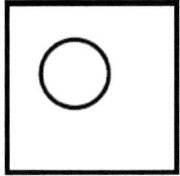

Figure 5. Target text frame with "domesticated" translation unit <Napoleon>, <Charles VIII>, etc.

In addition to the explicit domestication in examples 24–27 at least one of the analyzed target text translation units can be classified as implicitly "domestic", see example 28 (<på medeltiden> 'during the Middle ages'):

(28)   Det kanske är en fransk mus, som har kommit hit på medeltiden. (Runnquist 2000 [1966]: 34)

So far, the analysis of the translation of the source text translation unit <William the Conqueror> parallels the previous analysis of the source text translation unit <English>. However, in order to account for example 29, in which <William the Conqueror> is replaced by the target text translation unit <Christopher Columbus>, the analysis needs to be expanded:

(29)   navernoe priplyla vmeste s Kolumbom." (Kononenko 2000)

In this example, the source text explicitly "domestic" translation unit <William the Conqueror> is replaced by a "foreign" target text translation unit, which, however, does not refer to the same historical character as the source text, but to something which is equally "foreign" to both the source and target language culture. In a similar way as examples 2–5 and 20–23 this can be interpreted as a "foreignization", but of a different type that cannot be described as "literal"

---

17   For a discussion of Nabokov's (1923) translation, including his domesticating strategies, see for example Connolly (1995: 19f.), Vid (2008), as well as – with a more critical evaluation – Sdobnikov / Petrova (2006: 392ff.).

translation[18]: the target text situation can be illustrated by Figure 6, where the "foreign" translation unit is located outside the target language frame, but *not* in the same place as the source text translation unit (cf. Figure 4).

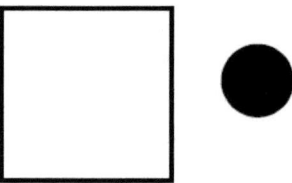

Figure 6. Target text frame with "foreign" translation unit <Christopher Columbus>.

5 The translation of the translation unit <'Où est ma chatte?'>

The discussion so far has been focused on the translation of the source text "domestic" translation units. However, in order to investigate more fully the concepts domestication and foreignization, the translation of source text "foreign" translation units also needs to be analyzed. Among the three source text F items, we will focus on Alice's utterance in French "Où est ma chatte?", and its possible translation into the target text language (cf. Table 1, translation units 6 and 7). The source text situation can be illustrated by Figure 7, where the "foreign" translation unit is located outside the source text language frame.

Figure 7. Source text frame with "foreign" translation unit <'Où est ma chatte?'>.

---

18 Cf. Venuti 1995: 200 on Ezra Pound's translations of Cavalcanti's poetry: "Pound's translations signified the foreignness of the foreign text, not because they were faithful or accurate [...] – but because they deviated from domestic literary canons in English".

In examples 30–31 Alice's French utterance is reproduced in the target text in the same linguistic form as in the source text, and, as in the source text, no translation is provided:

(30) Ou [sic] est ma chatte? (Nabokov 1976 [1923]: 18)
(31) Où est ma chatte? (Karau 2008)

This target text situation is illustrated by Figure 8, where the "foreign" translation unit is located outside the source text language frame: the context has changed, but the copied "foreign" translation unit has the same relation to this context as to the source text context.

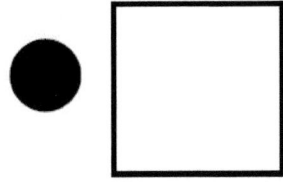

Figure 8. Target text frame with "foreign" translation unit <'Où est ma chatte?'>, copied from the source text.

In many target texts, however, a translation of the French utterance into the target language is added, see examples 32–34 (*gde moja koška, missä on kissani, dov'è la mia gatta*). The target text situation is illustrated in Figure 9, where an explicit relationship has been established between the "foreign" translation unit outside the target text frame, and the "domestic" translation unit inside it:

(32) – Où est ma chatte? / Èto predloženie bylo napečatano na samoj pervoj stranice Alisinogo učebnika, a značilo ono: "Gde moja koška?" (Oryol 1988: 25)[19]

---

19 Note, however, that the transliteration of the original Cyrillic text in the present article obscures the contrast between the copied sequence in French, written in the Latin alphabet, and the surrounding Russian context (including the translation of the French utterance into Russian) written in Cyrillic letters: "– Où est ma chatte? / Это предложение было напечатано на самой первой странице Алисиного учебника, а значило оно: «Где моя кошка?»". The same contrast, underscoring the "foreignness" of the French utterance, is also found in other target texts in languages with writing systems that are not based on the Latin alphabet, cf., for example Zhao 2000 [1922]: 34: "Où est ma chatte?", which is

(33)   – Où est ma chatte? Se oli näet hänen ranskankirjansa ensimmäinen lause ja merkitsee: "Missä on kissani?" (Kunnas / Manner 1972: 25)

(34)   – *Où est ma chatte?* – (che era la prima frase del suo libro di francese e, per chi non lo sapesse, significa: dov'è la mia gatta?) (Bossi 2007 [1963]: 28)

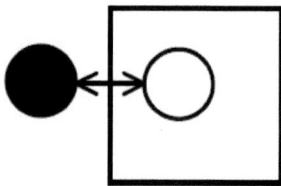

Figure 9. Target text frame with "foreign" translation unit <'Où est ma chatte?'> and its translation into the target language.

Another translation possibility is represented in example 35 'Where is my cat? she said in French', where the source text "foreign" translation unit has been replaced by its translation into the target language, with only a reference to its original "foreign" character, cf. Figure 10.

(35)   Var är min katta? sade hon på franska (Lundin 2005 [1977]: 20)

---

contrasted with its translation into Chinese "我的貓在哪裡" [wode mao zai na li] (for Zhao's translation of *Alice's Adventures in Wonderland* into Chinese, see Feng 2009). This writing system distinction can, of course, also be used for domesticating purposes, cf. Shcherbakov 1977: 44: "– У... э... ма шат? / Это была первая фраза в ее учебнике французского языка: «Где моя кошка?»" [U... è... ma šat? [...] Gde moja koška?], where the French phrase is reproduced in phonetic transcription with Cyrillic letters, and Jakhnin (Jakhnin 2002 [1991]: 33), who, after transcribing the French utterance with Cyrillic letters, adds a bilingual pun: "I vspomnila pervuju frazu iz učebnika francuzskogo jazyka: «U e ma šat?». Po pravde govorja, èto označalo: gde moja koška? No už očen' pohože bylo na čto-to pro myšat."

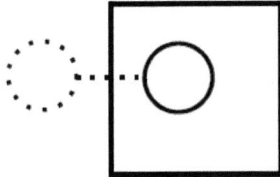

Figure 10. Target text frame with "domesticated" translation unit <'Var är min katta?'>.

In examples 36–37, the "foreign" source text French translation unit is not copied into the target text, but instead replaced by a different, but equally "foreign" phrase (in the context of the target language). Example 36 includes a translation into the target language (see Figure 11), whereas in example 37 (similarly as in the source text) no translation of the "foreign" translation unit is provided (see Figure 12).[20]

(36) *"Here is a cat"*, og det betyr: Her er en katt. (Hopp 1979: 20)
(37) *I am a cat!* (Kononenko 2000)

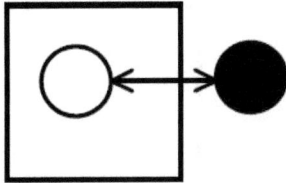

Figure 11. Target text frame with "foreign" translation unit <'Here is a cat'> and its translation into the target language <'Her er en katt'>.

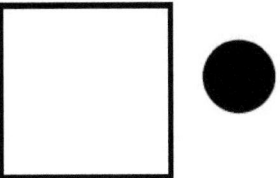

Figure 12. Target text frame with "foreign" translation unit <'I am a cat'> without translation into the target language.

---

20   Cf. the status of the English language in late twentieth-century Russia, which, it could be argued, has similarities with the status of French in nineteenth-century England.

Finally, in examples 38–39, two translations into French will be examined. The translation of a source text "foreign" translation unit into the very same "foreign" target language creates particular problems for both the translator and the reader when it comes to the relation between the "text world" and the "real world" (cf. above).[21] In example 38, the source text French phrase is copied into the target French language text with an added endnote 'in French in the text':

(38) "Où est ma chatte[1]?"// 1. "Où est ma chatte?": en français dans le texte. (Papy 2005 [1961]: 58, 190)

This target text situation is illustrated in Figure 13, where the "domestic" translation unit is located within the target text frame without any direct reference to anything "foreign". However, the status of the target text as a translation is underscored by the reference to the endnote, where the reader is *informed* of the existence of the French/English contrast in the source text.

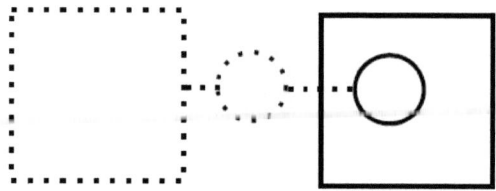

Figure 13. Target text frame with "domestic" translation unit <'Où est ma chatte'> and information about the source text language situation.

In example 39, on the other hand, the source text contrast between the French phrase and the English context is transferred into an Italian/French contrast, which can be illustrated by Figure 14:[22]

(39)   Dove è il mio gatto? (Bué 1869: 25)

---

21 For a detailed analysis of a similar, but more complicated case (the French dubbed dialogue of an originally British television series, set in France), see Delabastita (2010: 215–218).

22 Cf. Bué 1869: 25: "Je vais essayer de lui parler italien: "Dove è il mio gatto?" C'étaient là les premiers mots de son livre de dialogues."

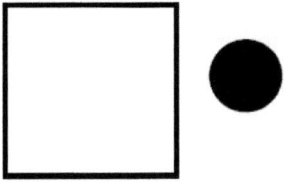

Figure 14. Target text frame with "foreign" translation unit <'Dove è il mio gatto?'>.

6 Conclusions

The analysis of the short excerpt from Lewis Carroll's *Alice's Adventures in Wonderland* and its translations has made it possible to identify a number of different types of translation of both "domestic" and "foreign" source text translation units. The corresponding target text translation units can be classified with reference to their source text origin: when the target text contains a "domestic" translation unit (cf. A–C, below), the following three types of translation have been identified:

A. In examples 6–19 the source text "domestic" translation unit is translated in such a way that it will *not* be seen as "foreign", but either explicitly (cf. examples 17–19) or implicitly (cf. examples 6–16) "domestic", cf. Figure 3, 5, above. This is the classic "domestication" case, which can also be described with terms such as "non-literal" or "free" translation, "dynamic equivalence", etc.

B. In example 35 ("Var är min katta? sade hon på franska (Lundin 2005 [1977]: 20)"), cf. Figure 10, the source text "foreign" translation unit has been translated into the target language, which thus exhibits the monolingual character that is typical of a "domesticated" translation.[23] A similar effect is demonstrated in the translation into French by Papy (example 38, see Figure 13), where the source text "foreign" translation unit <'Où est ma chatte?'> is copied into the French target text and in this context characterized as "domestic".

---

23 Cf. Sternberg 1981: 223f. on the "homogenizing convention" as one of the possibilities for translation of a polylingual source text.

C. In examples 32–34 (cf. Figure 9) the target text includes both a copy of the source text "foreign" translation unit <'Où est ma chatte?'> and its "domestic" translation into the respective target languages.

When the target text contains a "foreign" translation unit (cf. D–G, below), the following types of translation have been identified:

D. In examples 2–5 and 20–23 (cf. Figure 2, 4) the source text "domestic" translation unit (<English>, <William the Conqueror>) has been translated literally, resulting in a target text translation unit that can be classified as "foreign". This is the classic "foreignization" case, which can also be described with terms such as "literal" or "faithful" translation, "formal equivalence", etc.

E. In example 29 (cf. Figure 6) the source text "domestic" translation unit <William the Conqueror> is replaced by a "foreign" target text translation unit <Christopher Columbus>. This change from "domestic" to "foreign" can also be described with the term "foreignization", but a type of foreignization that seems to differ substantially from what is usually meant by the term "literal" translation.

F. In examples 30–34 (cf. Figure 8–9), the source text "foreign" translation unit <'Où est ma chatte?'> has been copied into the target text, retaining its "foreign" character in the new language context. This relationship between the source text and target text translation units can be described *both* as formal and dynamic equivalence, because both the actual wording and its "foreign" character is present in both the source and target text.

G. In examples 36–37 and 39 (cf. Figure 11, 12, 14) the "foreign" source text translation unit <'Où est ma chatte?'> is replaced by a different, but equally "foreign" translation unit in the target text (<'I am a cat'>, <'Here is a cat'>, <'Dove è il mio gatto'>).

By establishing and analyzing an inventory of attested translation solutions for both "foreign" and "domestic" translation units, I have tried to demonstrate that no simple equivalence exists between the traditional terms "literal" vs. "free" translation and the terms "foreignization" vs. "domestication" as used by Venuti and others. In addition, the results of the investigation suggest that "foreignization"/"domestication" is probably best not seen as an equipollent dichotomy, but rather as a privative opposition between *marked* "foreignization" and *unmarked* "domestication". However, this conclusion must at the present stage of the discussion be limited to the concepts "foreignization" and "domestication" and their use as labels for *translation techniques* according to the terminology proposed by Molina / Hurtado Albir (2002). They define translation techniques "as procedures to analyse and classify how translation equivalence works" and stress that such techniques are classified "by comparison with the original" and that they affect "micro-units of text" (Molina / Hurtado Albir 2002: 509). The question of the relationship between these "translation techniques" and the characterization of the Russian target texts of *Alice's Adventures in Wonderland* as "foreignized" or "domesticated" on the *textual* level is not possible to answer solely on the basis of the present analysis. The answer to this question would need to be informed not only by a detailed analysis of other "micro-units" that can be characterized as "foreign" or "domestic", but also through the consideration of the untypical character of the *Alice* text and the important distinctions between literary and non-literary texts, different source and target audiences, and individual and collective translation norms.

References

A. Source text and translations studied

1. Source text of *Alice's Adventures in Wonderland*
Carroll 2001 – Carroll, Lewis. *The Annotated Alice. Alice's Adventures in Wonderland and Through the Looking-Glass*. With an introduction and notes by Martin Gardner. London: Penguin.

2. Translations of *Alice's Adventures in Wonderland* studied
Anon. (1879) = *Sonja v carstve diva* (anonymous translation into Russian). Moskva: Mamontov.
Bossi, Elda (2007 [1963]) = Carroll, Lewis: *Alice nel paese delle meraviglie*. Translated into Italian by Elda Bossi. Firenze & Milano: Giunti.
Bué, Henri (1869) = Carroll, Lewis: *Aventures d'Alice au pays des merveilles* (translated into French by Henri Bué). London: Macmillan. Available at: http://www.rarebookroom.org/Control/freali/. Visited 10 November 2011.
Ceni, Alessandro (2003) = Carroll, Lewis: *Le avventure di Alice nel paese delle Meraviglie e Al di là dello Specchio*. Translated into Italian by Alessandro Ceni. Torino: Einaudi.

Demurova, N. (1991 [1967]) = Kèrroll, L'juis. *Alisa v strane čudes. Skvoz' zerkalo i čto tam uvidela Alisa, ili Alisa v zazerkal'e*. Translated into Russian by N. M. Demurova. Moskva: Nauka, 1991. Available at: http://lib.ru/CARROLL/carroll_1.txt. Visited 10 November 2011.

Frenkel (2006 [1923]) = Frenkel', A. (2006 [1923]): Kèrroll, L'juis. *Alisa v strane čudes*. Translated into Russian by A. D'Aktil' [A. A. Frenkel']. Moskva: OLMA Media Grupp.

Granstrem, M. (1908) = Kèrroll, L'juis. *Priključenija Ani v "mirě čudes"*. Translated into Russian by M. Granstrem. Sankt-Peterburg: Granstrem.

Hopp, Zinken (2010 [1979]) = Carroll, Lewis: *Alice i Eventyrland*. Translated into Norwegian by Zinken Hopp. Oslo: Aschehoug.

Jakhnin (2002 [1991]) = Jahnin (2002 [1991]): Kèrroll, L'juis. *Priključenija Alisy v Strane Čudes*. Translated into Russian by L. L. Jakhnin. Moskva: EKSMO-Press.

Karau, Jörg (2008) = Carroll, Lewis: *Alices Abenteuer im Wunderland. Hinter dem Spiegel und was Alice dort fand*. Translated into German by Jörg Karau. Available at: http://www.joergkarau-texte.de/PDF/Alices%20Abenteuer%20im%20Wunderland.pdf. Visited 10 November 2011.

Kononenko, A. (2000) = Kèrroll, L'juis. *Alisa v Strane Čudes*. Translated into Russian by A. Kononenko, 1998–2000. Available at: http://www.lib.ru/CARROLL/alisa_kononenko.txt. Visited 10 November 2011.

Kornijenka, Valentyna (2001) = Kerrol, L'jujis: *Alisa v Krajini Čudes*. Translated into Ukrainian by Valentyna Kornijenka. Available at: http://www.ae-lib.org.ua/texts/carroll_alices_adventures_in_wonderland_ua.htm. Visited 10 November 2011.

Kunnas, Kirsi / Manner, Eeva-Liisa (1972) = Carroll, Lewis: *Liisan seikkailut ihmemaassa*. Translated into Finnish by Kirsi Kunnas & Eeva-Liisa Manner. Jyväskylä: Gummerus.

Lundin, Harry (2005 [1977]) = Carroll, Lewis: *Alice i Underlandet. Spegellandet*. Translated into Swedish by Harry Lundin. Stockholm: En bok för alla.

Nabokov, V. (1976 [1923]) = Kèrroll, L'juis. *Anja v strane čudes*. Translated into Russian by V. Sirin [V. V. Nabokov]. New York: Dover.

Oryol (1988) = Orël, V. (1988): Kèrroll, L'juis. *Alisa v strane čudes*. Translated into Russian by V. E. Oryol. Moskva: Detskaja literatura.

Papy, Jacques (2005 [1961]) = Carroll, Lewis: *Les Aventures d'Alice au pays des merveilles*. Translated into French by Jacques Papy. Paris: Gallimard.

Parisot, Henri (1979 [1968]) = Carroll, Lewis: *Tout Alice*. Translated into French by Henri Parisot. Paris: GF Flammarion.

Pietrocòla-Rossetti, Teodorico (1872) = Carroll, Lewis: *Le avventure d'Alice nel paese delle meraviglie*. Translated into Italian by Teodorico Pietrocòla-Rossetti. London: MacMillan. Available at: http://www.rarebookroom.org/Control/itaali/. Visited 10 November 2011.

Reedijk, Cornelis / Kossmann, Alfred (1948) = Carroll, Lewis: *De avonturen van Alice in het wonderland*. Translated into Dutch by Cornelis Reedijk & Alfred Kossmann. Available through the *Amsterdam Slavic Parallel Aligned Corpus*, see http://home.medewerker.uva.nl/a.a.barentsen/page3.html.

Runeberg, Nino (1921) = Carroll, Lewis: *Alices äventyr i Underlandet.* Translated into Swedish by Nino Runeberg. Helsingfors: Schildt.

Runnquist, Åke (2000 [1966]) = Carroll, Lewis: *Alice i Underlandet.* Translated into Swedish by Åke Runnquist. Stockholm: Bonnier Carlsen.

Shcherbakov (1977) = Ščerbakov, A. (1977): Kèrroll, L'juis. *Priključenija Alisy v Strane Čudes. Zazerkal'e (pro to, čto tam uvidela Alisa).* Translated into Russian by A. A. Shcherbakov. Moskva: Hudožestvennaja literatura.

Selivyorstova (2010) = Selivërstova, D. (2010): Kèrroll, L'juis. *Alisa v Strane Čudes.* Translated into Russian by D. Selivyorstova. Moskva: Eksmo.

Skoumal, Aloys / Skoumalová, Hana (2000 [1961]) = Carroll, Lewis: *Alenka v kraji divů a za zrcadlem.* Translated into Czech by Aloys Skoumal and Hana Skoumalová. Praha: Academia.

Zakhoder (2007 [1971–1972]) = Zahoder, B. (2007 [1971–1972]): Kèrroll, L'juis. *Alisa v strane čudes.* Translated into Russian by B. V. Zakhoder. Moskva: Machaon.

Zhao, Yuanren (2000 [1922]) = Luyisi Kailuo: *Ailisi manyou qijing.* Ttranslated into Chinese by Zhao Yuanren [Yuen-Ren Chao]. Taibei: Jingdian chuanxun wenhua.

B. Secondary sources

Ambrosiani, Per (2010): "A Russian Tail? On the Translation of Puns in Lewis Carroll's *Alice's Adventures in Wonderland.*" In: Bengtsson, Anders / Hancock, Victorine [eds.] (2010): *Humour in Language. Textual and Linguistic Aspects* (= Stockholm Studies in Modern Philology. 15). Stockholm: Acta Universitatis Stockholmiensis. 30–63.

Cammarata, Adele (2007): *"La Gran natica dell'Aringa." I giochi di parole in* Alice's Adventures in Wonderland. *Traduzioni italiane a confronto.* 2 ed. @dic & Lulu.com. Available at: http://www.lulu.com/product/download/la-gran-natica-dellaringa---i-giochi-di-parole-in-alices-adventures-in-wonderland---traduzioni-italiane-a-confronto/677902. Visited 20 August 2009.

Connolly, Julian W. (1995): "Ania v strane chudes." In: Alexandrov, Vladimir E. [ed.] (1995): *The Garland Companion to Vladimir Nabokov.* New York: Garland. 18–25.

Delabastita, Dirk (2010): "Language, Comedy and Translation in the BBC Sitcom *'Allo 'Allo!*" In: Chiaro, Delia [ed.] (2010): *Translation, Humour and the Media,* vol. 2. London: Continuum. 193–221.

Evenepoel, Steefan / Van Poucke, Piet (2009): "Waar eindigt dat? Over cultuurspecifieke referenties en literair vertalen." In: Hinderdael, Michaël / Jooken, Lieve / Verstraete, Heili [eds.] (2009): *De aard heeft kamers genoeg. Hoe vertalers omgaan met culturele identiteit in het werk van Erwin Mortier.* Antwerpen – Apeldorn: Garant. 83–100.

Feng, Zongxin (2009): "Translation and Reconstruction of a Wonderland: *Alice's Adventures* in China." In: *Neohelicon* 36 (1), 237–251.

Horton, David (2002): "Describing Intercultural Transfer in Literary Translation: Alice in 'Wunderland'." In: Thome, Gisela / Giehl, Claudia / Gerzymisch-Arbogast, Heidrun [eds.] (2002): *Kultur und Übersetzung: Methodologische Probleme des Kulturtransfers*. Tübingen: Narr. 95–113.

Kibbee, Douglas A. (2003): "When Children's Literature Transcends its Genre: Translating Alice in Wonderland." In: *Meta* 48 (1–2), 307–321. Available at: http://www.erudit.org/revue/meta/2003/v48/n1/006977ar.pdf. Visited 10 November 2011.

Levý, Jiří (1969): *Die literarische Übersetzung. Theorie einer Kunstgattung*. Frankfurt am Main & Bonn: Athenäum.

Molina, Lucía / Hurtado Albir, Amparo (2002): "Translation Techniques Revisited: A Dynamic and Functionalist Approach." In: *Meta* 47 (4), 498–512. Available at: http://www.erudit.org/revue/meta/2002/v47/n4/008033ar.pdf. Visited 10 November 2011.

Nord, Christiane (1994): "It's Tea-Time in Wonderland: 'Culture-Markers' in Fictional Texts." In: Pürschel, Heiner *et al*. [eds.] (1994): *Intercultural Communication*. Frankfurt: Peter Lang. 523–538.

—— (1997): *Translating as a Purposeful Activity. Functionalist Approaches Explained*. Manchester: St. Jerome.

—— (2003): "Proper Names in Translations for Children: Alice in Wonderland as a Case in Point." In: *Meta* 48 (1–2), 182–196. Available at: http://www.erudit.org/revue/meta/2003/v48/n1/006966ar.pdf. Visited 2 August 2009.

Parker, Fan (1994): *Lewis Carroll in Russia: Translations of* Alice in Wonderland *1879–1989*. New York.

Pym, Anthony (1995): "Schleiermacher and the Problem of *Blendlinge*." In: *Translation and Literature* 4 (1), 5–30. Available at: http://usuaris.tinet.cat/apym/on-line/intercultures/blendlinge.pdf. Visited 10 November 2011.

Rushaylo, A. M. (1991) = Rušajlo, A. M. (1991): "Jubilej "Alisy v strane čudes"." In: Kèrroll, L'juis. *Priključenija Alisy v strane čudes. Skvoz' zerkalo i čto tam uvidela Alisa, ili Alisa v zazerkal'e*. Moskva: Nauka. Available at: http://lib.ru/CARROLL/carrol0_12.txt. Visited 10 November 2011.

Sdobnikov, V. V. / Petrova, O. V. (2006): *Teorija perevoda*. Moskva: Vostok Zapad.

Sternberg, Meir (1981): "Polylingualism as Reality and Translation as Mimesis". In: *Poetics Today* 2 (4), 221–239. Available at: http://www.jstor.org/stable/1772500. Visited 10 November 2011.

Venuti, Lawrence (1995): *The Translator's Invisibility. A History of Translation*. London and New York: Routledge.

Vid, Natalia (2008): "Domesticated Translation: The Case of Nabokov's Translation of *Alice's Adventures in Wonderland*." In: *NOJ / NOŽ: Nabokov Online Journal* 2. Available at: http://etc.dal.ca/noj/articles/volume2/08_Vid.pdf. Visited 10 November 2011.

Weaver, Warren (1964): *Alice in Many Tongues: The Translations of Alice in Wonderland*. Madison, Wisconsin: University of Wisconsin Press.

Yang, Wenfen (2010): "Brief Study on Domestication and Foreignisation in Translation." In: *Journal of Language Teaching and Research* 1 (1), 77–80.

Money flows into windows and doors or *Money flows like a river*? Identifying Translation Strategies by the Yardstick of Metaphorical Creativity

Alexandra Belikova
University of Eastern Finland, Joensuu

Abstract

This article seeks to improve existing approaches to the quantitative analysis of the degree of metaphorical creativity of journalistic texts, first used by political scientists and linguists to monitor political discourse, and also seeks to implement a new approach to the study of original and translated texts in the theoretical context of Lawrence Venuti's ideas of the two types of translation – foreignising and domesticising. The measurement of metaphorical conventionality/creativity of the source and the target texts is based on a technique entailing a set of objectively established features, and referring mainly to external sources (dictionaries, corpora) and to a minor extent based on the intuition and subjective language competence of the researcher.

It is assumed that there is a certain relation between the level of metaphorical conventionality/creativity and the strategy chosen by the translator. In particular, higher levels of the translation's metaphorical creativity than those of the original are an indicator of a foreignising strategy, and vice versa, maintaining or decreasing the degree of metaphorical creativity in translation indicates a domesticising adaptation of the metaphorical structure of the original text to the norms of the host culture, and a neutralisation of means of expression unusual for the recipient.

Based on the material of several articles from Finnish newspapers and their translations on the InoSMI website, which specialises in the translation of foreign publications about Russia, the proposed method is piloted to provide grounds for preliminary conclusions about the relation between the parameter described and the chosen translation strategy.

1 General provisions

Translation is an activity that incorporates an internal contradiction between the desire to maximise the accuracy in reproducing the form and the content of the original and a tendency to adapt the original to the needs, capacities, norms, language and culture of the recipient. Both general strategies – foreignisation and domestication – are used by translators to a greater or lesser extent, while translations resemble peculiar mosaic structures, which to varying extents incorporate both foreignising and domesticising solutions. It is unlikely that any translation is able to satisfy the requirements of the two systems simultaneously, and, as a rule, a translation exists as a kind of compromise between loyalty and infidelity to the original, the adoption and rejection of the text by a new reader, and a greater or lesser compliance with the rules of the target language. If foreignisation dominates, the translation is easily identified as such and is somehow different from original texts. If domestication is the dominant strategy, the translated text linguistically and by a number of other parameters does not stand out from the texts originally created in the language of the target culture.

2 General hypothesis and research problems

Translating from a minor language into a major one like English is mainly characterised by domestication – a large-scale adaptation of the text to the norms of the target culture, an elimination of foreign features, a neutralisation of "strange" forms of expression and translation and, generally, the translation becoming dissolved into a mass of original texts to the point of indistinguishability (Venuti 1995).

In this theoretical context, there is a serious methodological problem of how to operationalise abstract notions of foreignisation and domestication – the problem of how to transform the general idea into methodologically sound tools for the analysis of specific material. The present study attempts to give an operational meaning to the concepts of foreignisation and domestication used in the translation of metaphorical expressions.

The main hypothesis of the study is as follows: the translation of social and political metaphors from the Finnish language (minor) into Russian (major) is dominated by the domesticating strategy. Metaphors appear to be vulnerable objects, difficult or impossible to translate in terms of keeping a balance between the literal rendering of the metaphor and its image component. In translation, a metaphorical expression often retains its meaning, but loses its original image, or it keeps the original image, but loses part of its actual meaning. Preservation of both components of a metaphorical expression is difficult, and in a particular translation, one of the strategies usually prevails.

Verification of this hypothesis can be carried out at different levels, for example as a qualitative analysis of individual translation solutions, placing them on a tentative scale of domestication–foreignisation, but this paper focuses on a macro-level analysis, domestication–foreignisation ratio analysis and the overall level of metaphorical conventionality/creativity of the original text and the translation.

Each metaphorical expression can be ranked on the scale of conventionality/creativity, depending on how well entrenched in a language a metaphorical expression is; in other words, is it frequent or rare, are there dictionary entries or corpus hits representing this metaphor? The less frequent a metaphorical expression is and the more vivid and uncommon image it contains, the higher it ranks on the scale of creativity.

The level of metaphorical creativity of a single text reflects the ratio of different types of metaphors – from the dead to the creative ones – to their total. We proceed from the assumption that the maintenance or reduction of metaphorical creativity level in translation is a sign of a domesticising strategy, and an increase in metaphorical creativity in translation as compared to the original is a symptom of foreignisation.

Achieving the stated objective is possible with the following tasks:

a) developing an algorithm-based methodology to measure metaphorical conventionality/creativity by means of procedures presumably free from subjective intuition-based criteria;

b) analysing the metaphorical creativity in a body of original and translated texts on the basis of the method of calculating the level of metaphorical conventionality/creativity in political discourse.

3 Data

The research is based on newspaper and magazine articles in the Finnish language from the period 2005–2007 and their Russian translations made by well-qualified translators and published on the website www.inosmi.ru. InoSMI specialises in the translation of foreign articles on the problems of Russia, its domestic and foreign policy and its economy. Although the translations are predominantly from English, German and Spanish language sources, the editors do not overlook the publication of translations from other languages either.

The present study was carried out on the material of twenty articles from ten different sources: the newspapers *Helsingin Sanomat, Ilkka, Kaleva, Keskisuomalainen, Pohjalainen, Suomenmaa, Tiedonantaja, Turun Sanomat, Viikko-Eteenpäin* and the magazine *Suomen Kuvalehti* and their translations. The total size of the original texts was 10 075 word forms, and of the translated texts 14 830 word forms.

Measuring metaphorical expressins with the yardstick of creativity proposed here implies systematic use of dictionaries and corpora for both Russian and Finnish. The comparative reference corpora included the RNC (Russian National Corpus), in particular its newspaper subcorpus of more than 113 million word forms (http://ruscorpora.ru), and the Finnish-language newspaper subcorpus of the Language Bank, belonging to the Centre for Scientific Computing, Helsinki – Tieteen tietotekniikan keskuksen Kielipankki (http://www.csc.fi), which amounts to more than 131 million word forms. The analysis also involved original dictionaries, Russian (DMRL 2008; OSh 2007) and Finnish (KTS 2007; GUMM 1998), comparable in scope and time of publication.

4 Research method

The key concept of the metaphor in our study is viewed from the standpoint of conceptual metaphor theory, which determines its role as a cognitive tool that allows you to understand and structure one domain of reality in terms of another. In other words, the metaphor is a result of an interaction between two different structures of knowledge – the cognitive structure of the source and the cognitive structure of the target (Baranov 2003a), otherwise known as metaphorical projection or cognitive mapping. At the same time, specific ways of metaphorical mapping in different languages can either coincide or differ dramatically, depending not only on the universal human experience, but also on the national culture and the creative personality of a native speaker. Actual implementation of these differences is reflected in specific linguistic expressions, which we call metaphorical. The scheme of interaction between the cognitive source and target domains will be hereinafter referred to as a *metaphor*, and its linguistic expression – as a *metaphorical expression* (hereinafter – ME).

The evaluation of the metaphorical conventionality/creativity of the original and the translated text involves the following procedures:

• sampling of metaphorical expressions in the texts through the identification of metaphors methodology developed by a team of researchers led by J. Steen (Pragglejaz Group 2007; Steen *et al.* 2010);

• classification of MEs by a method for determining the degree of conventionality/creativity;

• evaluation of the metaphorical creativity of the original text and its translation in general, according to the De Landtsheer–Baranov's formula (De Landtsheer 1998; Baranov 2003b).

4.1 Retrieval of metaphorical expressions

When searching for metaphors we attempted to avoid reliance on the intuitions of the researchers and implement the Metaphor Identification Procedure (Pragglejaz Group 2007; Steen *et al.* 2010), a method of ME identification based on a careful word-by-word analysis of existing texts and a systematic comparison of their actual (contextual) and basic (dictionary entry) meanings. For this purpose, data from dictionaries of both languages were extracted.

The identification procedure was carried out as follows: a contextual meaning of each word or expression was defined and compared with the basic meaning in the dictionary. If the contextual meaning of the lexical unit or expression in the analysed text did not coincide with its basic one, it was considered a metaphorical expression. Metaphorical meaning may or may not be fixed in a dictionary as one of the secondary meanings of the word.

4.2 Classification of metaphorical expressions on the degree of conventionality/creativity

The idea of classifying metaphors on the degree of preservation of the original image is almost as old as the study of metaphors itself, so only a few papers do not mention the varying degrees of conventionality/creativity of metaphors and how they are divided into dead, sleeping, conventional and so on. However, since "Traité de stylistique française" by Charles Bally (1951 [1909]), these classifications have been based primarily on the researcher's intuition, and it wasn't until recent years that studies started to show a commitment to the development of a verifiable empirical way to assess the conventionality/creativity of metaphors (Steen *et al.* 2010; Pragglejaz Group 2007; Deignan 2005).

One of the tentative results of our research is the development an algorithmised model for determining the degree of conventionality/creativity of an ME based on binary logic, so that the analysis of materials with the help of this scheme involves minimal use of intuitive and introspective assessments. Preference is given to objective empirical methods of testing, such as referring to a corpus or a dictionary. The key works for the development of the algorithm were monographs (Goatly 1997; Deignan 2005; Kövecses 2000; Dobrovol'skij / Piirainen 2005).

A ready-made scheme appears as follows (Figure 1). A step by step procedure for assessing the conventionality/creativity of metaphorical expressions is described in detail in (Belikova 2012). In the course of classification, every ME found in ST and TT was firstly checked with explanatory dictionaries and, secondly, in case there were no suitable entries, it was searched for in existing corpora of Russian and Finnish.

Since the procedure for assessing the degree of conventionality/creativity of MEs according to the proposed scheme is quite time-consuming, it only makes it possible to process relatively short texts in which the number of MEs is not in the hundreds. For processing more extensive texts we used a simplified assessment of the conventionality/creativity of MEs with fewer taxa (Figure 2). Whenever a more sophisticated analysis was needed for any given ME an extended scheme was used (Figure 1).

Figure 1. Algorithm for estimating the degree of metaphorical expressions in terms of conventionality/creativity.

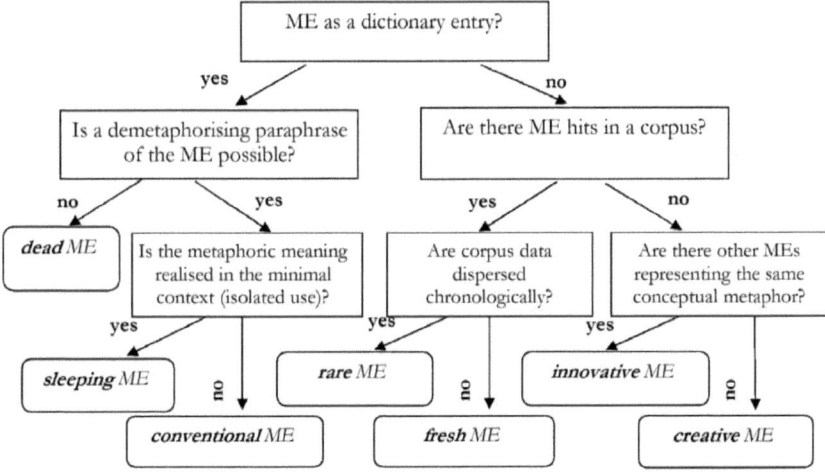

With the help of Figure 2, metaphorical expressions from twenty original articles and their translations were divided into five groups according to their level of conventionality/creativity: *dead, sleeping, conventional, irregular* and *unique*. Dead MEs were incorporated into the overall statistics only if in the parallel text they corresponded to a different ME with a higher creativity: sleeping, conventional, irregular or unique.

Figure 2. A simplified algorithm for estimating the degree of metaphorical expressions in terms of conventionality/creativity.

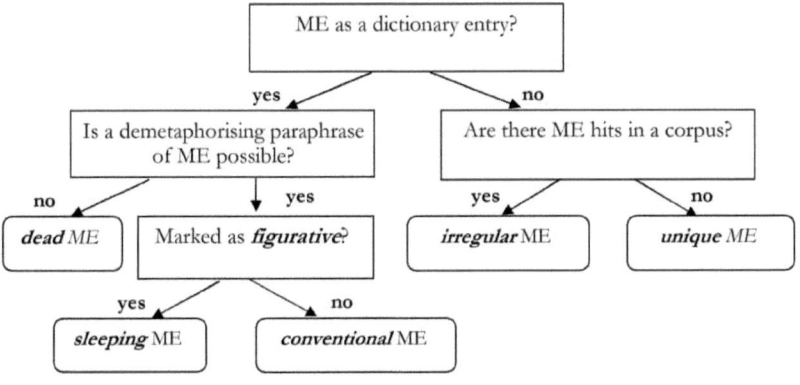

4.3 Establishing the metaphorical conventionality/creativity of the original text and translation

The calculation of the metaphorical creativity indicator (C) of the original text (hereinafter – ST) and that of its translation (hereinafter – TT) is performed according to the De Landtsheer–Baranov formula, used in works on metaphors in political discourse for a quantitative support of the hypothesis that creativity parameters of MEs in political discourse are linked to social and political crises (De Landtsheer 1998; Baranov 2003b). As adapted[1] for this study, the formula is as follows:

$$C = \frac{1*s + 2*k + 3*n + 4*u}{t}$$

where **s** is the number of sleeping MEs, **k** – conventional, **n** – irregular, **u** – unique, **t** – the total number of MEs in the text. **1, 2, 3** and **4** – coefficients of metaphorical conventionality/creativity, a specific value of which depends on the creativity of each group of MEs. The least creative (sleeping) MEs in the formula are of coefficient 1, and the most creative (unique) MEs are of coefficient 4 respectively. A very important disadvantage of the De Landtsheer–Baranov formula is that the criteria by which researchers divided MEs into groups are not stated, as in (Baranov 2003b: 2; Vertessen / De Landtsheer 2005: 13). Due to this fact, the use of the proposed formula in our study proved to be difficult, which, in fact, led to the need to develop our own criteria for assessing the degree of conventionality/creativity of MEs and to create a new classification (see section 4.2 and Belikova 2012).

---

[1] In the adapted formula, the number of terms constituting the numerator increased from three to four, according to the number of the selected taxa. In some studies (De Landtsheer 1998; Vertessen / De Landtsheer 2005), metaphorical expressions in terms of conventionality/creativity are divided into three groups: weak, normal and original/strong. In another study (Baranov 2003b) they are divided into erased, conventional and creative, and the formula for calculating the creativity of the text has the form of C (or I) = (1w+2n+3s)/ t, where **w, n, s** are corresponding types of MEs, and **t** is the total number of MEs in the text. In this paper, the MEs were divided into five groups (dead, sleeping, conventional, irregular and unique), but as the dead ME's creativity was appropriated by the coefficient of 0, the corresponding term in the numerator of the formula was omitted as not affecting the total value of the numerator.

The De Landtsheer–Baranov formula allows one to compare the metaphorical creativity of the original text and that of the translation, and to define the strategy at the level of the whole text. Enhancing metaphoric creativity in translation may be an indication of the translator using expressions for the most part close to the image of the original ME, but less frequent, less recognisable or even completely unknown in the target language. Conversely, a lower creativity level in translation indicates the translator's desire to use expressions that would not stand out from the overall context of the host culture as unusual, and would preserve the original level of ME conventionality/creativity, which often involves replacing the original image with one more common and widespread in the host culture. On this basis, we make an assumption about the connection between the parameter of the metaphorical creativity of the text and translation strategies: enhancing creativity in translation is a sign of a foreignising strategy in the translation, reducing creativity is a sign of a domesticating strategy.

5 Main findings

5.1 The quantitative ratio of metaphorical expressions in the original texts and translations

The calculations revealed that the total number of MEs in the ST and the TT is approximately equal: in the Finnish part – 466, in the Russian part – 457. The data on the absolute number of MEs, distributed according to the degree of their conventionality/creativity in accordance with the proposed model (see section 4.2, Figure 2) are shown in Table 1. Table 2 shows the same data in percentage terms.

Table 1 and Table 2 show that sleeping and conventional MEs predominate in both texts, their total accounting for 94 % of the original text, and 83 % in the translation of each text, respectively.

Table 1. Distribution of metaphorical expressions according to the degree of conventionality/creativity in the ST and TT (absolute ratio).

ME type	ST fin	TT rus
dead	12	31
sleeping	135	177
conventional	284	200
irregular	11	29
unique	4	20
TOTAL	446	457

Table 2. Distribution of metaphorical expressions according to the degree of conventionality/creativity in ST and TT (percentage).

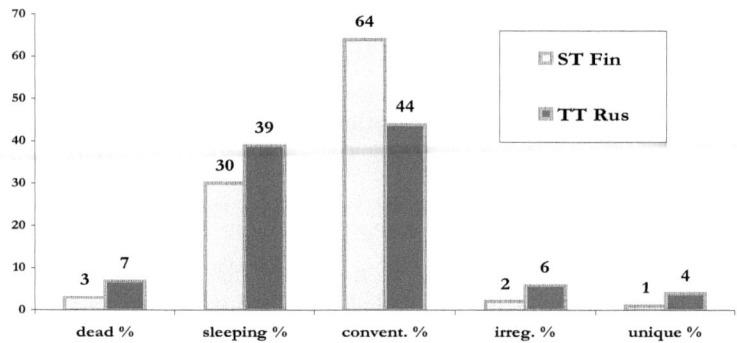

At the same time, the ratio of these two groups of MEs within the ST and TT is quite different. In the original Finnish text, the number of conventional MEs is more than double the number of sleeping MEs (64 % conventional and 30 % sleeping), whereas in translation they differ by an insignificant 5 percentage points (44 % conventional and 39 % sleeping MEs).

Thus, these data indicate that the translation from Finnish into Russian was accompanied by quite a noticeable quantitative redistribution within the two groups of metaphorical expressions: the number of sleeping metaphors increases (by 9 percentage points), the number of conventional ones is reduced (by 20 percentage points). Since in terms of creativity conventional MEs occupy a higher position than sleeping MEs, and their share of the total number of MEs in the translation is reduced, one may suggest that the level of metaphorical conventionality/creativity of the text as a whole is also reduced, which is also confirmed by the data obtained with the help of the formula for calculating the metaphorical creativity of the text.

5.2 The level of metaphorical conventionality/creativity of ST and TT

The quantitative data obtained from the sampling and classification of MEs are processed with the aid of the De Landtsheer–Baranov formula, which allows one to determine the coefficient of metaphorical conventionality/creativity of the text (see section 4.3), separately for original texts (C_{ST}) and translations (C_{TT}):

$$C_{ST} = \frac{1*135+2*284+3*11+4*4}{446} = 1.6861$$

$$C_{TT} = \frac{1*177+2*200+3*29+4*20}{457} = 1.6280$$

A decrease in the coefficient indicates a decline in the metaphorical creativity in translation, which can be considered an indirect proof of the initial assumptions concerning the removal of foreign features and a neutralisation of "strange" forms when translating from a minor language into a major one.

However, in this case claiming domestication to be a dominant strategy when translating from Finnish into Russian seems somewhat premature, since the described approach takes only one parameter into consideration – the level of conventionality/creativity of MEs. This approach does not account for the second, equally important component of the ME, namely the degree of preservation of the original metaphorical image in translation.

6 The image component of the ME in translation

How does the translator act, when faced with different ways of metaphorical mapping in SL and TL? To what extent is s/he free to choose how to translate a metaphor?

A translator has a different degree of freedom in deciding on a solution when reproducing different types of MEs in the translation. In particular, while dealing with dead metaphors as well as original metaphors the translator is left with practically no choice. A dead metaphor makes the translator use an established equivalent, whose image component is often different from the original: Fi. *kupin korva* (literally: ear of the cup) – Rus. *ручка чашки* (literally: handle of the cup); Rus. *игольное ушко* (literally: ear of the needle) – Fi. *neulansilmä* (literally: eye of the needle), Fi. *äly tulee iltajunassa* (literally: understanding comes on the night train) – Rus. *задним умом крепок* (literally: strong with one's hind mind). Creative MEs bearing a seal of the author's personality and based on the metaphorical system of the source language are rendered literally, since a different solution, i.e. the rejection of the unique original image exceeds the limits of translation and is regarded as a breach of translation ethics. This example of one of Tatyana Tolstaya's short stories translated into Finnish and English shows how closely the translator follows the author's creative image:

Rus. *Всего-то и было: Крым, тринадцатый год,* **полосатое солнце** *сквозь жалюзи* **распиливает на брусочки** *белый выскобленный пол...* (Т. Толстая. Милая Шура)

Fi. *Kaikkea sitä olikin: Krim, vuosi kolmetoista,* **raidakas aurinko pilkkoi säleiksi** *valkoiseksi hangatun lattian...* (Tolstaja 1989: 37; transl. by Marja Koskinen)

Eng. *It was so brief: the Crimea, 1913,* **the striped sun** *shining through the blinds* **sawing** *the white scraped* **floor into sections**... (Tolstaya 1990: 37; transl. by Antonina W. Bouis)

As a result, the real space of translation choice is a rich intermediate zone of sleeping, conventional and perhaps irregular MEs which are stable and preserve the duality of perception of the metaphorical image. For example, the expression that appeared in the Finnish newspaper Helsingin Sanomat **Rahaa virtaa** *Äiti Venäjälle* **ikkunoista ja ovista** (Helsingin Sanomat 03.09.2006, Itsevarmuus palasi Kremliin) is translated literally by the InoSMI translator: *Поток денег в Россию-матушку, да такой, что* **они текут в окна и в двери** 'A cashflow into Mother Russia so intense that **money flows into windows and doors**' (www.inosmi.ru/inrussia/ 20060905/229738.html), although to describe the intensity of cashflow into the state treasury one could have used a more conventional Russian expression **Деньги текут рекой** 'Money flows like a river'. What is the difference between these two translation solutions? When replacing the original Finnish image of money *flowing through windows and doors* with an image more familiar to Russian readers *flows like a river,* the translation maintains the same level of ME creativity as that of the original, because the Finnish *virrata ikkunoista ja ovista* 'to flow through windows and doors' and the Russian *течь рекой* 'to flow like a river' are marked by the dictionaries as **figurative** and therefore are conventional. If the translator's choice is in favor of preserving the original image, as is done on the InoSMI website, the level of ME creativity in the translation increases sharply. The original conventional ME becomes unique in the translation, and as a result the new reader's attention will be attracted by an expression which is unusual in Russian political discourse. Perhaps it is the effect of awakening the reader's attention that the translator anticipates when resorting to a foreignising strategy.

Naturally, the translator can remove the metaphor completely, for example by using a demetaphorising explication (paraphrasing) or by totally eliminating the ME. However, if the metaphor is preserved in the translation (there are 341 examples of a metaphor translated as a metaphor in our study), the translation solutions can be divided into six types. The classifying features of these types are: preservation of the original image ($I_{SM}=I_{TM}$) or its alteration ($I_{SM} \neq I_{TM}$), and maintaining the level of conventionality/creativity of the original ME ($C_{SM}=C_{TM}$), or its reduction ($C_{SM}>C_{TM}$) or its increase ($C_{SM}<C_{TM}$) (see Table 3).

Table 3. Translation solutions of ME (I – image, C – creativity of metaphorical expression, SM – source metaphorical expression, TM – target metaphorical expression).

1.	$I_{SM}=I_{TM}$ $C_{SM}=C_{TM}$	4.	$I_{SM} \neq I_{TM}$ $C_{SM}=C_{TM}$
2.	$I_{SM}=I_{TM}$ $C_{SM}>C_{TM}$	5.	$I_{SM} \neq I_{TM}$ $C_{SM}>C_{TM}$
3.	$I_{SM}=I_{TM}$ $C_{SM}<C_{TM}$	6.	$I_{SM} \neq I_{TM}$ $C_{SM}<C_{TM}$

These six types of translation are illustrated below on the foreignisation–domestication scale from foreignising to domesticating.

1. Foreignising translation: I=I, C<C. When saving the image component, the metaphorical expression in the translation is more creative and less familiar to the recipient.

(1a) *Jeltsinin suosikin Vladimir Putinin tultua valituksi Venäjän presidentiksi vuonna 2000 Kwasniewski alkoi johdonmukaisesti* **lämmittää** *Puolan ja Venäjän* **kanssakäymistä** *ja onnistuikin siinä alussa, joskin vain pikkuaskelin.* (Ilkka, 17.7.2005)
Literally: After Boris Yeltsin's favorite Vladimir Putin was elected Russian president in 2000, Kwasniewski began to consistently **warm up the relationship** of Poland and Russia and he succeeded at first, though only very gradually. (conventional ME)

(1b) *После избрания главой государства «назначенца» Ельцина – Владимира Путина, ставшего президентом России в 2000 году, Квасьневский начал* **разогревать связи** *между Польшей и Россией и достиг на первом этапе определенных успехов, хоть и небольших.* (InoSMI)
Literally: After Yeltsin's "appointee" Vladimir Putin was elected head of state and became Russian president in 2000, Kwasniewski began to **warm up the connections** between Poland and Russia, and achieved some success to begin with, albeit slight. (unique ME)

Figurative meaning of the verb *lämmittää* 'warm up' can be found in KTS and GUMM as a separate unit with a respective label; thus, this word in the context should be considered as a conventional ME, while Russian *разогревать* 'warm up' in (1b) does not have such an established figurative meaning reflected in a dictionary, and neither in RNC. The latter ME is unique in our terms, and consequently the creativity level of the unit is sufficiently enhanced in the TT.

2. Balanced translation: I=I, C=C. The translation preserves the original image and the degree of conventionality/creativity of the original ME.

(2a) **Viha** *vähemmistöjä kohtaan on Venäjällä* **syvään juurtunut.** (Helsingin Sanomat, 9.9.2006)
Literally: **Hatred for minorities** in Russia is **deeply rooted.** (conventional ME).

(2b) **Ксенофобия** *в России* **пустила глубокие корни.** (InoSMI)
Literally: **Xenophobia** in Russia has **become deeply rooted** (conventional ME).

Finnish dictionaries explain secondary meaning of *juurtua* 'kehittää juuria / take root' as 'saada luja jalansija, iskostua, syöpyä / become firmly established, consolidated' (KTS) and label it as figurative. Similarly Russian expression *пустить корни* 'to take roots' has a figurative meaning very close to the Finnish counterpart 'become firmly established, take a firm position' (OSh). Both the image and the conventionality/creativity level are the same in ST and TT; hence, this type of translation may be marked as neutral and taking a middle position between foreignisation and domestication.

3. Loyal translation: I=I, C>C. It is distinguished by the preservation of the original image component and a decrease in the metaphorical conventionality/creativity in translation.

In (3b) noun phrase *Kwasniewskin synti* 'Kwasniewski's sin' is rendered verbatim as *грех Квасьневского* leaving the original image untouched on the grounds of similarity between Russian and Finnish from that point of view (cf. Finnish *maksaa vanhoja syntejään* 'pay for old sins' (GUMM) and Russian *грехи молодости* 'sins of youth', *вспомнить о грехах прошлого* 'remember of the sins of the past' (OSh). But despite the similarity of image planes, the level of conventionality/creativity of ME in Russian translation is one step lower than in the original, since the former is labeled in a dictionary as figurative while the latter is not; in other words, Finnish conventional ME is translated into Russian with the sleeping ME.

(3a) *Kwasniewskin **synti** Kremlin silmissä oli osallistua Ukrainan tulenaran yhteiskunnallis-poliittisen tilanteen laukaisemiseen ja tien raivaaminen oranssivallankumoukselle...* (Ilkka 17.7.2005)
Literally: Kwasniewski's **sin** in the eyes of the Kremlin is his involvement in taking the heat off the flammable socio-political situation in Ukraine and clearing the roads for the Orange Revolution... (conventional ME)

(3b) **Грех** *Квасьневского в глазах Кремля – его участие в разрешении опасного общественно-политического кризиса на Украине и поддержка победителей "оранжевой" революции.* (InoSMI)
Literally: Kwasniewski's **sin** in the eyes of the Kremlin is his participation in the resolution of a dangerous socio-political crisis in Ukraine and his support of the winners of the Orange Revolution... (sleeping ME)

This approach is somewhat closer to domestication than the balanced translation approach.

4. Creative translation: I≠I, C<C. The replacement of the image component is accompanied by an increase in the translated metaphor's creativity.

(4a) **Kaiken huipuksi** *Moskova lopetti jatkotutkimukset II: n maailmansodan aikana venäläisten murhaamien lähes 22 000 puolalaisen upseerin ja älymystön edustajan kohtaloista.* (Ilkka 17.7.2005)
Literally: The **pinnacle** was the fact that Moscow cut off further investigation of nearly 22 000 Polish officers and intellectuals killed by Russians during the Second World War. (conventional ME)

(4b) *В качестве* **жирной точки** *в процессе поиска исторической справедливости Россия прекратила изучение вопроса, касавшегося судеб погибших от рук русских (на территории СССР) в годы Второй мировой войны почти 22 000 польских офицеров и представителей интеллигенции.* (InoSMI)
Literally: As **a fat full stop** in search of historical justice Russia discontinued investigating the issue concerning the fate of almost 22,000 Polish officers and intellectuals killed by Russians (the USSR) during the Second World War. (irregular ME)

Finnish ME *kaiken huipuksi* 'as a peak of all', which is marked in a dictionary with a label "figurative", belongs to conventional ME, whereas ME *в качестве жирной точки* 'as a fat full stop' in Russian translation, having nothing in common with the initial Finnish image, is not reflected in a dictionary and can be found only in RNC; thus, it is an irregular one.

5. Conventionally domesticising translation: I≠I, C=C. Maintaining the degree of ME conventionality/creativity with replacing the image.

(5a) **Kiistat** *toisen maailmansodan asetelmien ja tapahtumien luonteesta* **kärjistyvät** *voiton päivän juhlien lähestyessä.* (Turun Sanomat 16.3.2005)
Literally: Disputes about the nature of the balance of forces and events become sharp as the Victory Day is approaching. (conventional ME)

(5b) **Споры** *о расстановке сил и характере событий в годы Второй мировой войны* **накаляются** *в связи с приближением празднования Дня Победы.* (InoSMI)
Literally: The **debate** on the balance of power and the nature of the events during the Second World War **is heating up** in connection with the forthcoming Victory Day. (conventional ME)

In Finnish, a metaphor DISAGREEMENTS ARE SHARP/POINTED OBJECTS is manifested, whereas the Russian translation represents a metaphor DISAGREEMENTS ARE HOT OBJECTS, but the level of conventionality/creativity of both expressions is the same as they are listed in respective dictionaries and furnished with tags *figurative* (cf. Fi. kärjistyä *kuv.* 'become critical' (GUMM) and Rus. накалиться *перен.* 'become very heated, tense' (OSh)).

6. Radically domesticising translation: I≠I, C>C. Reduction in the level of conventionality/creativity, accompanied by a replacement of the image component.

(6a) *... sellaiset* **aloitteet, joihin** *Putinin kaudella olisi voitu* **tarttua**, *ovat jääneet tekemättä.* (Suomen Kuvalehti N 30, 2005)
Literally: ... The **initiatives** to **grasp at** during Putin's period were not implemented. (conventional ME)

(6b) ...*те* **инициативы**, *которые были высказаны за последние пять лет в годы нахождения Путина у власти и* **поддержать** *которые было бы необходимо, "повисли в воздухе"*. (InoSMI)
Literally: ...the **initiatives** that were announced over the past five years of Putin's presidency instead of receiving **support** "hung in the air". (sleeping ME)

Finnish original figurative ME *tarttua aloitteisiin* 'grasp at initiatives', representing a metaphor OPPORTUNITY IS AN OPERATING ARM, belongs to the class of conventional ME and is labeled as figurative in the reference dictionary, whereas its Russian counterpart is a sleeping one and exploits a metaphor INITIATIVE IS A RICKETY CONSTRUCTION; thus, both aspects of the ST expression have been changed to make metaphor less prominent in the TT.

The quantitative data on the different types of metaphors are summarised in Table 4.

Table 4. The translated metaphorical expressions in terms of preservation of the original metaphorical image and the level of conventionality/creativity (ME – metaphorical expression, SM – source metaphorical expression, TM – target metaphorical expression, I – image, C – conventionality/creativity of metaphorical expression).

$ME_{ST} \rightarrow ME_{TT}$ 341 (100 %)			
$I_{SM}=I_{TM}$ 186 (55 %)		$I_{SM} \neq I_{TM}$ 155 (45 %)	
$C_{SM}=C_{TM}$	29 %	$C_{SM}=C_{TM}$	17 %
$C_{SM}>C_{TM}$	15 %	$C_{SM}>C_{TM}$	17 %
$C_{SM}<C_{TM}$	11 %	$C_{SM}<C_{TM}$	11 %

As can be seen from Table 4, the translators only manage to maintain the value of both parameters, the metaphorical image and the level of conventionality/creativity, in 29 % of cases. In all other cases the translator either alters the image component, or changes the degree of conventionality/creativity of the ME. If a balanced translation is not possible, translators clearly choose to reject the original image (45 % vs. 26 %).

An increased creativity of the target MEs occurs in 22 % of cases; more frequently, the degree of creativity remains unchanged (46 %) or decreases (32 %).

The data obtained suggest that, if a balanced translation is difficult, in most cases translators of InoSMI prefer to sacrifice the original imagery of the text rather than increase the degree of its strangeness.

7 Conclusion

When translating from Finnish into Russian, the metaphorical density (the number of MEs) in the text remains virtually unchanged (in the original texts – 446, in translation – 457), but the level of metaphorical conventionality/creativity in the translated newspaper text is somewhat reduced.

In terms of conventionality/creativity, the vast majority of MEs in both original texts and translations are sleeping and conventional (a total of 93 % in ST and 83 % in TT), but their proportions in ST and TT are different. In Finnish original texts the number of conventional MEs is twice the number of sleeping ones, whereas in the translation these groups of MEs are practically equal.

Reducing the metaphorical creativity in translation can be considered only as indirect evidence of domesticating strategies implemented when translating from Finnish into Russian, as this study does not allow us to answer the question of whether foreignising and domesticating strategies are directly related to the level of metaphorical creativity of the text. Nevertheless, this initial assumption revealed some approaches characterising how Russian translators deal with media discourse texts.

8 Discussion

The observations correspond to the question of what happens to the metaphor in translation rather than why these modifications take place or why the number of sleeping MEs increases and the number of conventional ones decreases, or whether this is a unique feature of translations from Finnish into Russian or a universal feature of any translated text.

In this paper, these observations were interpreted in the context of the theoretical dichotomy of foreignisation–domestication: the reduction of conventionality/creativity of metaphors in translation and the translator's omission of the original imagery in favor of maintaining or lowering the level of creativity are seen as indicators of the translator's conscious or unconscious strategy for erasing "uncomfortable" features of the original, neutralisation of the culturally unfamiliar, which is especially noticeable in the translation from minor to major languages. The proposed method of analysis and a listing of variations of metaphor translations emerge here as a tool to operationalise the concepts of domestication and foreignisation.

However, one can admit that a reduction of metaphorical conventionality/ creativity in translation can be explained by laws of a higher order, such as translation universals, for example, conventionalisation/normalisation of the target language or its simplification. In this case, the translation of metaphor can be an interesting way to verify these theoretical ideas, still insufficiently tested in empirical research. The outcome can also be affected by a number of random factors related to the restrictions of the analysed material, such as the influence of an individual style of translation or editorial policy. Perhaps further research similar to that proposed here, including the material of other languages, will confirm or refute this assumption.

References

Baranov, Anatoly (2003a): "Deskriptornaja teorija metafory i tipologija metaforičeskih modelej." Available at: http://www.dialog-21.ru/Archive/2003/Baranov.htm. Visited 25.09.2011.

—— (2003b): "Politicěskaja metaforika publicističeskogo teksta: vozmožnosti lingvističeskogo monitoringa." In: *Jazyk SMI kak ob"ekt meždisciplinarnogo issledovanija*. Moskva. Available at: http://evartist.narod.ru/text12/09.htm#3_12. Visited 20.9.2011.

Bally, Charles (1951 [1909]): *Traité de stylistique française*. Geneve: Georg.

Belikova, Alexandra (2012): "Operationaalinen lähestymistapa metaforailmausten konventionaalisuuden arvioinnissa." In: Kemppanen, Hannu / Mäkisalo, Jukka / Belikova, Alexandra [toim.] (2012): *Kotoista ja vierasta mediassa*. Venäjästä suomeksi ja suomesta venäjäksi -workshop Joensuussa 7.–8.10.2010. 28–43. (= Publications of the University of Eastern Finland. Reports and Studies in Education, Humanities, and Theology. 4).

De Landtsheer, Christ'l (1998): "The political rhetoric of a United Europe." In: Feldman, Ofer / De Landtsheer, Christ'l [eds.] (1998): *Politically speaking: a worldwide examination of language used in the public sphere*. New York. 129–146.

Deignan, Alice (2005): *Metaphor and Corpus Linguistics*. Amsterdam: John Benjamins.

Dobrovol'skij, Dmitrij / Piirainen, Elisabeth (2005): *Figurative Language: Cross-Cultural and Cross-linguistic Perspective*. Amsterdam: Elsevier.

Goatly, Andrew (1997): *The Language of Metaphor*. London: Routledge.

Kövecses, Zoltan (2002): *Metaphor. A Practical Introduction*. Oxford: Oxford University Press.

Pragglejaz Group (2007): MIP: A method for identifying metaphorically used words in discourse. In: *Metaphor and Symbol*, 22 (1), 1–39.

Steen, Gerard J. / Dorst, Aletta G. / Herrman, J. Berenike / Kaal, Anna A. / Krennmayr, Tina / Pasma, Trijntje (2010): *A Method for Linguistic Metaphor Identification*. Amsterdam: John Benjamins.

Venuti, Lawrence (1995): *The Translator's Invisibility. A History of Translation*. London: Routledge.

Vertessen, Dieter / De Landtsheer, Christ'l (2005): "A Metaphorical Election Style? Patterns of symbolic language use in Belgian politics." A paper presented in the *ECPR Joint Sessions Workshop Metaphor in Political Science*. Granada, Spain, 14–19 April 2005. Available at: http://eis.bris.ac.uk/~potfc/Granada/Papers/Vertessen.pdf. Visited 20.10.2011.

Dictionaries and Corpora

DMRL = *Sovremennyj tolkovyj slovar' russkogo jazyka* (2008). S. A. Kuznecov [ed.] (2008). SPb.: Norint, Moskva: RIPOL klassik. (Dictionary of Modern Russian Language.)

Kielipankki = CSC – Scientific Computing Ltd. Available through the CSC – IT Center for Science Ltd, see http://www.csc.fi/kielipankki/.

RNC = *Nacional'nyj korpus russkogo jazyka*. [Electronic resource]. http://ruscorpora.ru. (Russian National Corpus.)

OSh = Ožegov, S. I. / Švedova, N. Y. (2007): *Tolkovyj slovar' sovremennogo russkogo jazyka*. Moskva: OOO "A TEMP". (Dictionary of Modern Russian Language.)

GUMM = MOT *Gummerus Uusi suomen kielen sanakirja* 1.0. (1998). Kielikone Oy: Gummerus Kustannus Oy.

KTS = *Kielitoimiston sanakirja* 2.0. (2007). Kotimaisten kielten tutkimuskeskuksen julkaisuja 149. Helsinki: Kotimaisten kielten tutkimuskeskus ja Kielikone Oy.

Domestication and *Foreignization* in Figurative Idiom Translation[1]

Esa Penttilä and Pirkko Muikku-Werner
University of Tampere
University of Eastern Finland

Abstract

Figurative idioms are intralinguistic peculiarities that are part and parcel of each particular language reflecting its special structural properties and cultural reality. When we try to translate a source language figurative idiom with a corresponding figurative idiom in the target language, we often come across various difficulties that derive from the fact that figurative idiom meaning is in many ways ambiguous. In this article, we divide idiom meaning into two: the core meaning and the additional meaning. This division helps us show what role some of the aspects of foreignization and domestication play in figurative idiom translation and also how multifarious a phenomenon the translation of figurative idioms in general can be. Although the strategies that are usually recommended for idiom translation mainly seem to be domesticating, we will at the end of this article briefly consider the possibility that sometimes a foreignizing strategy could offer useful solutions to translation problems.

1 Introduction

Literary translation sets challenges for the translator, since it always has to do with translating culture in addition to translating mere language (see e.g. Bassnett / Levefere 1998). One of the special areas where problems may become even more evident than in some others is the translation of idioms. In this article we will discuss some of these challenges by paying special attention to figurative idioms and the various aspects related to their translation. At the same time we restrict the term **idiom translation** to refer to cases where a source language (SL) figurative idiom is translated by a target language (TL) figurative idiom. This means that we

---

[1] We would like to express our thanks to the two anonymous referees of this manuscript, whose comments greatly helped us clarify our thinking. Any possible flaws that still remain we are solely responsible for.

leave out cases where the meaning of an idiom would be explained in other, non-figurative terms or a figurative idiom would be translated by a literary expression; although these are possible ways of translating a figurative idiom, they are not within the scope of this discussion.

With their creativity of expressions and multidimensional nature, figurative idioms contain various features that are important for their expressivity. They may, for example, favor unusual word order, contain special vocabulary, alliteration, even rhyme, and all these features play a role in the overall function of the idiom in its native culture. Moreover, figurative idioms include a fascinating combination of social observation, history, and humor, which varies from culture to culture. When they are translated, translators have a difficult task in trying to figure out how and to what extent these language-specific and culture-specific aspects could be rendered to another language. Sometimes the task is easy, if the SL and the TL cultures share the specific cultural aspects included in the phrase, but often the case is not so simple. Even similar physical observations are not always expressed in the same linguistic manner, since cultural knowledge and cultural experiences vary; each language organizes the world in a slightly different manner. Many figurative idioms simply have no semantically synonymous formal equivalents in other languages, and this does not make the translator's life any easier.

In this article, we aim to discuss the various dimensions of figurative idiom translation from the point of view of domestication and foreignization. We pay special attention to the culture-specific aspects of figurative idioms and how these features affect translation. Our material comes from Finnish and English and has been gathered from various idiom dictionaries, some bilingual, some monolingual.[2] Since idioms are sometimes listed as translation equivalents in bilingual dictionaries, the equivalents can to some extent be regarded as recommendations for idiom translation. It is interesting to see how the various culture-specific aspects of the SL figurative idioms are retained in their TL counterparts. After all, the basic

---

2   The English idioms discussed in this article have mainly been picked from *Collins COBUILD Dictionary of Idioms* (2002) and the Finnish ones from Muikku-Werner *et al.* (2008). We have also consulted the following dictionaries and vocabularies: Parkkinen (2005), Westlake *et al.* (2006), Wiren (2007), and Pouttu-Delière (2009). The sample sentences presented in the article have been collected from the Internet.

translation unit is culture rather than the word, sentence, or text, as Bassnett and Lefevere (1990: 4) point out.

Our discussion partly relates to literary translation, which has of course been studied from various perspectives (see e.g. Bassnett / Levefere 1998). There are also various contrastive studies on idioms, especially figurative idioms (see e.g. Cignoni *et al.* 1999; Deignan / Potter 2004; Nguyen 2009; Korpela 2010; Niemi *et al.* 2010), but study of idioms from the perspective of translation strategies is fairly rare (see e.g. Abu-Ssaydeh 2004; Penttilä / Muikku-Werner 2010), and this is where our contribution is aimed at.

2 Basic concepts

This article is based on three basic notions that are mentioned in the title: domestication, foreignization, and figurative idiom. The first two of these are usually linked to Venuti (1995), although he himself acknowledges their origin with Schleirmacher quoting his emblematic words on the two translation methods that he claims are the only ones that exist: "[e]ither the translator leaves the reader in peace, as much as possible and moves the author towards him, or he leaves the author in peace, as much as possible and moves the reader towards him" (Lefevere 1977: 74). Venuti also acknowledges his debt to Berman (1984; 1985). We, however, borrow our definitions directly from Venuti (1995). By **domestication** we refer to the translation strategy, in which the translator aims at "ethnocentric reduction of the foreign text to target-language cultural values" (Venuti 1995: 20). This means that when a figurative idiom that contains SL-specific elements is translated into TL, it is adapted so that its SL-specific cultural elements will be changed to corresponding TL-specific cultural elements. The possible political or colonial aspects that are sometimes related to domestication are not of interest here, but view the notion more or less neutrally.

By **foreignization** we refer to a translation strategy that puts "ethnodeviant pressure on [target-language cultural] values to register the cultural and linguistic difference of the foreign text, sending the reader abroad" (Venuti 1995: 20). In our case, this means that, when translators use this strategy, they retain the possible SL-specific cultural elements in the translated figurative TL-idioms as close to the original as possible.

Naturally, it deserves to be mentioned that domestication and foreignization are not categorically dichotomous notions but should rather be regarded as opposite ends of a continuum that covers various degrees of more or less domesticating and foreignizing translation strategies. This is what we will be concentrating on in our analysis as well.

When we define our third basic notion, **figurative idiom**, we first need to define what an idiom is; it is a language-specific multiword, conventionalized expression whose meaning is not a combination of the meanings of its parts (see e.g. Makkai 1972; Fernando 1996; Moon 1998; Langlotz 2006). This means that although an idiom appears to be structurally compositional, its meaning is not compositionally derived from its parts, and this sets an idiom into a class of its own among linguistic expressions both formally and semantically. In addition to this, a figurative idiom has one further restriction: it contains a metaphorical figure of speech, which adds an extra layer to its meaning and often makes the phrase semantically ambiguous. For example, the phrase *kick the bucket* carries both the literal meaning 'to hit a pail with one's foot' and 'to die'. However, it is only the latter meaning that can be regarded as idiomatic, and this meaning is what we refer to when we talk about **the meaning of the idiom**. This meaning can further be divided into two different dimensions. The non-literal, non-compositional core meaning that the figurative idiom carries and that is listed as its meaning in an idiom dictionary could be referred to as **the core meaning of an idiom**. It is the meaning that can usually be regarded as more or less similar between an SL idiom and its figurative translation equivalent in TL. In addition to the core meaning, a figurative idiom has a further dimension that includes, for example, the various social connotations that derive from the meanings of their component parts, historical references, proverbiality, colloquiality, pragmatic restrictions, alliteration, rhyme and humor, all of which play a role in bringing out the cultural aspects of a figurative idiom (see e.g. Nunberg *et al.* 1994; Barkema 1996; Penttilä 2006). These aspects are difficult to determine in detail but add a special layer to the core meaning and could be referred to as the **additional meaning of an idiom**. It is with respect to this dimension that figurative SL idioms and their figurative TL equivalents often differ in meaning. This can be seen, for example, in Pouttu-Delière (2009), a figurative idiom dictionary containing semantic equivalents in six languages, where the additional meanings of idiom equivalents often differ from each other, although the core meanings would be the same. It is also this dimension of idiom meaning that may lead to problems referred to as "culture bumps" by Leppihalme (1994) in her study on the translation of allusions, and it is particularly this dimension that we will be concentrating on in this article. Together the core meaning and the additional meaning of an idiom form the overall meaning that could be referred to as **the extended meaning of an idiom**. Semantic equivalence between an SL and a TL idiom usually applies to the core idiom meaning only but could sometimes also involve the extended idiom meaning, especially between languages of closely related cultures.

Before we proceed further, there is still one point that we want to make. In the literature, idioms are sometimes distinguished from proverbs. In this article, however, we do not make a difference between idioms and proverbs, but include both in the class of figurative idioms. In fact, some of the examples that we will be discussing in the following pages could just as well be defined as proverbs.

3 Translation strategies of idioms

It has traditionally been thought that the recommended translation strategy for idioms would be substitution, i.e. that an SL idiom would (and should) be translated by a corresponding TL idiom (with a different form but a more or less similar meaning). This is the tacit assumption, for example, in bi- or multilingual idiom dictionaries and the translation equivalents listed there. The strategy, however, does not necessarily apply to real-life, where idioms are translated with various strategies (see e.g. Nedergaard-Larsen 1993; Abu-Ssaydeh 2004; Pedersen 2005).

In his study of subtitle translation, Pedersen (2005) lists six main translation strategies that can be used for "culturally-challenging" expressions, or expressions that contain an extralinguistic culture-bound reference (ECR), as he terms the phenomenon (see also Vinay / Darbernet 1992 [1958]; Leppihalme 1994; Nedergaard-Larsen 1993). Although Pedersen's ECRs form a wider category than figurative idioms, his classification applies to figurative idioms as well. The strategies he lists can be placed on a continuum from the most foreignizing to the most domesticating according to Figure 1.

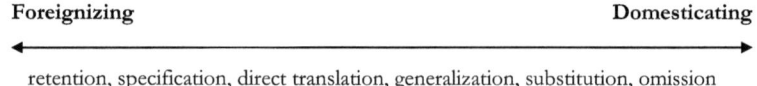

retention, specification, direct translation, generalization, substitution, omission

Figure 1. Pedersen's (2005) translation strategies placed on a continuum from most foreignizing (SL-oriented) to most domesticating (TL-oriented). The figure is an adapted simplification of Pedersen's (2005: 4) original illustration.

Of these six categories, retention and omission can be left out from our discussion, since they do not have to do with figurative idiom translation in the sense that we have defined the notion. Retention refers to a strategy where a culture-specific element is retained in its original SL form in the translation, so it is not replaced by its TL equivalent. It could be pointed out that this strategy is actually possible with some figurative idioms that contain supranational slogan-like catchwords, such as *alea jacta est* or *I'll be back*, but since the phenomenon is so marginal with respect to culture-specific translation problems that we are interested in, we will take no further heed of it. Omission, on the other hand, refers to omitting the culture-specific problematic elements altogether; therefore it does not involve idiom translation in our sense and will be disregarded in our further discussion. So, basically there are only four main translation strategies that Pedersen (2005) lists that can be discussed in terms of idiom translation strategies in our sense: specification, direct translation, generalization, and substitution. The first two of these can be roughly regarded as foreignizing and the last two as domesticating.

When we take a closer look at Pedersen's (2005) classification, we notice that he divides most of his translation strategies further into subclasses, some of which are useful for discussing the different aspects of figurative idiom translation. Especially the division of direct translation into calque translation and shifted direct translation and the division of substitution into cultural substitution[3] and

---

3   Pedersen (2005: 6–7) divides cultural substitutions into transcultural ECR translations and TL ECR translations, but from the point of view of our discussion this division is not necessary, so we will simply talk about cultural substitution, in which SL-specific cultural

paraphrase are useful for our discussion. Or actually, it is the first three of these substrategies that are important for us. Paraphrase is disregarded from further discussion, since it is not idiom translation in our sense but has to do with explaining the meaning of an idiom in other words, with a nonidiomatic expression. In the following, we will take a look at each of the three first-mentioned subcategories in more detail.

Calque translation refers to a strategy where a figurative idiom containing SL-specific cultural elements is translated word-for-word, which means that the cultural references remain the same; they are simply transferred from SL to TL. This strategy can clearly be regarded as foreignizing. Calque translation is typical of those culturally-challenged idioms that contain elements residing in the transcultural area between two or more cultures; this involves, for example, the translation of biblical idioms and idioms in widely-spread multicultural (or supranational) literary classics such as Shakespeare and Moliere. An example of this could be seen in (1).

(1) En. *cast the first stone* ~ Fi. *heittää ensimmäinen kivi* lit. 'cast the first stone'

Here the original culture-specific action, punishing someone by stoning, which has not been part of the Finnish legal customs, has been retained in the translation. This is actually a typical translation strategy with sacred texts, which have been regarded as the verbatim word of God, which should of course be retained word-for-word (Serban 2006: 47).

The second strategy, shifted direct translation, refers to a case where the translation is more or less word-for-word but where some of the SL-specific cultural elements are replaced by elements that are more familiar in TL culture. In this way, the strategy includes an optional cultural shift and can be regarded as residing somewhere between a foreignizing and a domesticating strategy. An example can be seen in (2), which includes typical translation equivalents in English and Finnish.

(2) En. *have goose pimples* ~ Fi. *olla kananlihalla* lit. 'have chicken pimples'

elements are translated with cultural elements that are more familiar in the TL culture. For our discussion, it is irrelevant whether these cultural elements are transcultural or TL-culture specific.

In this figurative idiom, the phrase is basically translated word-for-word, but the culture-specific animal species, goose, is replaced by chicken, which has traditionally been a much more typical domestic animal in Finland.

Cultural substitution is clearly a domesticating translation strategy. It is a strategy in which SL-specific cultural elements are replaced in translation by TL-specific cultural elements. For example, a figurative SL idiom that refers to a phenomenon that is not known in TL culture is translated with a figurative TL idiom that refers to a phenomenon that is well-known in TL culture. Cultural substitution could be regarded as the recommended default strategy for idiom translation. It is a strategy that can easily be used if a figurative idiom contains SL-specific elements that are unknown or rare in TL culture, if only there exists a corresponding TL idiom that renders the same core meaning. An example of this can be seen in (3).

(3) En. *go fly a kite* ~ Fi. *suksi suolle* 'go ski to the marsh'

In Finland flying a kite has traditionally been a rare activity restricted to the small – and largely Swedish-speaking – upper class, and therefore an expression in Finnish in which you request someone to go and fly a kite does not convey the strong connotative meaning that the original idiom carries in its own culture. In Finland, skiing on the other hand has been an essential part of the culture and Finnish marshes are known to be places where it is more difficult to move than on solid ground, and therefore if someone asks one to go ski on the marsh, the strength of the utterance is immediately clear to a native Finnish speaker. Moreover, the Finnish idiom contains alliteration, which is one of the special features of Finnish figurative language. In English, the phonological similarity between *fly* and *kite* most likely has a similar effect.

4 Idiom translation with respect to culture-specific aspects

We will now move on to discuss the different changes that can be induced on culture-specific elements in figurative SL idioms when they are translated with more or less corresponding figurative TL idioms. Of course changes do not always occur, and often there is no need for them. For example, if the original idiom contains culture-specific items that are part of the common cultural heritage shared by both SL and TL speakers, then there is no need to make any amendments in the translation. We will pay particular attention to the dimension of domestication and foreignization and to the changes that occur when different translation strategies are used. Our discussion takes as its starting point the translation strategies provided by Pedersen (2005), but we proceed by presenting examples that reflect various aspects of figurative idiom translation, many of which have not been mentioned so far. Part of our discussion is in line with Pedersen's classification, but part of it helps us introduce new idiom translation strategies that have not been mentioned so far.

4.1 Foreign phenomenon rendered into a familiar one

As already mentioned, substitution can be regarded as a domesticating translation strategy, and there is a clear need for it in idiom translation. When SL idioms contain phenomena that are missing from TL culture, or are very rare in it, the connotations and social and historical references that the original idiom conveys cannot be rendered by merely translating it word-for-word. It is necessary to try to find other means to express a similar meaning. One of the possible differences concerns the context of the utterance. For example, in some cultures operas can be such an essential part of the general culture that even common people can be expected to know that the final aria signifies the end of the show. In Finland, however, opera has been restricted to a fairly limited number of people and has not achieved the same general status as, for example, the church. Therefore the opera-related English idiom exemplified in 4 could well be replaced by a Finnish semantic equivalent that carries the same core meaning but has church as its context. It could at the same time be asked whether the Finnish figurative image has a somewhat democratizing effect on the figurative idiom, since even in the English-speaking world opera is probably associated with the elite rather than the commonalty.

(4) En. *it isn't over until the fat lady sings* ~ Fi. *se ei ole kirkossa kuulutettu* lit. 'it has not been announced in church yet'

In example 5, on the other hand, the original idiom refers to a custom that could be regarded as foreign in the Finnish context. Although people drink tea in Finland as well, the social value of tea drinking is nothing compared to the British Isles. In that sense a word-for-word translation again cannot really convey a similar extended meaning as the original idiom has in its source culture. However, there is a corresponding figurative idiom in Finnish that has more or less the same core meaning and does not contain any references to a foreign custom but refers to a common, shared experience. The possible translation is illustrated in example 5.

(5) En. *a storm in a teacup* ~ Fi. *myrsky vesilasissa* lit. 'a storm in a water glass/glass of water'

The idiom *myrsky vesilasissa* is fairly likely a translation idiom in Finnish. After all, both German and Russian contain the same idiom, *ein Sturm in Wasseglass* and *burja v stakane vody*, respectively. By the way, it is interesting that this idiom also occurs in Russian, although in Russia tea drinking has traditionally played a much more significant role than in Finland. One can also speculate that there is a somewhat flattening effect in the Finnish idiom when compared with the English one. In the British culture tea has a very important role in the fundamental safety of the whole nation; whenever there is a crisis, the Brits have a cup of tea. Therefore a storm in a teacup can be regarded as something earth shattering and shaking the basic values of the society, whereas the Finnish storm in a glass of water could never be thought of as having a similar connotation.

4.2 Specification

As already mentioned, specification is a translation strategy that can be regarded as domesticating. In specification, a more general element in an SL idiom is replaced by a more specific one in a TL idiom. Among the easiest elements that one can replace in SL-specific idioms are elements that occur at a general level, or basic level, as it is termed in cognitive linguistics (see e.g. Taylor 2004). For one reason or another, specification is a phenomenon that often occurs in translation and specification[4] can also be regarded as one of so-called translation universals (see e.g. Pápai 2004; Puurtinen 2004). One may feel that a hyperonym is too flat and mild and therefore a hyponym may help in communicating the figurative image behind the idiom better. An example of this is seen in 6, which contains two proverbial idioms that could be regarded as translation equivalents.

---

4   In the discussion on translation universals, the term that is used for what we call specification in this article is usually explicitation.

(6) En. *A bird in the hand is worth two in the bush* ~ Fi. *parempi pyy pivossa kuin kymmenen oksalla* lit. 'better (to have) a partridge in hand than ten on a branch (of a tree)'

The specification here has to do with the species mentioned in the proverb. While the English expression contains a reference to a generic bird, its Finnish counterpart mentions a specific bird species, a partridge. By the way, the Finnish idiom (as the English one as well) is fairly old, which is emphasized by the fact that it contains an archaic word *pivo* 'hand'; the word can be regarded as practically unknown to most present-day speakers of Finnish.

A similar specifying effect as in 6 can be noticed in example 7, where the word *fuel* referring to a general concept is replaced by the word *bensa* referring to a more specific concept.

(7) En. *add fuel to the flames* ~ Fi. *kaataa bensaa liekkeihin* lit. 'pour petrol to the flames'

4.3 Intensification

Since intensification resembles specification in the sense that it involves adding an extra effect to the translation, it could be regarded as a domesticating strategy. It may adapt the idiom to the TL culture, for example, by modifying it so that the phrase better fits the observations made in the TL culture. An example of this was seen already in example 6, where *two* birds in English have become *ten* partridges in Finnish. One of the factors behind this change may reside in the pessimism that has been found to be typical of Finns, who use it as a strategy of protecting themselves from unpleasant surprises and disappointments (Keltikangas-Järvinen 1996: 224). When one exaggerates the uncertainty of future events, it is easier to accept the present; one firm accomplishment is better than ten uncertain wishes that are extremely unrealistic.

Another example of this strategy can be seen in (8), where a fairly neutral expression is replaced by a very strong, even a taboo, expression.

(8) En. *don't put the cart before the horse* ~ Fi. *älä mene perse edellä puuhun* 'don't climb the tree with your arse first'

The two figurative idioms in this example cannot necessarily be regarded as immediate translation equivalents, but their core meanings may be regarded as more or less similar, and they have been listed as equivalents in Westlake *et al.* (2006: 60–62), a humorous bilingual idiom dictionary. Stylistically, however, there is a great difference between the two idioms, since the Finnish idiom is extremely vulgar, whereas the English one is neutral. It is interesting to see how a somehow regressive or backward activity can be conceived so differently in English and Finnish cultures. If translators use a dictionary where these two, or other similar pairs of idioms, are regarded as equivalents, they need to be well aware of the stylistic and other relevant differences between the listed expressions.

4.4 Added esthetics

References to concrete real word phenomena are often domesticated in figurative idiom translation, but sometimes domestication may also concern the way things are expressed. For example, in Finnish the mere joy of expression, an endeavor to produce an esthetically delightful and witty expression is present, for example, in various forms of folk culture including proverbs and idioms. Since it is a feature that could be regarded as typical of Finnish oral culture, it can be viewed as a domesticating aspiration, when this type of esthetic delight is emphasized in idiom translation into Finnish. We have already seen an example of this in 6, and another example is presented in (9).

(9) En. *pot calling the kettle black* ~ Fi. *pata kattilaa soimaa, musta kylki kummallakin* lit. 'pot reproaching kettle, both have black sides'

Here the figurative TL idiom is almost a direct translation of the SL idiom, but there are a few aspects that add to the esthetics of the translated idiom and make it better adapted to the TL culture. In Finnish the idiom contains alliteration, but it does so also in English. *Soimata* 'reproach', however, is a somewhat special word, since it is a literary low-frequency verb, the use of which creates an interesting contrast with the ordinary, everyday nature of pot and kettle, thus adding special esthetics to the idiom.

Another example of a figurative Finnish idiom that corresponds to an English one but adds alliteration to the TL expression, can be seen in (10).

(10) En. *break one's word* ~ Fi. *syödä sanansa* lit. 'eat one's word'

Alliteration, by the way, is not typical of Finnish idioms only, but has been found to reside in idiomatic expressions in other languages as well (Gries 2011: 492–493). Nevertheless, the role that alliteration plays in Finnish folk poetry is extremely strong, as the Finnish national epic, *The Kalevala*, indicates.

4.5 A possible strategy: foreignization through calque translation?

This last section of our discussion is devoted to a translation strategy that is not used much at present: calque translation, or a word-for-word translation of figurative idioms, which clearly is a foreignizing translation strategy. It introduces the foreign images embedded in the original expression to the awareness of the TL audience, which may sometimes make the translation stand out in its context as somewhat strange.

At present, calque translation could be regarded as a nonpreferred, even stigmatized, strategy of idiom translation. For example, none of the idiom dictionaries that we have looked at lists calques as translation equivalents, except in those cases where the shared figures of speech most likely derive from the common cultural origin. After all, in the old translations of the Bible and the literary classics we often find *calques* that have become adapted to the expressive power of our native tongue.

In the following lines we would like to entertain a few thoughts that have to do with the possibility of calque translation of figurative idioms especially in cases where the strategy would bring out special effects in the figurative idiom that would not be possible with a more domesticating strategy. Such cases would include situations 1) where there is no corresponding figurative idiom with similar meaning in TL, 2) where the form of the SL idiom is important, in which case the message may get distorted, if the SL idiom is substituted with a corresponding TL idiom, or 3) where the figurative image reflected by the idiom is somehow semantically significant. It has already been mentioned that with sacred texts, in particular, foreignizing translation strategies could be useful, since at least some people prefer archaic, even strange, translations, which they feel are "more appropriate in view of the supernatural character of the message" (Serban 2006: 51). It also seems that – probably due to the overwhelming influence of English – everyday Finnish has assimilated directly translated figurative English idioms into itself, so that they are not as unusual as one might think. The next few examples (11–13) illustrate directly translated loan idioms that are commonly found in Finnish newspapers and therefore common at least in that genre. They are not from translated texts, but texts originally written in Finnish. The figurative idioms, however, are clearly translated loans from English, since none of them have originally existed in Finnish, but their word-for-word equivalents exist in English.

(11) Fi. *Mutta edelleen on meidän venekunnalla apina selässä ja saldo avaamatta* lit. 'But still our crew has a monkey on its back and the account unopened' ~ En. *to have a monkey on one's back* 'have a serious problem that makes your life difficult' (http://www.pandalook.fi/index.php?option=com_content&view=article&id=94:team-pandalook-6-ahvenanmaalla&catid=38:2011&Itemid=86)

(12) Fi. *Matti Vanhasen johtama hallitus on tällä hetkellä kuin rampa ankka* lit. 'The cabinet led by Matti Vanhanen is at the moment like a lame duck' ~ En. *lame duck* 'weak and unable to act (because the successor will soon be inaugurated)' (http://www.hs.fi/politiikka/artikkeli/Hein%C3%A4luoma+Vanhasen+hallitus+on+rampa+ankka/1135236928502)

(13) Fi. '*Tämänkertainen vaali ei taida olla minun kuppini teetä*', Heinäluoma pohtii. lit. 'The present election doesn't seem to be my cup of tea, Heinäluoma speculates' ~ En. *it's not my cup of tea* 'something that one is not enthusiastic about or interested in' (http://www.uusisuomi.fi/kotimaa/114765-demari-lipponen-muutti-kisan-%E2%80%93-%E2%80%9Dylivoimaista-osaamista%E2%80%9D)

Although all these examples, have been picked up from texts originally written in Finnish, it is not by any means clear that the figurative idioms in them would be understood by all Finnish speakers. If someone who is not familiar with the idiom in example 11 encounters it for the first time, it may be very difficult to decipher its negative meaning – especially if the person likes monkeys. Even the context may not necessarily help the interpretation. However, the idiom is commonly used in sports commentaries, although outside that context it may not be common. So, one has to belong to a certain ingroup, i.e. to follow sport, in order to know the idiom and to be able to interpret it. If one is not a sports fan, the meaning may remain a mystery. Lameness on the other hand, which is present in example 12, is something that can be regarded as unequivocally harmful and therefore the idiom is more transparent than the idioms in examples 11 and 13. As already pointed out, tea does not play a significant role in the Finnish culture, but Finns regard coffee as much more important. Therefore the idiom in example 13 does not necessarily communicate a similar meaning in Finnish as it does in English – the semantically equivalent Finnish idiom would rather be *se ei ole minun heiniäni* lit. 'it is not my hay'.

At this point, it should be mentioned that, although foreignized figurative idioms may at times be problematic for TL speakers to understand, foreignized idiom translations also enrich the idiom repertoire of TL. One of the factors behind this phenomenon may be the speakers' wish to associate with a prestige group of some kind. In her study on anglicisms in contact adds, Passi (1990) suggests that the following factors may lead to their use: some users of anglicisms aim to increase their status by emphasizing their education and good knowledge of foreign languages; some may have a need to show off; some use anglicisms as a (secret) code; some aspire to raise attention; and some may wish to appear humorous. There is also certain magic in foreign names and words, since we are often supposed to be more fascinated by something unfamiliar than by something familiar. It appears plausible that similar motives may lead to foreignized *calque* translations. It may also be asked how much domestication in general is needed in a country like Finland, where the level of education is high and the Anglo-American culture is so prevalent in the media. However, it may also be asked, and with good reason, whether *calque* translation is an aspect of the present globalization trend that may lead to depriving small, individual cultural communities of their special cultural identities?

5 Conclusion

As the above discussion has shown, a figurative idiom does not simply carry its core meaning but also has various additional properties that can be regarded as forming its additional meaning. It is with respect to these additional meanings that translation equivalents of figurative idioms with the same core meaning usually differ, and they need to be considered when translating figurative idioms from one language to another.

Very often – and probably as recommended – figurative idioms are translated by using a domesticating strategy, which renders foreign cultural references into more familiar ones and thus makes the expressions easier for TL speakers to understand. By emphasizing aspects that are typical of the native way of expression, a translator may adapt the figure of speech to better suit the TL culture. In this process, at least the following changes are possible: 1) a foreign element in the expression could be replaced by a familiar one, 2) the expression could become more specific, 3) the image embedded in the idiom could be intensified and gain heightened drama, or 4) the esthetics and humor value in the idiom could be increased. Naturally, at the same time, the extended overall meaning of the idiom changes to some extent at least.

Although a domesticating translation strategy at present seems to be the recommended – or almost the only – one with figurative idioms, there may at times be reasons for adopting a more foreignizing translation strategy instead. Some of the additional properties that figurative idioms carry may be communicated better by using a foreignizign strategy. Especially in cases where the additional idiom meaning is somehow important for the overall meaning of the text, a calque translation that renders the figurative image word for word might be a useful solution. Various translation loans, for example, from the Bible indicate that such a foreignizing translation strategy was more openly accepted earlier, and it deserves to be considered at present as well – especially since the transcultural area in language use is constantly increasing due to improved foreign language skills.

It is a demanding task for a translator to balance between the domesticating and foreignizing ends of the strategic continuum while trying to find the most suitable translation for SL idioms. In many cases, domestication helps to bring out many of the special (and communicatively important) properties for those who are unfamiliar with SL. However, foreignization can sometimes be a useful method for translating idioms (see also Penttilä / Muikku-Werner 2011). At least in certain, especially informal, circles *calque* translation of English idioms seems to be a fairly common phenomenon.

This article presents a work in progress and the topic certainly deserves further investigation and discussion. One possible step for a further study is to examine how people from different age groups understand old and more recent *calque* translations of idioms. The difference between genders is also worth investigating, since some of the directly translated idioms seem to exist in fairly closed, gender-specific circles. Neither should one forget the role of the artistic or esthetic effects that are part of idiom translation.

References

Abu-Ssaydeh, Abdul-Fattah (2004): "Translation of English idioms into Arabic." In: *Babel* 50 (2), 114–131.

Barkema, Henk (1996): "Idiomaticity and Terminology: A Multi-Dimensional Descriptive Model." In: *Studia Linguistica* 50 (2), 125–160.

Bassnett, Susan / Levefere, André (1990): "Introduction: Proust's Grandmother and the Thousand and One Nights: The 'Cultural Turn' in Translation Studies. In: *Translation, History, Culture: A Source Book*. London: Routledge. 1–13.

—— (1998): *Constructing Cultures: Essays on Literary Translation*. Clevedon: Multilingual Matters.

Berman, Antoine (1984): *L'épreuve de l'étranger: Culture et traduction dans l'Allemagne romantique*. Paris: Gallimard.

—— (1985): "La traduction et la lettre ou l'auberge du lointain." In: *Les tours de Babel*. Mauvezin: Trans-Europ-Repress. 35–150.

Cignoni, Laura / Coffey, Stephen / Moon, Rosamund (1999): "Idiom variation in Italian and English: Two corpus-based studies." In: *Languages in Contrast* 2 (2), 279–300.

Collins Cobuild Dictionary of Idioms (2002). 2nd edition. London: Harper Collins.

Deignan, Alice / Potter, Liz (2004): "A corpus study of metaphors and metonyms in English and Italian." In: *Journal of Pragmatics* 36, 1231–1252.

Fernando, Chitra (1996): *Idioms and Idiomaticity*. Oxford: Oxford University Press.

Gries, Stefan Th. (2011): "Phonological similarity in multi-word units." In: *Cognitive Linguistics* 22 (3). 491–510.

Keltikangas-Järvinen, Liisa (1996): "Suomalainen kansanluonne." In: Laaksonen, Pekka / Mettomäki, Sirkka-Liisa [eds.] (1996): *Olkaamme siis suomalaisia*. Kalevalaseuran vuosikirja 75–76. Helsinki: Suomalaisen Kirjallisuuden Seura. 216–225.

Korpela, Maria (2010): *Ruumiinosannimet suomen ja unkarin idiomeissa*. Master's thesis. Turku: University of Turku.

Langlotz, Andreas (2006): *Idiomatic Creativity*. Amsterdam & Philadelphia: John Benjamins.

Leppihalme, Ritva (1994): *Culture Bumps: On the Translation of Allusions*. Helsinki: University of Helsinki. (= English Department Studies. 2).

Makkai, Adam (1972): *Idiom Structure in English*. The Hague: Mouton.

Moon, Rosamund (1998): *Fixed Expressions and Idioms in English: A Corpus-Based Approach*. Oxford: Clarendon Press.

Muikku-Werner, Pirkko / Jantunen, Jarmo / Kokko, Ossi (2008): *Suurella sydämellä ihan sikana: Suomen kielen kuvaileva fraasisanakirja*. Helsinki: Gummerus.

Nedergaard-Larsen, Birgit (1993): "Culture-bound problems in subtitling." In: *Perspectives: Studies in Translatology* 2, 207–242.

Nguyen, Van-trao (2009): *Expressing Idioms in English and Vietnamese: A Contrastive Analysis*. Queensland: The University of Queensland.

Niemi, Jussi / Mulli, Juha / Nenonen, Marja / Niemi, Sinikka / Nikolaev, Alexandre / Penttilä, Esa (2010): "Body-part idioms across languages: Lexical analyses of VP body-part idioms in English, German, Swedish, Russian and Finnish." In: Ptashnyk, Stefaniya / Hallsteinsdóttir, Erla / Bubenhofer, Noah [eds.] (2010): *Korpora, Web und Datenbanken. Corpora, Web and Databases. Computergestützte Methoden in der modernen Phraseologie und Lexikographie. Computer-based Methods in Modern Phraseology and Lexicography. Baltmannsweiler*: Baltmannsweiler: Schneider Verlag Hohengehren. 67–76.

Nunberg, Geoffrey / Sag, Ivan A. / Wasow, Thomas (1994): "Idioms." In: *Language* 70 (3), 491–538.

Pápai, Vilma (2004): "Eplicitation: A universal of translated text?" In: Mauranen, Anna / Kujamäki, Pekka [eds.] (2004): *Translation Universals: Do they Exist?* Amsterdam & New York: Benjamins, 143–164.

Parkkinen, Jukka (2005): *Aasinsilta ajan hermolla*. Helsinki: WSOY.

Passi, Mia (1990): *Anglicisms in Columns*. Master's thesis. Joensuu: University of Joensuu, Department of Translation Studies.

Pedersen, Jan (2005): "How is culture rendered in subtitles?" In: *MuTra 2005 – Challenges of Multidimensional Translation: Conference Proceedings*. Available at http://www.euroconferences.info/proceedings/2005_Proceedings/2005_Pedersen_Jan.pdf.

Penttilä, Esa (2006): *It Takes an Age to Do a Chomsky: Idiomaticity and Verb Phrase Constructions in English*. Unpublished PhD Thesis. Department of English, University of Joensuu.

Penttilä, Esa / Muikku-Werner, Pirkko (2011): "English gatecrashers in Finnish: Directly translated English idioms as novelties of Finnish." In: Kujamäki, Pekka / Kolehmainen, Leena / Penttilä, Esa / Kemppanen, Hannu [eds.] (2011): *Beyond Borders: Translations Moving Languages, Literatures and Cultures*. Berlin: Frank & Timme. 247–265.

Pouttu-Delière, Päivi (2009): *Kielikuvia ja fraaseja 6 kielellä*. Jyväskylä: Gummerus.

Puurtinen, Tiina (2004): "Eplicitation of clausal relations: A corpus-based analysis of clause connectives in translated and non-translated Finnish children's literature." In: Mauranen, Anna / Kujamäki, Pekka [eds.] (2004): *Translation Universals: Do they Exist?* Amsterdam & New York: Benjamins. 165–176.

Serban, A. (2006): "Translation and Genre: Sacred Texts." In: *Encyclopedia of Language and Linguistics*. Amsterdam: Elsevier. 47–53.

Taylor, John R. (2004): *Linguistic Categorization*. 3rd edition. Oxford: Oxford University Press.

Venuti, Lawrence (1995): *The Translator's Invisibility: A History of Translation*. London & New York: Routledge.

Vinay, Jean-Paul / Darbelnet, Jean (1995 [1958]): *Comparative Stylistics of French and English: A Methodology for Translation*. Translated and edited by Juan C. Sager and M.-J. Hamel. Amsterdam & Philadelphia: John Benjamins.

Westlake, Paul / Partti, Krista / Pitkänen, Eeva-Liisa (2006): *Se ei ole minun cup of tea*. Helsinki: WSOY.

Wirén, Veijo (2007): *Suomi-englanti idiomi- ja fraasisanakirja*. Helsinki: Arthouse.

Measuring *Foreignization* in Literary Translation: An Attempt to Operationalize the Concept of *Foreignization*

Piet Van Poucke

University College Ghent and Ghent University, Belgium

Abstract

One of the decisions a literary translator has to make before getting to work is what overall translation strategy he or she wishes to follow, i.e. whether to translate in a more *foreignizing* or *domesticating* way. And even after having made this decision neither of the two strategies can be followed in a pure and consistent way, as all literary translations, by the very nature of translation, inevitably contain a mix of different translation shifts that are either foreignizing or domesticating. Consequently, most studies on foreignization are conducted on a rather qualitative basis, taking into account and discussing in detail only some specific variables of the translator's strategy, but not really *measuring* the *degree of foreignization* of a translation.

In this paper an attempt is made to construct a quantitative model for assessing translations on a foreignization-domestication scale, based on the different existing taxonomies of translation shifts, and taking into account not only lexico-semantic, but also syntactic and stylistic variables (cf. Chesterman 1997) in a microstructural analysis. In order to check the relevance of this quantitative model a limited case study is provided on three literary translations of Fyodor Dostoevsky's *Besy* into Dutch and English.

1 Introduction

Ever since the start of human translation activities the concepts of *domestication* and *foreignization* have been diametrically opposed, although this specific terminology came into use only in the 1990s, when Venuti (1995) introduced the two terms in his seminal *The Translator's Invisibility*. Since then many researchers have conducted investigations into the two concepts but the large amount of papers and monographs written on the subject only constitute an obvious confirmation of how broadly and sometimes even contradictory these concepts have been interpreted by different authors in different times. Consequently, this paper first tries to open up this discussion and establish a clear definition of the main concepts.

In this paper we will also attempt to operationalize the concepts of *domestication* and *foreignization* in order to be able to *measure* the degree of foreignization of a literary translation. Translations often seem to disclose their nature at first sight and, indeed, a thorough and motivated qualitative analysis can usually reveal the domesticating or foreignizing character of a translation. However, it is clearly more difficult to make conclusions about tendencies in literary translation across the borders of time and space without using quantitative methods. Can we state, for instance, that Russian literature is translated into Dutch more domesticatingly than English literature? Or is Dutch literary translation more foreignizing in the 1960s than in the 1990s? A model that would allow us to attach a *degree of foreignization* to every single literary translation made would make it possible to compare larger amounts of translation at the same time and to detect certain tendencies in the prevailing *strategies*[1] of literary translation. So a quantitative model has to be constructed that takes into account the different levels at which translation strategies interfere in the original text during the process of translating.

2 Translation strategies

In order to measure the degree of foreignization of a translation we should, above all, establish a clear definition of what we consider to be foreignization and domestication. According to Venuti (1995: 20) "<f>oreignizing translation signifies the difference of the foreign text, yet only by disrupting the cultural codes that prevail in the target language." It is "a form of resistance against ethnocentrism and racism, cultural narcissism and imperialism" (ibid.). Foreignizing translations are, in this regard, translations that remain close to the original, not only on a lexico-semantic but also on syntactic and stylistic levels. Referring to Schleiermacher (2004 [1813]: 49) we can say that translations are foreignizing when they leave the writer in peace as much as possible and move the reader toward him.

---

1   In this paper the term *translation strategy* is used to indicate the translator's overall approach to a text, in contrast to the term *translation shift*, indicating the method or procedure used by the translator in a specific case.

We speak about domesticating translations when, on the other hand, "the translator works to make his or her work invisible, producing the illusory effect of transparency that simultaneously masks its status as an illusion: the translated text seems natural, i.e. not translated" (Venuti 1995: 5). These types of translations bring the writer toward the reader (cf. Schleiermacher 2004 [1813]: 49) and adjust the target version of the original to the taste and expectations of the target public. In order to realize this effect the literary translator has a broad range of different translation *shifts* at his disposal. In this paper the term *translation shift* is used to indicate the changes which occur in translation, i.e. "departures from formal correspondence in the process of going from the SL^2 to the TL" (Catford 1965: 73). Different translation studies' scholars refer to the same shifts by using the terminology *strategies* (Baker 1992; Chesterman 1997; Grit 1997), *methods* (Vinay / Darbelnet 2000 [1958]) or *procedures* (Vinay / Darbelnet 2000 [1958]; Newmark 1988), but we prefer the term *shifts*, as proposed by Catford (1965) and van Leuven-Zwart (1989; 1990) in her two pioneer articles on *Translation and Original: Similarities and Dissimilarities*.

3 Foreignizing and domesticating translation shifts

Translation studies have a long tradition of research on the various translation shifts the translator has at his disposal in order to transfer the message of the ST into another language. Several attempts have been made by now to describe and sometimes classify the shifts, irrespective of the language pair involved in the translation process (Vinay / Darbelnet 2000 [1958]; Catford 1965; Vlahov / Florin 2006 [1970]; Newmark 1988; Leuven-Zwart 1989, 1990; Baker 1992; Chesterman 1997; Grit 1997). Most of these scholars, however, do not make a division of translation shifts into foreignizing or SL-oriented and domesticating or TL-oriented translation shifts.

One of the earliest attempts to divide the most frequently used translation shifts into foreignizing and domesticating tools is the taxonomy constructed by the Canadian linguists Jean-Paul Vinay and Jean Darbelnet in 1958 in their *Methodology for Translation*. They make a clear distinction between *direct* or *literal translation* and *oblique*

---

2   In this paper the following abbreviations are used: SL = source language; TL = target language; ST = source text; TT = target text; SC = source culture; TC = target culture.

translation in those cases where the translator has to fill a gap in the TL by "corresponding elements" (Vinay / Darbelnet 2000 [1958]: 84). They condense the different translation shifts to just seven: on the one hand the *direct* shifts Borrowing, Calque and Literal translation and, on the other hand, the *oblique* shifts Transposition, Modulation, Equivalence and Adaptation (Vinay / Darbelnet 2000 [1958]: 85–92). Omission, one of the shifts which could be either foreignizing or domesticating, is not considered in the taxonomy of Vinay and Darbelnet (see 5.4).

Sergej Vlahov and Sider Florin (2006 [1970]: 109–110), in considering the different shifts for the translation of culture-specific items (or *realia*), do make a division into the SL-oriented Transcription (транскрипция) or Transliteration (транслитерация), on the one hand, and the TL-oriented Translation (перевод) or Substitution (замена), on the other hand, but this division is clearly too broad to be useful as a foreignization-domestication dichotomy.

Kitty van Leuven-Zwart (1989) does not make a distinction between SL and TL-oriented translation shifts either, but she does define three categories of microstructural shifts in translation of narrative texts, based on the different levels of relationship between the units of translation in both source text and target text. She also introduces specific terminology. In the case of *modulation* (159), when the synonymy between the translation units in ST and TT is broken, the translation shift is less far-reaching than in the case of what she calls *modification* (165), when the relationship between the source and the translation is one of contrast. The most radical shifts are categorized by van Leuven-Zwart as *mutation*, suggesting the "lack of any aspect of conjunction" (168), which is the case when clauses or phrases are either added or deleted, or when the translator makes a "radical change of meaning" (169).

The theory of Diederik Grit (1997) limits itself to the translation of realia only, but the categories of shifts described by him are, apparently, applicable to other translation problems as well. Without making a distinction between SL and TL-oriented translation shifts he organizes his seven different shifts in such a way that they could be considered as being put on a scale ranging from most foreignizing to most domesticating, with *retention* (Du. handhaving) on the one (SL-oriented) side of the scheme and *omission* (Du. weglating) as being the most domesticating (or TL-oriented) way of translating culture-specific items (45–47). Andrew Chesterman

(1997: 94–112), on the other hand, singles out no less than 30 different translation *strategies*, 10 syntactic, 10 semantic and 10 pragmatic *strategies*.

A serious attempt to bring the various translation shifts together into one larger scheme, with a clear distinction between SL-oriented and TL-oriented shifts was made by Jan Pedersen (2005: 1) in his paper on the translation problems caused by "Extralinguistic Culture-bound References" in general, but more specifically in subtitling. Actually, Pedersen made two different attempts because he included a new taxonomy in his (2007) paper on "Cultural Interchangeability: The Effects of Subtitling Cultural References in Subtitling". His hesitation about where to include the shifts *official equivalent, omission* and *specification* into the two schemes (2005: 4; 2007: 31) clearly illustrates the problems with labeling and establishing the degree of foreignization of the various translation shifts. Further on in this paper we will look at this issue in a more exhaustive way.

4 Continuum or field?

One of the questions that could be asked at this point is whether these schemes can be rewritten and transformed into a continuum of translation shifts, which could be used as a tool for measuring the degree of foreignization of the strategy chosen by the translator of a literary work. In other words, is it possible to make a distinction between strongly foreignizing, slightly foreignizing, slightly domesticating, strongly domesticating and perhaps even *neutral* translation shifts? And if this is possible, are we then able to construct a scale ranging from 1 to 10 with more or less foreignizing shifts?

This is exactly what Ligita Judickaitė (2009) tried to do in her analysis of foreignizing and domesticating translation shifts in the Lithuanian subtitles of the cartoon *Ratatouille*, based on Pedersen's classification from 2005. Her continuum, from most foreignizing to most domesticating shifts, contains the following 10 items: Preservation – Addition – Naturalization – Literal Translation – Cultural Equivalent – Omission – Globalization – Translation by a more concrete word – Creation – Equivalent (Judickaitė 2009: 36).

In our opinion the construction of a pure continuum of translation shifts is rather utopian in essence because of the incomparability of the nature of the shifts. On what grounds can we, for instance, decide that a *Cultural Equivalent* is slightly less foreignizing than *Literal Translation*, but more foreignizing than *Omission* and how can this difference be operationalized in order to establish the reigning translation strategy in literary works?

The relative nature of these translation shifts forces the researcher, in our opinion, to reformat the different shifts into four or five larger *fields*, each of which includes one or more shifts. Those fields could be defined as *Strong Foreignization* (F), *Moderate Foreignization* (f), *Moderate Domestication* (d), *Strong Domestication* (D) and perhaps even *Neutral Translation* (0), with Strong Foreignization and Strong Domesticating being more radical and, therefore, clearly appearing more rarely than their moderate counterparts, as illustrated in Figure 1.

Between the two triangles of Foreignization and Domestication we are left with a blank area where Neutral Translation (0) should go.

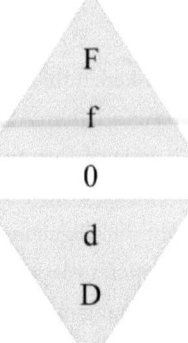

Figure 1. The division of translation shifts into foreignizing and domesticating *fields*.

5 An alternative model

Each of the translation shift fields apparently contains various translation shifts. In the following an attempt will be made to classify them into five clusters.

5.1 Strong Foreignization

If we look at Strong Foreignization as a set of shifts that retain both form and meaning of the translated ST items and, in other words, stay as closely as possible to the ST, then we should distinguish between the lexico-semantic and the syntactic-stylistic levels. Translation shifts on the former level include all forms of borrowing (retention, preservation, transcription, transliteration, loanwords, loan-based neologisms) and, on the latter level, we observe the explicit and marked retention of word order, phrase structure or clause structure in those cases when alternatives are not only possible but also more idiomatically accepted in the TL. Strong Foreignization in literary translation immediately confronts the reader with features that are strange to his or her TC: culture-specific items and elements in the ST discourse that the reader is unfamiliar with.

5.2 Moderate Foreignization

The Moderate Foreignization field includes shifts that cause minor changes in either form or meaning, but nevertheless stay close to the ST on a lexico-semantic or syntactic-stylistic level. Shifts that fall within the scope of Moderate Foreignization are deliberate literal (or direct) translation (in the case of calques, for instance, when more idiomatic alternatives are available in the TL but are not used by the translator) as well as what Pedersen (2005: 3) calls *official equivalents*. Specification, explicitation or addition, when the form of the original is retained but extra information is added to the term in order to explain the meaning of a culture-specific item, without substituting it by a more familiar item in the TC, also have to be classified as examples of Moderate Foreignization.

On a syntactic and stylistic level, Moderate Foreignization can be found in *transposition*, a shift defined by Vinay and Darbelnet (2000 [1958]: 88) as "replacing one word class with another without changing the meaning of the message", a shift they themselves consider to be *oblique*, i.e. more TL-oriented. Whether *transposition* should be regarded as either (moderately) foreignizing or (moderately) domesticating depends on the specific situation and the linguistic characteristics of SL and TL. Whenever the translator has no choice but to change the word class in the TT because of syntactic restrictions in the TL and, apart from the word class, nothing else is changed in the text, then we consider the shift as being moderately foreignizing because only the form, but not the meaning, of the original is changed. This does not mean, however, that the translator cannot use *transposition* as a domesticating translation shift as well, for instance when (s)he turns the shift into a systematic way of adapting the ST to the expectations of the TC audience.

Other examples of Moderate Foreignization include the retention of stylistic features, such as alliteration, repetition, rhythm and rhyme.

Moderate Foreignization largely corresponds with what Van Leuven-Zwart defines as *modulation*, when, using her terminology, "an aspect of disjunction" occurs between the ST and the TT (van Leuven-Zwart 1989: 159), that is, however, not strong enough to be considered deliberately domesticating.

5.3 Moderate Domestication

The largest set of translation shifts is probably that of Moderate Domestication which includes all shifts that adapt the original text to some idiomatic and stylistic norms of the TL, i.e. when significant changes in form or meaning are encountered in the translation when compared with the ST. In the different taxonomies used in this paper these translation shifts have been mentioned under a multitude of different names: Transposition, Modulation (Newmark; Vinay / Darbelnet), Equivalence (Newmark; Vinay / Darbelnet), Generalization, Substitution (Pedersen), Trope Change (Chesterman), Cultural Substitution (Baker), Paraphrase (Baker; Chesterman) and others, but they all have in common that the TT is adapted to the taste and expectations of the public. Van Leuven-Zwart uses the term *modification* to classify this kind of translation shift.

On a syntactic level Moderate Domestication also comprises what Chesterman (1997: 98) calls *cohesion change*: a shift "that affects intra-textual reference, ellipsis, substitution, pronominalization and repetition, or the use of connectors of various kinds". As a counterpart to Moderate Foreignization the loss of alliteration, repetition, rhythm or rhyme should be considered as a stylistic feature of Moderate Domestication.

5.4 Strong Domestication

When no trace of the ST can be found in the translation, neither of the original form, nor the original meaning, we consider the translation shift as being Strongly Domesticating. This is the case when we find examples of *mutation* in the translation. According to van Leuven-Zwart (1989: 168) a text is *mutated* in the case of "*addition* of clauses or phrases, *deletion* of clauses or phrases, and *radical change of meaning*", which means there is no connection at all between the ST and the TT in translation.

Indeed, in those cases when information is added to the original text or when the meaning of the original is radically changed, we can safely consider the translation shift to be Strongly Domesticating. The reader is confronted with a translation that not really reflects the original and most probably the added information contains features typical for the TL or TC. A special case of Strong Domestication is omission, which is reflected in the different positions this translation shift is accorded in the taxonomies used in this paper. Van Leuven-Zwart (1989: 168–169) considers *deletion* as an example of *mutation*, when it is completely impossible to establish a link with the ST, while Judickaitė (2009: 38–39) accords it a place somewhere near the center of her continuum, judging that this shift "does not include the process of translation in its traditional sense". Pedersen (2005: 9; 2007: 31), on the other hand, seems to be undecided on where to put this shift in his scheme, although he considers it to be more TL-oriented than SL-oriented.

Omissions can, of course, be of different size and weight, ranging from the omission of one insignificant detail to a whole episode, but if we decide to stick to the definition of foreignization as a translation strategy that stays as faithful as possible to the ST, then there is no alternative but to consider omission to be Strongly Domesticating, because no trace of the original is left in the TT, which means that the reader is not brought to the writer at all and (s)he is denied contact with an item that held, instead, some significance for the author of the ST. In those cases when entire episodes from the ST are deleted in the TT, however, *measuring* the degree of foreignization, as described in our model (see 6) becomes rather pointless as the *degree of foreignization* will be extremely negative but, instead, we should look at the reasons for omitting larger amounts of text in the TT: are we dealing with an adaptation (e.g. children's literature), or with a case of censorship or any other kind of *patronage*, as Lefevere (1992: 15–25) called the powers outside the literary system that exert influence on the system itself?

5.5 Neutral Translation

The question remains whether Neutral Translation exists and how it can be defined. We decided to include Neutral Translation in the model, covering all cases of translation whenever the translation remains *unmarked*, i.e. those cases where the translator did not really meet a translation problem and was able to use the most *obvious* choice of words, that is, in a manner of speaking, the first suggestion presented to the translator who is looking up an entry in a dictionary.

When, recapitulating the extremely simplified example of Vinay and Darbelnet (2000 [1958]: 92), the French sentence "Le livre est sur la table" is replaced by "The book is on the table" in English, no real shifts in form nor meaning happen, since these two sentences do look perfectly acceptable in both languages, and no meaning is added nor omitted in either language, regardless of the direction in which the sentence has been translated: from English into French or vice versa. In these cases the two languages seem to have perfect matches for each other's discourse and translations can be made in both directions, regardless of which of the two is to be considered the SL or the TL.

This kind of Neutral Translation becomes more difficult to spot when we are dealing with language pairs that are less related to each other, for instance when one language uses articles or case endings and the other doesn't, but this does not mean we cannot define a perfectly *neutral* TL version of a particular expression in the SL, taking into account all grammatical and syntactic restrictions of the language pair involved. When different idiomatic alternatives are available to the translator in the TL, then we should always be able to distinguish *neutral* translation from those cases of (too) *literal translation*, which we should label as Moderate Foreignization.

6 Comparison of ST and TT on the level of transemes

Having constructed a model that includes the main translation shifts in a simplified scheme, we should be able to determine the isolated translators' decisions on a microstructural level. Returning to our initial challenge to measure the degree of foreignization of a literary translation by comparing different TL versions of one SL literary text, it is clear we still have to bring the information on individual decisions together in one larger scheme. In order to be able to count the different shifts we first have to define *units of translation*, the smallest elements in which to divide both the ST and the TT.

In this paper we take *transemes* as the starting-point for investigating translations on a microstructural level. A *transeme* is defined by van Leuven-Zwart (1989: 155) as the "comprehensible textual unit" into which the source and target texts have to be divided as basic units of comparison, as "sentences are generally too long and words too short to be easily compared" (id.). Van Leuven-Zwart derives these units from Dik's *Theory of Functional Grammar* (1989), based on *state of affairs transemes* (a predicate + its arguments), on the one hand, and *satellite transemes* (adverbial specifications or amplifications of the state of affairs transeme), on the other hand (van Leuven-Zwart 1989: 156). In this paper we will refine and expand the notion of *transemes* into the smallest textual unit that forms a whole for translational purposes. Within the scope of this paper, we will also look beyond pure lexico-semantic units, to include stylistic and syntactic features, e.g. alliteration, repetition, sentence length and marked word order.

By dividing the ST into lexico-semantic, stylistic and syntactic transemes we can make a detailed microstructural comparison of the ST with different translations into several languages, thus establishing, for each of the translation shifts, a degree of foreignization according to the model and the criteria explained in the previous section. As this process is, of course, very labor-intensive and time-consuming, the analysis of the ST and TT should be limited to "a few passages chosen at random" (van Leuven-Zwart 1989: 155), assuming that the translation strategy chosen by the literary translator remains consistent throughout the whole translation which is, indeed, not always the case, but any research method based on a sample taken at random has to deal with this risk.

Having compared an equal number of transemes in both ST and one or more TT, the degree of foreignization (DF) of a translation can be measured by bringing the quantitative results of the microstructural analysis of the transemes into the following model:

$$DF = 5F+2f+(-2)d+(-5)D$$

where "F" is the number of translation shifts that should be considered as strongly foreignizing (5.1), and "f" represents the number of cases of moderate foreignization (5.2), "d" moderate domestication (5.3) and "D" strong domestication (5.4) respectively. We suggest this model with constants 2 and 5 (instead of the more obvious 1 and 2) in order to give more weight to the extremities of strong foreignization and domestication. This seems only logical as we are looking at the overall result of the translation process, compared to the original text. While most cases of moderate foreignization and domestication could go unnoticed by a reader familiar with the ST, both strong foreignization and domestication represent major operations that do influence the character of the TT and should, therefore, count for more.

The number of cases of neutral translation (5.5) is not taken into account but they do, of course, influence the final result of the calculations because they straighten out the extremes of the translation strategies. The more cases of neutral translation in the translation, the less extreme the final degree of foreignization will be. The number of cases of neutral translation also enters into it when the average degree of foreignization is calculated: DF/N, with N = the total number of transemes the research results are based on.

7 Case study

In order to check the validity of this quantitative model a case study has been carried out based on three different translations of the Russian novel *Besy* (*Devils* or *Demons*) by Fyodor Dostoevsky, two translations into Dutch (D1 and D2) and one into English (E):

(D1) *Boze Geesten* (Evil Spirits), translated by Hans Leerinck (1959), first published in 1959;

(D2) *Duivels* (Devils), translated by Hans Boland (2008), first published in 2008;

(E) *Devils*, translated by Constance Garnett (2005), first published in 1916.

The oldest Dutch translation (D1) is published in the prestigious and canonical *De Russische Bibliotheek* (The Russian Library) series, which is renowned for the high quality of the (mostly rather foreignizing) translations. The D1 translation, indeed, seems to be, at first sight, rather foreignizing with long *Dostoevskian* sentences and a vocabulary that seems rather outdated in Dutch today.

Boland, the translator of the newest Dutch version (D2), on the other hand, deliberately chose a more domesticating translation strategy and he even wrote an essay on his translation choices which has been published as a separate volume, entitled *Zeer Russisch zeer. Over Dostojevski's Duivels (On Dostoevsky's Devils)*. Boland (2008: 68–69) explains, among other things, why he decided to translate the title of the work as *Duivels* (Devils), although previous Dutch translations, including the more or less canonical D1, were entitled either *Demonen* (Demons) or *Boze Geesten* (Evil Spirits).

The English translation by Garnett can justly be considered as canonical in English-speaking countries, which explains why the translation was published in 2005 in the Wordsworth Classics series without any reference to the fact that this translation actually dates back to 1916.[3] The translation seems, at first sight, very faithful to the Russian original in respecting the specific style of the Russian novelist.

The first 201 transemes in the Russian ST have been compared at a microstructural level with the different translations according to the aforementioned criteria. This case study is of a rather limited size, but the first results of the investigation, nevertheless, indicate some clear tendencies in the three translations, as will be illustrated by the examples in the following paragraphs.

(1) R: Вместо введения: / несколько подробностей из биографии / многочтимого / Степана / Трофимовича / Верховенского.[4] (1)[5]

---

3   The 2005 edition, in fact contains one extra chapter, translated by Michael Nicholson, that had been left out in the first translation by Garnett (2005).
4   The sign / is used to indicate the division between transemes.

D1: In plaats van inleiding (f): enige details uit de biografie (f) van de hooggeachte (f) Stepan (F) Trofimowitsj (F) Werchowenski (F).

D2: In plaats van een inleiding (f): enige biografische gegevens (d) over de zeer geachte heer (D) Stepan (F) Ø (D) Verchovenski (F).

E: Introductory (D). Some details of the biography (f) of that highly respected gentleman (D) Stephan (f) Trofimovitch (F) Verhovensky (F).

The D1 translation almost literally follows the Russian original regarding the choice of words, word order and style. The name, patronymic and surname of the novel's hero are literally transcribed, which means these shifts should be considered as strongly foreignizing (F). The D2 translation is less consistent. The first names and surname are equally transcribed (F), but the patronymic is deliberately omitted (D) on the argument that Dutch culture does not use patronymics anyway and, therefore, they should not be used in translations either (Boland 2008: 71). On the other hand, the translator of the D2 version adds the word "heer" (mister) to the adjective "highly respected", while this was not strictly necessary in Dutch (D). The English translation also combines foreignizing and domesticating features: transcription of patronymic and surname (F), adaptation of the name (f, because the *Stepan* of the original is replaced by a more English sounding *Stephan*, but not by the domesticating *Steven* or *Stephen*), omission of the "Вместо" (instead of) (D) and addition of the word "gentleman" (D).

The way translators make use of borrowings and loanwords in literary translation is one of the elements that give an indication about the translation strategy chosen (see 5.1). In example (2) Leerinck (D1) and Garnett (E) deliberately stick close to the original "пьедестал" (which is a loanword itself in Russian!) although they had an alternative available ("voetstuk" in Dutch and "base" in English).

(2) R: пьедестала (3)
     D1: piedestal (F)
     D2: voetstuk (0^6)
     E: pedestal (F)

---

5   The numbers between brackets refer to the paragraphs in the original Russian text from where the samples are taken.

6   0 is used to indicate "neutral translation".

An example of *radical change of meaning* (see 5.4) is to be found in the Dutch translations of some ancient linear units:

(3) R: в какие-нибудь два вершка росту (3)
     D1: ongeveer twee duim lang (D)
     D2: nauwelijks twee duim groot (D)
     E: only three or four inches high (f)

The Russian "два вершка" actually equals about 3.5 inches, but in both Dutch translations the height (of the Lilliputians the narrator is talking about) is reduced to 2 inches (a "duim" is an inch), while the original information is retained in Garnett's translation, although she actually has to use an explicitation to render the information from the original as faithfully as possible.

Stylistic features are taken into account as well in our microstructural analysis. The alliteration in example (4) is retained only in the D1 version, while one of the two elements of the alliteration is simply omitted in the other two translations. In the fifth example only the D1 translation retains the literal repetition of the expression "так-сказать" which, in our opinion, is essential to render the characterization of the novel's narrator in a true Dostoevskian manner.

(4) R: беспрерывной и благородной склонности (3)
     D1: voortdurende en verheven neiging (f)
     D2: Ø gecultiveerde neiging (D)
     E: Ø generous propensity (D)

(5) R: так-сказать <...> так-сказать (3)
     D1: om zo te zeggen <...> om zo te zeggen (f)
     D2: laten we maar zeggen <...> liever gezegd (d)
     E: so to say <...> so to speak (d)

A final example illustrates the translators' decisions on a stylistic level:

(6) R: потому что прекраснейший был человек (3)
     D1: want hij was een prachtvent (d)
     D2: Hij was nou eenmaal een doodgoeie ziel (d)
     E: for he was a most excellent man (f)

In this case the translation shifts, in both Dutch versions, concern the linguistic register of the ST because neither "vent" (*fellow* or *chap*, in D1) nor "ziel" (*soul*, in D2) reflect the neutral character of the Russian word "человек", that simply means "man". The same goes for the translation of the adjective "прекраснейший" which has been translated literally in English ("most excellent"), but adapted in Dutch into "splendid (fellow)" in D1 and even "extremely kind-hearted (soul)" in D2.

An analysis of the translation choices for all 201 transemes in our sample yields the results given in Table 1.

Table 1. Division of translation shifts in translations D1, D2 and E, according to the quantitative model.

Transemes 1-201	F	f	0	d	D	DF
D1 (1959)	8	64	111	16	2	126
D2 (2008)	4	13	103	62	19	-173
E (1916)	5	47	106	31	12	-3

Despite the limited extent of the case study, some very clear conclusions can be drawn about the degree of foreignization of all three translations. The intuitional impression about the translation strategies in the two Dutch translations is actually confirmed by the statistical data in Table 1. The *canonical* D1 translation, indeed, scores a much higher degree of foreignization than the modern D2 translation. But the English version, that seemed faithful to the Russian original at first sight, actually holds the middle between the two Dutch versions in any of the aspects of the model. The 12 cases of strong domestication, mainly omissions, do compensate for the 52 transemes that were translated rather foreignized, which means the Garnett translation is less balanced than the other two. Most cases of foreignization in her translation relate to literal translations and the preservation of the specific Russian word order, which gives the reader a good impression of the ST written by Dostoevsky but on the other hand, the large number of omissions do have consequences for how the reader perceives the text. They reflect well the fleeing strategy the translator followed whenever she was confronted with specific translation difficulties that exposed her rather moderate knowledge of the Russian language.[7]

8 Conclusions

In this paper we attempted to operationalize the concepts of domestication and foreignization, based on a microstructural analysis of transemes and starting from a simplified model that comprises 5 fields of translation shifts, including lexico-semantic, syntactic and stylistic features. The case study on three translations of Dostoevsky's "Besy" suggests that the model is indeed usable on small corpuses and that translations from different periods and target cultures can be compared within the model.

Still a number of questions remain. Firstly, we should bear in mind that a diachronical analysis might be hindered by changing linguistic norms over time. Words in translation that seem marked to the reader now might have been the neutral choice of word at the time when the translation was made, forcing the researcher to change his/her assessment from (f) into (0). When investigating the foreignization/domestication question a researcher should most probably make a distinction between a foreignizing translation now and the text at the time of publishing.

A second problem, which makes translation less *measurable*, confronts the researcher when larger passages in the TT are affected by one major strategic decision by the translator. When the translator omits larger amounts of text, when fragments in other languages are left untranslated or when dialects and slang are deliberately and throughout the text normalized in translation we cannot easily include this kind of translator's decision in a quantitative model. The same goes for those cases when large amounts of text have been omitted and/or radically changed because of external decisions, irrespective of the translator, i.e. in the case of censorship or other kinds of patronage.

---

7 Garnett's somewhat limited knowledge of Russian is confirmed in a recent article by Amanda Hopkinson (2011) on the history of literary translation in the United Kingdom.

Nevertheless, the case study shows the relevance of a quantitative model for translation studies' research. Thanks to the fact that the model can be applied, at once, to translations into different languages, it can be used as a tool to investigate tendencies in translation on a macrostructural level, across the borders of cultures and languages and even across the borders of time, when taking into account the linguistic evolutions in the TL.

References

Baker, Mona (1992): *In Other Words. A coursebook on translation.* London and New York: Routledge.
Boland, Hans (2008): Dostojevski, F. M. *Duivels.* Amsterdam: Athenaeum. Translated by Hans Boland.
—— (2008): *Zeer Russisch zeer. Over Dostojevski's "Duivels".* Amsterdam: Triade.
Catford, J. C. (1965): *A Linguistic Theory of Translation.* London: Oxford University Press.
Chesterman, Andrew (1997): *Memes of translation.* Amsterdam and Philadelphia: John Benjamins.
Dik, Simon (1989): *The Theory of Functional Grammar.* Dordrecht: Foris.
Garnett, Constance (2005): Dostoevsky, Fyodor. *Devils.* London: Wordsworth Classics. Translated by Constance Garnett.
Grit, Diederik (1997): "De vertaling van realia." In: *Filter* 4 (4), 42–48.
Hopkinson, Amanda (2011): "Literair vertalers in Groot-Brittannië." In: *Filter* 18 (3), 21–26.
Judickaitė, Ligita (2009): "The Notions of Foreignization and Domestication applied to Film Translation: Analysis of Subtitles in Cartoon *Ratatouille*." In: *Jaunųjų Mokslininkų Darbai* 2 (23), 36–43. Available at: http://old.su.lt/filemanager/download/6470/Judickaite.pdf. Visited 17 November 2011.
Leerinck, Hans (1959): Dostojewski, F. M. *Boze geesten.* Amsterdam: van Oorschot. Translated by Hans Leerinck.
Lefevere, André (1992): *Translation, Rewriting and the Manipulation of Literary Fame.* London and New York: Routledge.
Leuven-Zwart, Kitty van (1989): "Translation and Original: Similarities and Dissimilarities", 1 and 2. Part 1. In: *Target* 1 (2), 151–181.
—— (1990): "Translation and Original: Similarities and Dissimilarities", 1 and 2. Part 2. In: *Target* 2:1, 69–95.
Newmark, Peter (1988): *A Textbook of Translation.* New York, London, Toronto, Sydney and Tokyo: Prentice Hall.
Pedersen, Jan (2007): "Cultural Interchangeability: The Effects of Substituting Cultural References in Subtitling." In: *Perspectives: Studies in Translatology* 15 (1), 30–48.
—— (2005): *How is Culture Rendered in Subtitles?* Paper presented at *MuTra 2005: Challenges of Multidimensional Translation.* Available at: http://www.euroconferences.info/proceedings/2005_Proceedings/2005_Pedersen_Jan.pdf. Visited 17 November 2011.

Schleiermacher, Friedrich (2004 [1813]): "On the different Methods of Translating." In: Venuti, Lawrence [ed.] (2004): *The Translation Studies Reader* (2nd edition). London and New York: Routledge. 43–63.

Venuti, Lawrence (1995): *The Translator's Invisibility. A History of Translation.* London and New York: Routledge.

Vinay, Jean-Paul / Darbelnet, Jean (2000 [1958]): "A Methodology for Translation." In: Venuti, Lawrence [ed.] (2000): *The Translation Studies Reader.* London and New York: Routledge. 84–93.

Vlahov, Sergej / Florin, Sider (2006 [1970]): *Neperevodimoe v perevode.* Moskva: R. Valent.

"... thou, my Rose, ...": Translating the Direct Address of Shakespeare's Sonnet into Russian

Elena Rassokhina

Umeå University, Sweden

Abstract

Shakespeare's Sonnet 109 belongs to the large group of sonnets that seem to be addressed to an unnamed young nobleman. The poet addresses his beloved friend as 'thou, my Rose' in the couplet of Sonnet 109. The main problem encountered in the couplet is posed by the contradiction between a feminine grammatical gender of the target noun *roza* in the Russian language, on the one hand, and a male addressee, on the other. The couplet has challenged Russian translators in different ways and I analyze this in the light of the dichotomy foreignization/domestication. Fourteen translations of the sonnet have been considered. Translators had to choose one of the strategies (domesticating, foreignizing, and a third strategy that combines both characteristics) in their approach to solving the problem. The result shows that almost all of the interpretations contain a certain degree of domestication which means that this strategy has been the most pervasive in the history of the sonnet's translation into the Russian language.

Sonnet 109

O never say that I was false of heart,
Though absence seemed my flame to qualify;
As easy might I from my self depart
As from my soul, which in thy breast doth lie:
That is my home of love. If I have ranged,
Like him that travels I return again,
Just to the time, not with the time exchanged,
So that myself bring water for my stain.
Never believe, though in my nature reigned
All frailties that besiege all kinds of blood,
That it could so preposterously be stained
To leave for nothing all thy sum of good;

For nothing this wide Universe I call,
Save thou, my Rose; in it thou art my all.[1]

1 Introduction

Shakespeare's Sonnet 109 belongs to the large group of sonnets (1 through 126) that seems to be addressed to an unnamed young nobleman with whom the speaker has an intense romantic relationship. The poet addresses his beloved friend as 'thou, my Rose' in the couplet of Shakespeare's Sonnet 109:

For nothing this wide Universe I call,
Save thou, my Rose; in it thou art my all.

The main problem encountered in the couplet is posed by the contradiction between a feminine grammatical gender of the target language noun *roza* in the Russian language and a male addressee to whom this word is directed. The couplet has challenged Russian translators in different ways and I analyze this in the light of the dichotomy domestication/foreignization. These concepts are from Lawrence Venuti (1995), who states that the domesticating approach involves the process of the identification of domestic values by the reader. This identification is adopted in order to minimize the strangeness of the original foreign text. The domesticating translation aims to present the readers of the target text with the illusion that it was originally written in the target language in order to make it fluent and, using Venuti's word, to make it 'transparent'.

A foreignizing translation, on the other hand, challenges the target language reader by breaking target language conventions, that is, the translator deliberately retains something of the foreignness of the source text. A foreignizing translation is not transparent and traces of the foreign are left as much as possible within the translated text, thus making the reader feel the linguistic and cultural differences.

Thus, the presence or absence of elements of foreignness in a target language text can serve as a criterion for judging whether the translation is domesticated or foreignized. It has been argued, however, that any translation will use a combination of these strategies in practice because, as Paloposki and Oittinen

---

1   This sonnet is quoted from the edition by S. Booth (1977: 94–95).

noted, "two seemingly opposing strategies can be aiming for similar effects" (2000: 375). Likewise, the Spanish translation scholar Dora Sales Salvador suggests, that "in the contradictory, yet complementary dialectic between exoticising (foreignising) and familiarising (domesticating), the ideal solution would be to find a medium term, an in-between space, respecting otherness but able to transmit and communicate to the target culture" (Rollason 2010: 4).

Bearing in mind that domestication/foreignization strategies approach translation from a cultural perspective, it is obvious that the main reason that translation exists is the existence of different languages and, therefore, the language barrier. As Komissarov states, "the idea of linguistic transfer is implicit in the very name of the phenomenon and a definition of the translating process usually makes some reference to language or languages" (1991: 33). This means that both the linguistic features of the languages (in our case English and Russian) and the traditional cultural perceptions and associations connected to the source language *rose* and the corresponding Russian word *roza* have to be taken into account. After providing the necessary grammatical, historical and cultural overview, I will take a closer look at examples of the actual Shakespearian line in Russian translation in order to explore what the concepts of domestication and foreignization mean in relation to this linguistic problem. The study also attempts to estimate the dominant translation strategy that has been used to deal with this particular linguistic, but culturally-charged item. The aim of this study is not to assess the correctness of translations but to describe the translational products from two different perspectives.

2 Grammatical, historical and cultural background

Sonnet 109 has been translated into the Russian language more than ten times.[2] The main difficulty that is encountered by translators in the couplet is posed by the direct address "my Rose", which corresponds to *moja roza* in Russian. Consequently, the literal translation of *thou, my Rose* into Russian would be *ty, moja*

---

2   For a chronological overview of the translators up to 2010, see Pervushina (2010: 342ff.). For an overview of the sonnet's translations into Russian, see http://www.shakespeare.ouc.ru/sonnet-109-ru.html.

roza. However, this straightforward translation proves to be problematic in relation to the poetic context of Shakespeare's poem. One of the major difficulties arising from the translation process concerns the grammatical gender of nouns.[3]

Russian nouns are classified into three genders (masculine, feminine and neuter) that have syntactic consequences. The gender of a Russian noun is revealed by agreement, that is, when an adjective, or a relative, a third-person or a possessive pronoun adopts a different form because of the gender of the noun it modifies. The Russian noun *roza*, which we encounter in Sonnet 109, belongs to the feminine grammatical gender and affects the form of the preceding possessive pronoun *moja* (my). At the same time, it is generally accepted that the first 126 of Shakespeare's sonnets are addressed to a young nobleman and focus on the speaker's romantic relationship with him. This specific cultural element has caused translators some difficulties in relation to grammatical issues. For example, it has been noted that in Sonnets 1 and 99 Shakespeare uses the possessive pronoun *his* to refer to the noun *Rose* (see the first word in line 4, my emphasis):

> From fairest creatures we desire increase,
> That thereby **beauty's *Rose*** might never die,
> But as the riper should by time decrease,
> ***His*** tender heir might bear his memory…
>
> (Sonnet 1)

> ***The Roses*** fearfully on thorns did stand,
> One blushing shame, another white despair;
> A third, nor red nor white, had stol'n of both,
> And to **his** robb'ry had annexed thy breath, …
>
> (Sonnet 99)

This grammatical detail became an issue for a special gender-oriented discussion among Russian critics and translators. Yeliferova (2009) notes, that in Sonnet 99 the word 'Rose' "suddenly becomes masculine". The explanation that she offers is

---

[3] In an analysis of recent studies of grammatical gender, Kremer notes that a strong disagreement among scholars about whether English has a category of noun gender is caused by divergent definitions of the term 'gender' (Kremer 1997: 64). I use the term 'grammatical gender' following Corbett's definition: "Saying that a language has three genders implies that there are three classes of nouns which can be distinguished syntactically by the agreement they take" (Corbett 1991: 4).

that the rose has always been a traditional substitute for a beloved female in all cultures; therefore, it is "quite logical" that the word takes the masculine gender because Shakespeare's addressee is a male.[4] Sharakshane (2009), one of the latest translators of the whole sonnet cycle into Russian, and who includes an accompanying commentary on each sonnet, claims that the capitalization of the noun *Rose* in the Quarto edition suggests its personification. Furthermore, he states that in English poetry the rose usually becomes masculine when it is personified.[5] I would argue that these statements need some correction and verification.

It is worth noting, that Old English had a system of grammatical gender that is similar to Modern German or Russian: every noun belonged to one of three grammatical genders (masculine, feminine or neuter). According to the Anglo-Saxon Dictionary, which deals with all the words that occur in poetry and prose during the period between the 5th and 11th centuries, the noun *rose* belonged to the feminine gender (Hall 1984: 142). During the Middle English period (between the late 11th and the late 15th century) the language was in transition and began to lose its gender system, and the shift away from grammatical gender had been completed long before the Elizabethan era (Barber 2000: 160). Therefore, the word *rose* must have dropped its grammatical feminine gender by the time the word occurs in Shakespeare's texts.

A further issue concerns the possessive pronoun *his*, which refers to the noun *rose* in the sonnets. The pronoun *his* does not make *rose* masculine, but reflects another process of language change that was occurring at the very time Shakespeare was writing. As Barber explains, *his* was a traditional possessive form of *it*, and "not until the end of the sixteenth century do we encounter *its*. It is very rare in Shakespeare, occurring only in works published late" (Barber 2000: 187). However, *its* was in common use in the 1620s, while *his* was limited to the possessive of *he*. Shakespeare took advantage of the emerging gender implications of the pronoun in Sonnet 109 and used *his* with the primary meaning 'its', thus linking the rose as a symbolic flower to the young man, the sonnet's addressee.

---

4 "Roza kak 'ona' – tradicionnyj substitut vozljublennoj. A u Šekspira adresat sonetov – junoša, poetomu vpolne logično i roza okazyvaetsja v mužskom rode" (Yeliferova 2009).
5 "[...] v anglijskoj poèzii, pri personifikacii, roza prinimaet mužskoj rod" (Sharakshane 2009).

Despite these grammatical processes during the Elizabethan era, the rose as a plant was a cultural symbol of female beauty. The long history of the rose as a symbol of femininity goes back to Greek mythology, where it was an attribute of Aphrodite and Venus, and later became associated with the Virgin Mary (Impelluso 2004: 118). According to the *Dictionary of Subjects and Symbols in Art*, the rose was still sacred to Venus during the Renaissance, when one "linked the rose to Venus because of its beauty and fragrance, comparing the pricking of its thorns to wounds of love" (Hall 1979: 268). The flower occupied a special place in Elizabethan thought because the rose was also an important emblem of the Tudor dynasty. Shakespeare used the image of the rose frequently in his plays and returns to it in the sonnets. The comparison of the young man with a rose is a constant motif throughout the first sequence of the sonnets, despite the word's feminine associations.[6] However, it should be noted that in the Quarto edition of 1609 the word *Rose* is always emphasized by the capitalization of the initial letter (in Sonnet 1 even with the italicization of the word)[7], a detail that "may signal a wider field of reference, encompassing both genders and, possibly, a metaphysical ideal of beauty" (Duncan-Jones 2010: 112). Crystal, who describes the practice of using capital letters in the Early Modern English of Shakespeare's time, writes that "there was a huge amount of variation in the way individual words were capitalized" (Crystal 2008: 49) because the conventions were still developing. While there is much inconsistency in Shakespeare's use of capitals in the Folio, Crystal states that the 1609 Quarto edition of Sonnets is the only place where an intention behind the use of capitals can be suspected. "There is no obvious system behind the usage, other than the possibility that individual words have been capitalized to suggest extra prominence, and this is a matter of individual interpretation, line by line" (Crystal 2008: 52). In reference to Sonnet 109, Booth states that *my rose* is "a common appellation of affection in which rose is emblematic of perfection and understood as 'the best'" (Booth 1977: 354). Thus, as a form of address, *rose* may stand for the general idea of the human beauty's paragon, a simile of youth, which can be applied to both women and men. In *Richard II*, for instance, the Queen uses

---

6   See Sonnets 1, 35, 54, 67, 95, 98, 99.
7   It should be noted, however, that in Sonnet 35 the capitalized *Rose* is placed at the beginning of line 2, thus following the practice of using initial capitalization of a line of verse, which was standard in print by Shakespeare's time (see Crystal 2008: 49).

the epithet "my fair rose" for Richard (*R2*: 5.1.8) in the scene that includes their parting. In *Hamlet*, Ophelia describes Hamlet as "the expectancy and rose of the fair state" (*Hamlet* 3.1.151), which implies that she sees the Prince as the heir to the throne.

This may also be seen as a reflection of the concept associated with the Great Chain of Being that was widely recognized during the Renaissance.[8] A monarch, who occupied the highest position among human beings, could only be compared to things that had the same royal positions in their different realms. Forker states that "[r]oses, being at the top of the floral hierarchy in the Great Chain of Being, were naturally associated with kings", and refers to the red and white roses which played such a significant historical role in the Wars of the Roses (Forker 2002: 416).[9] Consequently, the noun *rose*, which is used as a substitute for the young friend in the sonnets, does not seem to contradict the courteous poetic tradition of the Elizabethan Age.

3 Comparison of the Russian translations

As we have seen, the English tradition allows the use of *rose* as a way of referring to both a male and a female addressee. However, the fact that the poet addresses his male friend by means of the direct address *my Rose* in Sonnet 109, contrasts sharply with the traditional Russian association of the flower with female beauty, which is strongly supported in the grammar of the Russian language.[10] The difficulty that arises for a Russian translator is how to translate the source language's direct address *my Rose*, whose literal translation into Russian would be *moja roza*, which is grammatically feminine.

Table 1 summarizes the possible options available for translators. The horizontal lines correspond to three possible representations of the addressee's sex: male, indefinite (the addressee's sex is not specified), or female. These three options may

---

8   On the concept of the Great Chain of Being see Tillyard (1966).
9   Cf. Hotspur in *Henry IV* says: *To put down Richard, that sweet lovely rose, / And plant this thorn, this canker, Bolingbroke?* (1.3. 175–176). Bolingbroke, as opposite to the lawful Richard II, is called for thorn and canker, one of the lowest plants in the kingdom of flora.
10 On the poetic usage of rose in Russian literature see Veselovsky 1939: 132–139.

be analyzed using the dichotomy domestication/foreignization as two basic strategies for solving the problem (Venuti 1995). The first sequence of the Sonnets (1–126) is dedicated to a young man but, according to Spiller (1992: 150), the sequence only contains about twenty-five poems in which the male sex of the addressee is clear. Sonnet 109 does not belong to this group.

In the practice of translation, a translator may consider whether to adopt a more foreignizing or more domesticating approach and to what extent this should be carried out (cf. above). It should be noted that the practice of a male author of a love poem addressing a man instead of a fair maiden cannot be considered to be characteristic of Russian literary tradition.[11] For this reason the use of a clearly masculine form of address in the translation may be interpreted as foreignization. On the other hand, an implied female addressee would be perceived to be natural by Russian readers within the context of the sonnet; therefore, this translation choice could also be perceived as domestication. Moreover, I would claim that even the use of the common, indefinite way of addressing the sonnet's love object in the Russian translation will likely be perceived as female-oriented, i.e. domesticated, because of the lack of male-oriented literary experience.

Apart from the male/female identity of the sonnet's addressee, translations may also differ in relation to the solutions for the direct address 'rose' as a textual micro-unit: a) *roza* (the literal translation of 'rose'), b) a masculine substitute for the noun *roza* (e.g. *cvetok* – a flower), or c) an omission of the actual word.

---

11   There were some reflections of homosexuality throughout the history of Russian literature before the beginning of the 20th century, but it was usually condemned as a sin. As Karlinsky states, "The two giants of Russian nineteenth-century literature, Tolstoy and Dostoevsky, were men of the Victorian age who regarded all forms of sexuality as impure, distasteful and dangerous" (2002). The theme of homosexual love enjoyed considerable attention nationwide during the short period of the first decade of the 20th century, but all the gains were reversed by the Revolution of 1917. During the Soviet regime no gay-themed works were published.

Table 1. The possible options available for translating the direct address 'Rose' into the Russian language.

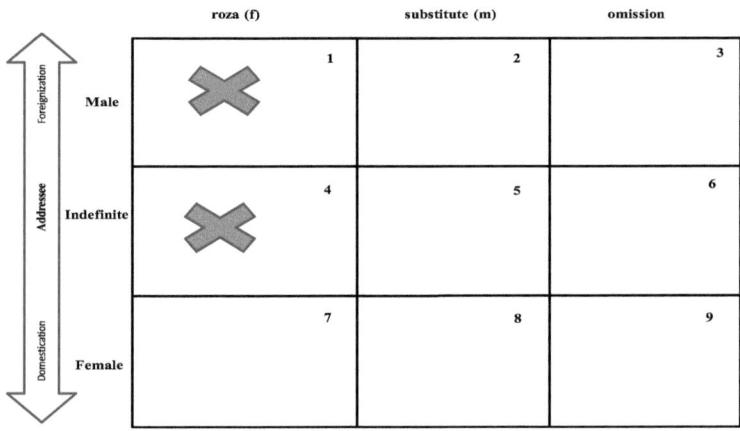

These three different types of translation solutions are indicated in the columns of Table 1. They may be described as translation techniques that, according to Molina and Hurtado Albir (2002: 508), occupy a special place in problem solving – while "strategies are part of the process [of translation], techniques affect the result".

There are 14 different translations included in the analysis, and they cover the period from 1880 to 2009. Table 1 provides the key for the analysis of the translations. However, as is the case with any simplified model, it cannot include all the possible aspects – these will be discussed below. The literal translation of the sonnet's direct address requires an indefinite (common) addressee and the feminine address *roza*, and can be positioned in section 4 of the table. Another hypothetical option, which may also be considered to be the literal translation because it could be seen as a reflection of the translator's intention to mark the sex of the person addressed, allows for a male addressee and the same feminine direct address *roza*. This option will occupy section 1. However, such word combinations as those suggested by the original are unlikely to occur in the Russian language (this is indicated by crosses in sections 1 and 4).

The first attempt to translate the whole cycle of Shakespeare's sonnets into the Russian language was made at the end of the 19th century by Gerbel. The translator presented a rather radical solution to the problem; that is, omitting *roza* totally, and then readdressing the sonnet to a woman.

Da, esli ne tebja, to nikogo svoeju	Yes, if not you, then no one (I) dare
Vo vsej vselennoj ja nazvat' uže ne smeju.	to call "mine" in the whole universe.[12]
(Gerbel 1880)	

The Russian feminine possessive pronoun *svoeju* (mine) that is used above indicates that the addressee is a woman.[13]

The strategy of "feminizing" the sonnet's addressee has also been chosen by Marshak (1948), the most recognized translator of the cycle, and whose interpretations are considered classic in Russia. Using Venuti's words, Marshak "brings the author back home" (Venuti 1995: 20), minimizing the strangeness of Sonnet 109 for Russian readers.

Čto bez tebja prostornyj ètot svet?	What is this wide universe without you?
Ty v nëm odna. Drugogo sčast'ja net	You are the only one in it. There is no
(Marshak 1948)	other kind of happiness.

Marshak totally omits any reference to a flower and instead employs the sentence *Ty v nëm odna*. The word *odna* (the one) in this phrase takes a feminine form and indicates that the poem is addressed to a female person.[14] Thus, both Gerbel and Marshak use the most domesticating strategy in translating the sonnet: they do not employ the direct address and use the feminine grammatical gender for the addressee.

Two recent translations by Badygov (2005) and Kozarovetsky (2000) avoided including the literal translation of *roza*, but, unlike Marshak, they did this without

---

12   All back-translations are mine – E.R.
13   The verbal evidence of Gerbel's redirection of the poet's feelings toward a female addressee has been found in a further 22 sonnets. See Pervushina (2009: 93).
14   Marshak readdressed 14 sonnets to a female (Pervushina 2009: 214).

readdressing the sonnet to a woman.[15] Still, the Russian reader will probably assume that the sonnet is addressed to a female in accordance with the established literary tradition in which the sonnet is associated with love poetry that is to a lady. Therefore, in spite of the fact that the translators chose to stay neutral, I would consider the omission of the direct address as a domesticating strategy and place both versions in section 6, but closer to the domestication pole of the continuum.

Ničtožen dlja menja ves' ètot mir,　　　　The whole world means nothing to me,
No bez tebja ja odinok i sir.　　　　　　　But I am lonely and poor without you.
(Badygov 2005)

Ves' mir mne kažetsja liš' pustotoju,　　　The whole world seems empty to me,
I tol'ko ty cvetëš' sred' suhostoja.　　　　And only you are blooming among dead
(Kozarovetsky 2000)　　　　　　　　　　wood.

In order to avoid tension between the male addressee and the feminine gender of address, Vinonen (1964) and Kushner (1989) replaced *roza* with the noun *cvetok* (flower) which is masculine. This translation strategy is well suited for Venuti's definition of domestication as "an ethnocentric reduction of the foreign text to target-language cultural values" (Venuti 1995: 20).

Čto mir! Hodil ja po ego dorogam,　　　　The world! I have walked down its roads,
I znaju: tak že pust' on, kak širok.　　　　And (I) know: it is as empty as it is wide.
Liš' ty ego i krasiš', moj cvetok.　　　　　You alone make it more beautiful, my flower.
(Vinonen 1964)

Ne stal by žit' ja v ètom carstve lži,　　　 I wouldn't live in this kingdom of lies,
Kogda b ne ty, cvetok moej duši!　　　　If not for you, the flower of my soul!
(Kushner 1989)

The word *cvetok*, which is a part of the noun phrase *cvetok moej duši* (flower of my soul) may serve as an example of the strategies being combined. The noun does not disagree with Russian cultural values, because it is masculine, and it may also be applied to both a woman and a man. Furthermore, in this context it also acquires

---

15　We encounter the combination *moj drug* (my friend) in line 5 of Badygov's version, but this kind of address may also be used to address both men and women.

the meaning of being 'the best part of an object', an emblem of perfection, which comes closer to the understanding of the *rose* in the original text. These two interpretations can be placed in the middle section of the table.

The majority of Russian translators in the history of the translation of Sonnet 109 choose to use the literal translation of 'rose' (*roza*) in their versions. Fofanov translated the sonnet as early as in 1904 and used *roza* in the couplet.

I ver' – vselennuju ja ni vo čto ne stavlju,	Believe – I think little of the universe,
Tebja, o roza, ja odnu ljublju i slavlju.	I love and praise only you, o rose.
(Fofanov 1904)	

Even though the author does not readdress the sonnet to a woman as openly as Gerbel did before him, the link between the feminine numeral *odna* and *roza* gives the strong impression that there is a female being addressed. For this reason I place Fofanov's translation in the table as an example of domesticating translation.

During the last decade, many translators have striven to use the direct address *roza* in their versions:

Ves' mir ničto. Moročil on, draznja.	The whole world is nothing. It was confusing (and) teasing.
Ty – roza. Vsë ty v mire dlja menja.	You are the rose. You mean everything to me in the world.
(Mikushevitch 2004)	
O, roza, ja kriču – pust' belyj svet	O, rose, – I'm crying – Let the universe
Hranit tebja, – v nëm bol'še sčast'ja net.	To save you [since] there is no more happiness in it.
(Kuznetsov 2004)	
Vselennaja ničtožna, – tak skažu ja.	The universe is miserable, – I'll say so.
V tebe, o rosa, mir svoj nahožu ja.	In you, o rose, I found my world.
(Sharakshane 2009)	

In these examples the feminine address *roza* is likely to be perceived by the target reader as being addressed to a female. However, following Shakespeare's original, the translators do not provide the reader with any clear indication of the sex of the person addressed by *roza*. As a result, these three translations can be placed in the same section as Fofanov's version, but closer to section 4, because of their higher degree of literalness.

Fradkin (1990) has found another compromise solution by using *roza*, but at the same time linking it with the masculine hypernym *cvetok*. The addressee, therefore, loses his/her obvious sexual identity.

Prekrasnej vo vselennoj net cvetka;	There is no flower in the world more fair
Ty – roza, čto odna vo vse veka.	than you;
	You are the rose that is the only one for all
(Fradkin 1990)	time.

Finkel' (1977) developed this idea further by translating the English 'rose' with a noun phrase *rozy cvet* (the rose's bloom), where the head noun *cvet* is masculine:

Ne nužen mne ničtožnyj ètot svet,	I do not need this miserable world,
Mne nužen ty, o nežnoj rozy cvet!	I need you, o, the tender rose's bloom!
(Finkel 1977)	

The Russian reader of Finkel's translation can identify domestic values because in this context the phrase *rozy cvet* acquires the meaning 'the best part of an object', an emblem of perfection, and this is close to the meaning of the original (compare to the commonly used Russian expressions *cvet nacii* (flower of the nation), *cvet intelligencii* (the intellectual elite), *vo cvete let* (in the prime of life).

Stepanov (2003) has found a further solution by using the noun *roza* together with another noun, namely the masculine word *drug* (friend): a masculine noun, that may suggest a male addressee for a Russian reader, but also allows a female one as well.

Bez miloj rozy, bez tebja, moj drug,	Without the sweet rose, without you, my
Ves' mir ničto, i pusto vsë vokrug.	friend,
	The whole world is nothing, and it is empty
(Stepanov 2003)	everywhere.

These three interpretations combine features of both domestication and foreignization because they tend to preserve the original flavor while exhibiting no traces of stiffness, which makes it possible to place them in the middle section of the table.

Chaikovsky was the second author after Gerbel to undertake the task of translating the whole sonnet cycle into Russian in 1914, and introduced a different perspective of the addressee's sex. Unlike his predecessor, who readdressed the sonnet to a female, Chaikovsky chose to emphasize the "right" sex of the addressee by using the word *rózan*, which is a masculine synonym of *roza* that today has fallen out of use.[16]

Net v mire ničego milej tebja,	There is nothing nicer than you in the world,
O rózan moj, ty mne i vsë, i vsja!	O, my rose, you are everything for me!
(Chaikovsky 1914)	

This translation is an example of how a translator tries to challenge target language conventions by employing the masculine word (*rózan*) in order to satisfy the literalness of translation. The strangeness of this interpretation is obvious for the Russian reader of today, which, in terms of Venuti's theory, may serve as a criterion for describing it as foreignizing.

4 Conclusion

Chronologically, the target texts represent 130 years of the translation history of the sonnets into Russian. The direct address *Rose* in Sonnet 109 has proved to be problematic for the translators. The difficulty includes taking into account both the grammatical features of the target language and the traditional cultural perceptions and associations connected to both the source language *rose* and the target language *roza*. This problem challenged Russian translators in different ways and those have been considered as representations of domestication and foreignization in the sense of the dichotomy proposed by Venuti.

---

16 The word *rozan* was marked as old-fashioned in 1978 edition of Ožegov's *Slovar' russkogo jazyka*, though I cannot be sure if it was unusual to the same degree at the time of Chaikovsky translation.

A comparison of the translation strategies has been applied in the analysis of fourteen interpretations made in the target language. One of specific domesticating solutions was readdressing the sonnet to a woman because the normative tradition in Russian love poetry assumes that if a man is present as a lyric subject, then a woman is seen only as an addressee, and vice versa. This strategy was applied in early translations by Gerbel and to a lesser extent by Fofanov, and later by Marshak. A group of three of the most recent translations made by Mikushevitch, Kuznetsov and Sharakshane seem to prefer the domesticating strategy as well, but strive toward some indefiniteness in the question of the sex of the person addressed.

Table 2. Distribution of the translations.

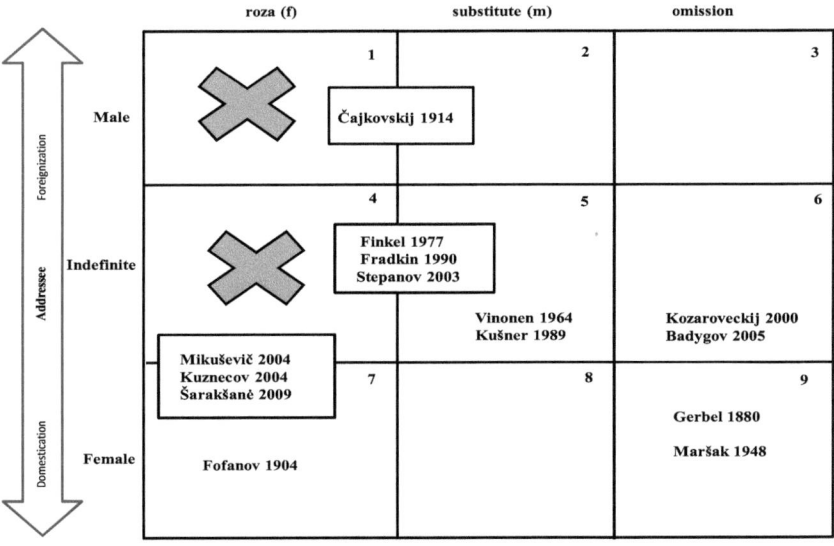

Several interpretations combine features of domesticating and foreignizing strategies (see Table 2). Translators such as Badygov, Kozarovetsky, Vinonen and Kushner chose to avoid using the literal translation of *roza* and instead replaced it with a masculine noun, thus trying to escape the direct feminine associations that *roza* implies. Another group of translators (Finkel, Fradkin, Stepanov) consciously aim to retain the strangeness of the foreign text. They chose to preserve *roza* in their versions, while using methods to reduce the feminineness of the sonnet caused by the address. Nevertheless, the Russian reader will probably assume that the sonnet is addressed to a female. For this reason these translations can be placed somewhere in-between the two poles of the basic strategies but closer to the domesticating one. Finally, the remaining translation by Chaikovsky is the only one that is foreignized, using Venuti's terminology. According to the results, domestication has been the most pervasive translation strategy throughout the whole history of the translation of this sonnet's direct address, even though there have been some variations in the approaches. I would claim that there is a certain degree of domestication in every translation (except one) because of the differences between the linguistic and cultural peculiarities reflected in the source and the target texts.

References

A. Source texts and translations studied

1. Source texts

Booth, Stephen [ed.] (1977): *Shakespeare's Sonnets*. New Haven, London: Yale University Press.

Duncan-Jones, Katherine [ed.] (2010): *Shakespeare's Sonnets*. London: Bloomsbury. (= The Arden Shakespeare).

Forker, Charles R. [ed.] (2002): Shakespeare, W. *King Richard II*. London: Thomson Learning. (= The Arden Shakespeare).

Kastan, David Scott [ed.] (2002): Shakespeare, W. *Henry IV. Part I*. London: Thompson Learning. (= The Arden Shakespeare).

Taylor, Neil / Thompson, Ann [eds.] (2006): Shakespeare, W. *Hamlet*. London: Thompson Learning. (= The Arden Shakespeare).

2. Russian translations of *Sonnet 109*

Badygov (2005) = *Uil'jam Šekspir. Sonety*. Translated by R. Badygov. Moskva: Vodolej Publishers. Available at: http://lib.meta.ua/book/23837/.

Chaikovsky (2010 [1914]) = Čajkovskij, M. (2010 [1914]): *Šekspir. Sonety*. Translated by M. Chaikovsky. Moskva: Olma Media Grupp. Available at: http://lib.ru/SHAKESPEARE/shks_sonnets19.txt.

Finkel (2010 [1977]) = Finkel', A. (2010 [1977]): *Šekspir. Sonety*. Translated by A. Finkel. Sankt-Peterburg: Izdatel'stvo Ivana Limbaha.

Fofanov (2001 [1904]) = *Šekspir Vil'jam. Komedii, sonety*. Translated by K. Fofanov. Samara: "ABC". Available at: http://www.azlib.ru/f/fofanow_k_m/text_0030.shtml.

Fradkin, I. (2003 [1990]) = *Uil'jam Šekspir. Sonety.* Translated by I. Fradkin. Sankt-Peterburg: Dean. Available at: http://lib.ru/SHAKESPEARE/sonnets15.txt.

Gerbel (2001 [1880]) = Gerbel', N. (2001 [1880]): *Vil'jam Šekspir. Sonety.* Translated by N. Gerbel. Sankt-Peterburg: Kristall. Available at: http://az.lib.ru/s/shekspir_w/text_0330.shtml.

Kozarovetsky (2009) = Kozaroveckij, V. (2009): *Šekspir U. Sonety.* Translated by V. Kozarovetsky. Moskva: NPC "Praksis".

Kushner (2004 [1989]) = Kušner, B. (2004 [1989]): "Sonet 109." In: *Sonety. Antologija sovremennyh perevodov.* Sankt-Peterburg. Azbuka-klassika. Available at: http://lib.meta.ua/book/22706/.

Kuznetsov (2004) = Kuznecov, A. (2004): Sonety Šekspira. Translated by A. Kuznetsov. In: *Dal'nij vostok* 5, 161–205. Available at: http://lib.ru/SHAKESPEARE/sonets5.txt.

Marshak (2006 [1948]) = Maršak, S. (2006 [1948]): *Uil'jam Šekspir. Sonety.* Translated by S. Marshak. Moskva: AST.

Mikushevitch (2004) = Mikuševič (2004): *Uil'jam Šekspir. Sonety.* Translated by V. Mikushevitch. Moskva: Vodolej Publishers. Available at: http://lib.ru/SHAKESPEARE/shks_sonnets16.txt.

Sharakshane (2009) = Šarakšanè (2009): *U. Šekspir. Sonety. Perevod s angl. A. Šarakšanè.* Moskva: "Menedžer". Available at: http://sonnets-best.narod.ru/Commentary_podstr_page.htm.

Stepanov, S. (2003) = *Uil'jam Šekspir. Sonety.* Translated by S. Stepanov. Available at: http://lib.ru/SHAKESPEARE/sonets4.txt.

Vinonen, R. (1971 [1964]) = "Uil'jam Šekspir. Sonety." Translated by R. Vinonen (sonnets 48, 66, 73, 109, 116, 121, 130). In: *Sel'skaja molodëž'* 2, 62–63. Available at: http://lib.ru/SHAKESPEARE/shks_sonnets31.txt_with-big-pictures.html.

B. Secondary sources

Abbott, Edwin A. (1966): *A Shakespearean Grammar.* New York: Dover.

Barber, Charles (2000): *The English Language: A Historical Introduction.* Cambridge: Cambridge University Press.

Booth, Stephen (1977): *Shakespeare's Sonnets.* New Haven, London: Yale University Press.

Corbett, Greville G. (1991): *Gender.* Cambridge: Cambridge University Press.

Crystal, David (2008): *Think on My Words: Exploring Shakespeare's Language.* Cambridge: Cambridge University Press.

Yeliferova (2009) = Eliferova, Marija (2009): "'Bagira skazala...' Gender skazočnyh i mifologičeskih personažej anglojazyčnoj literatury v russkih perevodah." In: *Voprosy literatury* 2, 254–277. Available at: http://magazines.russ.ru/voplit/2009/2/eli12.html. Visited 2 September 2011.

Hall, James (1979): *Dictionary of Subjects and Symbols in Art.* London: Murray.

Hall, John R. Clark (1984): *A Concise Anglo-Saxon Dictionary.* Toronto: University of Toronto Press in association with the Medieval Academy of America.

Impelluso, Lucia (2004): *Nature and its Symbols.* Santa Monica CA: Getty Publications.

Karlinsky, Simon (2002): Russian Literature. In: Summers, Claude J. [ed.] (2002): *An Encyclopedia of Gay, Lesbian, Bisexual, Transgender, and Queer Culture*. West Adams Chicago, IL. Available at: http://www.glbtq.com/literature/russ_lit.html. Visited 3 April 2012.

Kremer, Marion (1997): "Person Reference and Gender in Translation: A Contrastive Investigation of English and German." Tübingen: Gunter Narr. (= Language in Performance. 14).

Komissarov, V. N. (1991): "Language and Culture in Translation: Competitors or Collaborators?" In: *TTR: traduction, terminologie, redaction*, vol. 4 (1), 33–47.

Lyons, John (1968): *Introduction to Theoretical Linguistics*. Cambridge: Cambridge University Press.

Molina, Lucía / Hurtado Albir, Amparo (2002): "Translation Techniques Revisited: A Dynamic and Functionalist Approach." In: *Meta* 47 (4), 498–512.

Paloposki, O. / Oittinen, R. (2000): "The Domesticated Foreign." In: Chesterman, Andrew / Gallardo San Salvador, Natividad / Gambier, Yves [eds.] (2000): *Translation in Context: Selected Contributions from the EST Congress*, Granada, 1998. Amsterdam: John Benjamins. (= Benjamins Translation Library. 39).

Pervushina (2010) = Pervušina, Elena (2010): *Sonety Šekspira v Rossii: perevodčeskaja recepcija XIX–XX vekov*. Vladivostok: Izdatel'stvo Dal'nevostočnogo universiteta.

Quirk, Randolph / Greenbaum, Sidney / Leech, Geoffrey / Svartvik, Jan (1972): *A Grammar of Contemporary English*. London: Longman.

Rollason, Christofer (2010): "Beyond the Domestic and the Foreign: Translation as Dialogue." In: Bhaduri, S. / Basu, A. [eds.] (2010): *Perspectives on Comparative Literature and Culture in the Age of Globalization*, London, New York, New Delhi: Anthem Press. 29–39. Available at: http://yatrarollason.info/files/TranslationasDialogue.pdf. Visited 26 February 2011.

Sharakshane (2009) = Šarakšanè, Aleksandr (2009): "Sonet 1." In: *U. Šekspir. Sonety. Perevod s angl. A. Šarakšanè*. Moskva: "Menedžer". Available at: http://sonnets-best.narod.ru/Commentary_podstr_1.htm.

Spiller, Michael. R. G. (1992): *The Development of the Sonnet: An Introduction*. London: Routledge.

Tillyard, E.M.W. (1996): *The Elizabethan World Picture: A Study of the Idea of Order in the Age of Shakespeare, Donne and Milton*. Harmondsworth: Penguin Books.

Venuti, Lawrence (1995): *The Translator's Invisibility. A History of Translation*. London and New York: Routledge.

Veselovsky (1939) = Veselovskij, Aleksandr (1939): "Iz poètiki rozy." In: Veselovskij, A. N. *Izbrannye stat'i*. Leningrad: GIHL.

Fear of *Foreignization*: "Soviet School" in Russian Literary Translation

Alexandra Borisenko
Moscow State University, Russia

Abstract

In Russia the opposition of *foreignizing/ domesticating* translation is little known and rarely used. Instead *literal translation* is opposed to *realistic translation*, and these terms have strong idealogic connotations. The discussion about the conflicting translation methods goes back to 1920–1930's, and as every conflict of the Soviet era, it became political rather then literary or academic. After Perestroika, the situation changed dramatically: the number of titles went up, circulation numbers plummeted, target audiences became more varied, so did the approaches to translation. However, all this diversity and freedom had no consequences for aesthetic expectations of the reading public and critics; standards of literary translation are frozen in the same shape as they had been in Soviet times.

1 Foreignization v. literalism

Foreignization and *Domestication* are underused terms in Russian translation studies; the whole concept is perceived as foreign and somewhat suspicious. There is even no accepted translation of the terms: sometimes an awkward transliteration *forenizacija/domestikacija* is used, sometimes the more meaningful opposition *očuždenie/osvoenie*. For many Russian scholars the fancy Western word *foreignization* is just a disguise for *literalism* (*bukvalizm* as it is called in Russian). And therefore there is nothing to discuss – everybody knows that literalism is bad.

First of all: is foreignization really the same thing as literalism? No, it is not. Literalism is not the only tool that can give a translation a "foreign" flavor. There is a curious book by Vadim Rudnev: *Winnie-the Pooh and the Philosophy of Everyday Language* (Rudnev 1996). In this book, A. A. Milne is presented as a sophisticated writer whose work has deep implications for adult readers, and the translation of the book, attached to this opus, is intentionally foreignized by translator Tatyana

Mikhailova – no doubt, in accordance with Rudnev's specifications. Rudnev wants the reader to forget the children's book, known by heart, and to see a completely new work, complicated and strange. Accordingly, the translation does everything possible to estrange reader from the familiar tale. Thus, constant use of *present historicum*, which is not used in the original, is supposed to "add stylistic weight" to the text. Milne's long chapter titles (Chapter 1 ...*in which we are introduced to Winnie-the-Pooh and some bees, and the stories begin;* Chapter 2 ...*in which Pooh goes visiting and gets into a tight place, etc.*) are replaced by short ones (*Bee, Hole* etc.) According to Rudnev, this is done to make the book sound more like William Faulkner's novels. This intentional and elaborated foreignization has very little regard for accuracy; in fact, it is an extremely loose translation. This is, of course, a rare case, a trailblazing experiment, but it shows very clearly that foreignization can do without literalism and the two are not necessarily associated.

By the way, in the same book Rudnev suggests another opposition: analytic translation v. synthetic translation. *Analytic* translation is like Brecht's theater, where spectators never forget that they are watching a performance; *synthetic* translation is like Stanislavsky's theater, where spectators shed real tears and 'believe' in everything they see on stage (Rudnev 1996). This opposition is very close to the foreignization/domestication concept, but it has never been accepted by Russian translation theory.

Russian translation theory is still using the old dichotomy of loose/literal translation, or uses even vaguer terms, such as *literalism (bukvalizm)* and *realistic translation*. Needless to say, this choice of words does not help develop a coherent translation theory.

2 The beginning of Soviet translation project

To understand this unfortunate situation, we must go back and look at the history of translation in Russia. In the 19th century and in the early 20th century, translation process in Russia was very much the same as everywhere in Europe: there was domesticating mainstream, and foreignizing experiments, often related to literalist approach.[1] The mainstream translation norm by the turn of the 19th century was very loose indeed: sometimes even the name of the original author was omitted; it was normal to replace foreign names with Russian ones, to add and omit passages, to change phrases; English novels were often translated via the mediation of French. That was the inheritance, received by the Soviet state.

The young state was full of ambitious projects: mass literacy was one of the noblest. The next logical step was to give these new readers all the treasures of world literature. In 1919, under supervision of Maxim Gorky, a new publishing house was founded – it was called *World Literature*. This publishing house survived only until 1927, but the idea of mass-publishing of all the world's masterpieces remained very popular. In 1967–1977 a series *World Literature Library* was published, consisting of 200 volumes, 300.000 copies each. Print runs in Soviet era were enormous, though the number of titles was somewhat limited.

By the time Gorky's publishing house *World Literature* appeared, it had become obvious that something should be done about translations. Old translations were unsatisfactorily loose, and editing often made them worse. New translations were often done by people who knew languages, but were not professional translators – in fact, Gorky gave jobs to many representatives of the "old intelligentsia", who otherwise would have starved in post-revolutionary collapse. Of course, as it happens with inexperienced translators, many of them resorted to beginner's literalism. Osip Mandelstam was among those who opposed this translation tendency: "Pedantic checking against the original recedes into the background compared to the incomparably more important cultural task, that each phrase sound Russian, in agreement with the original's spirit"[2] (Mandelshtam 1929).

The need for some kind of school, of methodology was obvious, and *World Literature* publishing created a workshop for translators and published a brochure *Principles of Literary Translation* (1919). It included very contradictory advice by Nikolai Gumilyov, Fyodor Batyushkov and Kornei Chukovsky. Soon afterwards,

---

1   For example, Pushkin's friend Pyotr Vyazemsky translated the novel *Adolphe* by Benjamin Constant in a very literalist manner, trying to distort Russian language for the task, to give it new forms and new options. This translation was much ridiculed, as it often happens with experiments of this sort, and provoked lively discussions (Levin / Fedorov 1960: 63).

2   Hereinafter quotations are translated by the author of the present article.

Batyushkov starved to death, and Gumilyov was executed, so the next edition of the book was written by Chukovsky alone. Later, he reworked it into a famous book, *Translation as Fine Art* (1941). This book – witty, well-written, with lots of examples – is still a bestseller. "It is not reproducing a letter with a letter that should be done in translation, but (I'm prepared to repeat it a thousand times!) a smile with a smile, music with music, soulful intonation with soulful intonation" (Chukovsky 1968: 51).

3 Academia publishing house and the *bukvalists*

For *World Literature* this manifesto of domesticating translation was a natural choice. But it was not the only publishing house in Soviet Russia, and in the 1920's centralization was not yet complete. Another publishing house of the 1920's and 1930's was *Academia* (1921–1937), first located in Petrograd, later transferred to Moscow. It had very different principles and goals.

The term *bukvalizm* in its specific, pejorative use was later associated with this publishing house, its elitist editing policy, and strong views on translation. *Academia* did not see "workers and peasants" as their target audience. They cared about paper, fonts, illustrations, layout and, of course, translations. The people who worked there felt very strongly about translation liberties of the recent past, and they intended to be as accurate as possible. They also tended to accompany translations with elaborated commentary, footnotes, forewords etc.

Their *method of technological accuracy* stated that stylistic peculiarities of the original should be faithfully reflected in translation: repetitions, metaphors, inversions etc. They refused to smoothen up awkwardness or tone down sentimentality. Probably the most vivid example of their work was the translation of Charles Dickens's *Pickwick Papers* – translated by Yevgeny Lann (1933) and annotated by the famous philosopher Gustav Shpet. The commentaries constitute a very important part of this work – the translators tried to bring into the Russian version the material world of the book, with its complicated legal system (solicitors, barristers, attorneys), transport (dogcarts, gigs, hansom cabs), etc. The illustrated commentary explained all new words and described English everyday life in minute detail. In 1937 Shpet was executed for "anti-Soviet activity" and until very recently the translation was published without the commentary and without any mention of Shpet's name.

Of course, the term *foreignization* would much better describe *Academia*'s principles than the word *literalism* – their translations were not particularly literal, but they definitely had a certain foreignizing effect. It was certainly an elitist approach to literature, which contradicted the very spirit of Soviet enlightenment. *Academia* soon became the target for some translators of looser, more domesticating persuasion. The word *bukvalizm* became a label, a curse word, a condemnation.

4 The crusade of realistic translation

The most influential and fierce enemy of *bukvalists* was Ivan Kashkin, a famous translator, one of the founders of "Soviet school", main theorist of *socialist realism* in translation. He was a talented and knowledgeable man, a teacher of many outstanding professionals and an indomitable polemist. His criticism of *bukvalist* translation was tireless and merciless, if often unfair. Unfortunately, as every conflict of the Soviet era, this opposition quickly became political. Any foreignizing techniques were undesirable in the Soviet Union, where everything "strange" in a literary text was considered ideologically hostile and every book was aimed at the broadest possible audience, so Kashkin had a convincing case. He continued to refer to the interests of the "Soviet reader" which were obviously violated by literalists.

In those times a critic could easily become an informer – it was quite easy to go to prison for wrong ideas and methods, for ideologic "mistakes", for "political shortsightedness". Besides, translators often fought for their place under the sun – it was probably the only moment in history when literary translators were very well-paid, and with enormous print-runs and relatively few published titles, it was very difficult to get the job. There were clans, there was rivalry. There was no place for pluralism.

A good example of "ideologic criticism" was provided by the translation of *Don Juan* by Georgy Shengeli (Shengeli, RGALI). He was another "literalist", and his translation of Byron's famous narrative poem was severely criticized by Ivan Kashkin. Among other things, Kashkin stressed the fact that Shengeli distorted the image of Suvorov. This accusation was very serious – Suvorov was one of Stalin's favorite historical figures. In fact, Shengeli was extremely lucky that Stalin died soon after this discussion; otherwise he could have paid with his life for such negligence. In fact, Kashkin does not even try to prove that Byron was complimentary about Suvorov. This would have been a hard task indeed. Here is one example:

> Suwarrow, who was standing in his shirt
> Before a company of Calmucks, drilling,
> Exclaiming, fooling, swearing at the inert,
> And lecturing on the noble art of killing, –
> For deeming human clay but common dirt,
> This great philosopher was thus instilling
> His maxims, which to martial comprehension
> Proved death in battle equal to a pension…

What Kashkin says is very typical and at the same time very curious: "Does the Soviet school of translation teach to insult the Soviet reader by keeping intact the distorted picture of the great general, or, even worse, distort it even more?" (Kashkin 1952: 266–268).

This gives us some clue to the otherwise extremely vague concept of *realistic translation*. Mikhail Gasparov, with characteristic acidity, explains it as follows:

> Ivan Kashkin, a fine translator in his practice, in theory proclaimed a somewhat strange view that the translator should translate not the text, but the reality reflected in this text (it was called *realistic translation*) – and, therefore, Shengeli committed an unforgivable error when he presented Suvorov in Don Juan as Byron had depicted him, and not as we know and remember the great commander (Gasparov 1988b: 359–367).

Another translator of Don Juan was Tatyana Gnedich – she started the work while being a prisoner in Gulag and worked on the text for many years. Andrey Azov proved in his thorough paper (2011) that Tatyana Gnedich took into account Kashkin's criticism of Shengeli, and was especially careful with Suvorov's image, softening Byron's lines.

By this time the word *bukvalizm* was a dangerous label, and translators tried to avoid it at all costs. The translator was supposed to be true to the writer's "spirit", to the "historic truth", to the "Soviet reader" – all three notions being extremely vague but sacred.

5 Theory and practice of Soviet translation school

It is understandable that demand for precision could not be popular with the Soviet system of severe censorship. Yekaterina Kuznetsova analyzed in her diploma paper (2011) many versions of Hemingway's novel *For Whom the Bell Tolls* with editors' and censors' corrections. This novel was first translated into Russian in 1941 but was not published until 1962, with many different attempts and variants in between. There are several examples of editing, related to the characteristics of Communists:

'You never think about only girls. I never think at all. Why should I? <u>I am Général Sovietique. I never think. Don't try to trap me into thinking</u>'.

— Вы думаете не только о девушках, а и о многом другом. А я вообще ни о чем таком не думаю. На что мне?

('You never think about only girls. I never think about such things ~~at all~~. Why should I? ~~I am Général Sovietique. I never think. Don't try to trap me into thinking'.~~)

Lister was <u>murderous</u> in discipline. <u>He was a true fanatic and he had the complete Spanish lack of respect for life. In a few armies since the Tartar's first invasion of the West were men executed summarily for as little reason as they were under his command. But</u> he knew how to forge a division into a fighting unit.

Листер был <u>особенно строг</u> насчет дисциплины, и он сумел выковать из дивизии настоящую боеспособную единицу.

(Lister was especially strict ~~murderous~~ in discipline. ~~He was a true fanatic and he had the complete Spanish lack of respect for life. In a few armies since the Tartar's first invasion of the West were men executed summarily for as little reason as they were under his command. But~~ and he knew how to forge a division into a fighting unit.)

As we can see, all changes in the text are made in accordance with the principles of *realistic translation*: we know that Communists are good, so the translation should not "distort" the image.

Interestingly, though, the victory of realistic method affected theory much more seriously than practice. Censorship aside, the Soviet school managed to overcome many usual limitations of domesticating translations. There always existed certain foreignizing, though not literalist tendencies which balanced out the naturalization of the text.

The educational intention behind the *World Literature* project implied detailed commentary and explanation of the foreign context – almost all translations were accompanied by footnotes, annotations, forewords, afterwords etc. (which was never a common practice for mass-market translations in the West).

Interest for foreign cultures and their "local color" was increased by isolation, by years of the iron curtain – foreign countries were inaccessible, attractive and exotic, and literary translation was probably the only window allowing a look into this magic world. So for many translators it was particularly important to preserve all the features of this world, and sometimes even of a strange tongue and strange way of thinking.

Translation also had an abnormal function of developing the Russian literary language – almost all Russian writers who experimented with new literary forms were banned or suspicious, so translators carried this burden on their shoulders. In fact, many translators in Soviet times acted as noble smugglers, who secretly brought a gulp of fresh air inside a besieged country. Foreign literature was precious because it was different – thus, foreignizing technics, emphasizing this difference, were widely employed.

In contrast to theoretic declarations, the best Russian translators did not strive to produce translations that read "as if they were written in Russian". Viktor Golyshev, one of the best translators of American literature, who translated Faulkner, Steinbeck, Wilder, Warren etc., said in an interview: "If your translation sounds completely Russian, you are sure to produce bullshit. There should be a gap between what you would like to say and what you have to say as an honest man. And this gap is where true discovery is hidden" (Golyshev 2003: 80).

Theory, on the other hand, was stuck in its Soviet illusion of a mission to be completed and the golden mean attained. Even now there is no satisfactory definition of *literalism*, or *realistic translation*, which nowdays is more often called *adequate translation*.

In translation textbooks *bukvalizm* is still defined as "translator's mistake", "slavish imitation of the original" or just "wrong method". Adequate translation is on the contrary "the right method", "good translation".[3]

The only voice that was raised in Soviet time in defence of *literalism* (or any other form of non-domesticating translation) was the voice of the scholar and critic Mikhail Gasparov, who had first pronounced literalism to be "not a curse-word, but a scholarly method". He also showed certain limitations of domesticating translation – including some very famous examples, such as Samuil Marshak's translation of Shakespeare's sonnets. Gasparov made an attempt to move the whole dispute outside the paradigm of political fight into a purely academic domain. He stated that there was no golden mean in translation, that different translations serve different purposes and different readers need different translations:

> A 'loose' translation wants the reader to not sense he is reading a translation; a 'literalist' translation wants the reader to remember it at all times. A 'loose' translation wants to bring the original closer to the reader, and therefore violates the style of the original; a 'literalist' translaion wants to bring the reader closer to the original, and therefore violates the reader's stylistic habits and tastes. […] A 'loose' translation aims at broadening the scope of the reader's knowledge about foreign-language literatures. A 'literalist' translation aims at broadening the scope of writer's skills using artistic devices developed in foreign-language literatures. A 'loose' translation is a translation for literary consumers; a 'literalist' translation is a translation for literary producers. (Gasparov 1988a: 48)

Gasparov was also the first to challenge the static model of translation with its notion of one ideal translation for all and forever. He introduced the dynamic concept, in which translation changes depending on the stage of relationship between the two cultures.

> Civilization meets civilization just as one person meets another. To get their contact going, they have to see something similar in each other; to get it to continue (and not wither away after first attempt), they have to see something dissimilar. Literary translation is one such form of civilizations getting acquainted with each other. (Gasparov 1988a: 47)

His ideas, first voiced in the early 1970's, still remain largely unrecognized by Russian mainstream translation theory and translation criticism.

---

[3] For example, see the following textbooks Komissarov (2002: 16); Barkhudarov (1975: 185).

6 Conclusions: New times, old battles

After the Perestroika, the situation on the translation and book market changed dramatically: the number of titles went up, circulation numbers plummeted, target audiences became more varied, as did the approaches to translation. Since the early 1990's there has been virtually no censorship in literature and translation. Paradoxically, all this diversity and freedom had no consequences for aesthetic expectations of the reading public and critics: standards of literary translation were frozen in the same shape as they had been in Soviet times, all clichés of Soviet times are very much alive.

Probably the most important of them is the sacred status of "perfect translations", which in the view of the readers replace and often surpass the original.[4]

Better knowledge of languages and foreign countries, access to all sorts of information naturally led to a shift in the relationship of Russian culture and Russian audiences with many Western literatures and individual texts. Inevitably new translations of famous books started to appear, only to be severely criticized by readers and critics alike. Probably the most striking example is a new translation of Salinger's opus by Max Nemtsov (2008): Salinger had been translated in the 1960's, mostly by a very good and very famous translator Rita Right-Kovalyova, and since then *The Catcher in the Rye* became "appropriated" by the Russian literature. There was an anecdote, widely spread by Sergei Dovlatov – allegedly, Gore Vidal proclaimed that Kurt Vonnegut lost a lot in the original compared to translations by Rita Right (Dovlatov / Volkova 1992: 70).

Nemtsov's translation was received with hostility. Remarkably, it was condemned *before* anybody had a chance to read it. The mere fact that someone dared translate Salinger again was not acceptable to the majority of readers and critics. Everyone compared the new translation with the old one, with the original completely out of the picture. Meanwhile, the old translation, for all its literary merits, was severely censored, smoothed out, domesticated, and it was only natural that a new one should appear. It was a foreignizing translation in many senses – often awkward,

---

[4] In Western history such a status was attached to the Vulgate, St. Jerome's Latin translation of the Bible: when Erasmus started comparing it with the original texts, it was perceived by many as heresy and sacrilege.

with many footnotes – probably more an exercise in close reading than a work of literature (Borisenko 2009). Still, for the Western reader it would have been just one more translation, not a big deal (recent years saw quite a number of new English translations of *War and Peace*, *Crime and Punishment*, and other Russian classics). But we in Russia have our own Salinger – and the original looses a lot in comparison – so why would we need close reading?

Here we come again to the same problem as with the literalist/adequate opposition: the idea of the only method, the only translation, the only way is still dominant in literary translation discourse. To think of it, this notion is completely absurd: is iambic verse better than trochaic? Should one win and the other loose? Do we want all poems sound the same? We still need to learn the lesson of our best translators (who were so different) and our best scholars – how to agree to disagree.

References

Azov, A. G. (2011): *Iz istorii otečestvennogo perevoda: "Don Žuan" Bajrona v perevode G. A. Šengeli.* Moskva: Moskovskij gosudarsvennyj universitet. Unpublished course project. Philological Faculty of Lomonosov Moscow State University.

Barkhudarov (1975) = Barhudarov, L. S. (1975): *Jazyk i perevod (voprosy obščej i častnoj teorii perevoda).* Moskva: Meždunarodnye otnošenija.

Borisenko, A. L. (2007): "Ne kriči: 'Bukvalizm!'". In: *Mosty* 14 (2), 25–34.

—— (2009): "Selindžer načineet i vyigryvaet." In: *Inostrannaja literature* 7. Available at: http://magazines.russ.ru/inostran/2009/7/bo16.html.

Gasparov, M. L. (1988a): "Brjusov i bukvalizm. In: *Poetika perevoda.* Moskva: Raduga. 29–62.

—— (1988b): "Neizvestnye russkie perevody bajronovskogo "Don Žuana"." In: *Izvestija AN SSSR. Serija literatury i jazyka* 4, 359—367.

Gasparov, M. L. / Avtonomova, N. S. (2001): "Sonety Šekspira – perevody Maršaka." In: Gasparov, M. L. [ed.] (2001): *O russkoj poezii.* Sankt-Peterburg: Azbuka. 389–409.

Golyshev (2003) = Rybkin, Pavel (2003): "Perevodnye kartinki." [Interview with V. Golyshev]. In: *Bol'šoj gorod* 40. 23 November 2003. Available at: http://www.bg.ru/article/3158/.

Dovlatov, S. / Volkova, M. (1992): *Ne tol'ko Brodskij. Russkaja kul'tura v portretah i anekdotah.* Moskva: RIK "Kul'tura".

Kashkin (1952a) = Kaškin, I. A. (1952): "Tradicii i epigonstvo." In: *Novyj mir* 12, 229.

—— (1952b): "Udači, poluudači i neudači." In: *Novyj mir* 2, 266.

Komissarov, V. N. (2002): *Lingvisticeskoe perevodovedenie v Rossii.* Moskva: Izdatel'stvo ETS.

Kuznetsova (2011) = Kuznecova, Ye. D. (2011): *Sposoby adaptacii perevodnogo teksta k ideologičeskim i cenzurnym trebovanijam*. Moskva: Moskovskij gosudarstvennyj universitet. Unpublished master's thesis. Philological Faculty of Lomonosov Moscow State University.

Lann, Yevgeny (1933) = Lann, E. L. (1933): *Dikkens, Čarl'z. Posmertnye zapiski Pikvikskogo kluba*. V 3 tomah. Translated by E. Lann. Moskva–Leningrad: Academia.

―― (1939): "Stil' rannego Dikkensa i perevod "Posmertnyh zapisok Pikvikskogo kluba"." In: *Literaturnyj kritik* 1, 57–58.

Levin, Ju. D. /Fedorov, A. V. (1960) = Levin, Ju. D. /Fëdorov, A. V. [eds.] (1960): *Russkie pisateli o perevode XVIII–XX vv*. Leningrad: Sovetskij pisatel'.

Mandelshtam (1929) = Mandel'štam, O. E. (1929): "Potoki haltury." In: *Izvestija*, 7 April 1929.

Nemtsov (2008) = Nemcov, Maksim (2008): *Dž. D. Selindžer. Sobranie sočinenij*. Translated by M. Nemtsov. Moskva: Èksmo.

Rudnev, V. P. (1996 [1992]): *Vinni-Puh i filosofija obydennogo jazyka*. Moskva: Russkoe fenomenologičeskoe obščestvo.

Chukovsky (1968) = Čukovskij, K. I. (1968): *Vysokoe iskusstvo*. Moskva: Sovetskij pisatel'.

Shengeli (RGALI) = Šengeli, G. A. *Kritika po-amerikanski. Otvet na stat'ju I. Kaškina "Tradicija i èpigonstvo"*. Rossijskij gosudarstvennyj arhiv literatury i isskusstva. F. 2861. D. 98. L. 66–167. [Archive materials].

Cultural and Political Contexts of Translating into Finnish in Soviet/Russian Karelia

Marja Jänis and Tamara Starshova

University of Eastern Finland, Joensuu

Petrozavodsk State University, Russia

Abstract

In this article translating into Finnish in Soviet/Russian Karelia is analyzed as a case study of translating into a minority language. Special attention is paid to the specific cultural and political contexts in which it is undertaken (Venuti 1998). The minority position is essential in studying what is translated, by whom and how (Meylaerts 2007). The results of the analysis are presented in a chronological order, describing the rise and fall of the translation activities that were fatally affected by dramatic and tragic events in the political history of Soviet/Russian Karelia. The concepts of domestication and foreignization are applied to discussing ways of translating words denoting new political and social phenomena. Finally the results of the analysis are placed into a wider framework of translation and minority: politics, interference by the majorities in defining the proper ways of translating, and the relativity of the concept of a minority language.

1 Introduction

This article deals with translating into Finnish in Soviet/Russian Karelia, the northwestern part of Russia/the Soviet Union bordering on Finland, where Finnish has always been a minority language. As Lawrence Venuti (1998: 143) states, minorities bring unpredictable variations to constants and standards of translating and specifying the minor situation requires not only analyzing language and textuality, but also reconstructing the cultural and political contexts. In this article we present a case study with special reference to those political and social changes that have affected translating into Finnish in Soviet/Russian Karelia. Our analysis follows the main aspects of translating into a minority language, as stated by Reine Meylaerts (2007: 298) in her article on multilingualism in Belgium: "(…) what can/cannot or must be translated, how and by whom (…)". We hope that our analysis will inspire research in similar or opposite cases of translating into minority languages. We will also consider the applicability of the concepts of domestication and foreignization to our material.

2 Background

A great amount of research exists about the development of the Finnish language and literature in Soviet/Russian Karelia (see e.g. Alto 1989; Anttikoski 2000; Austin 2009; Jalava 1990; Kangaspuro 2000, 2002; Klementyev / Kozhanov 2009; Takala 2009; Ylikangas 2004; Zakharova 2009; Vavulinskaya 2009). Ideological and political aspects of language policy are widely discussed in this research, but the role of translation has not been analyzed, which is not unusual in analogous research on linguistic development in multilingual societies (see e.g. Meylaerts 2007: 298). Our study is based on material collected by Tamara Starshova on translation history, translators and discussions about translation in Soviet/Russian Karelia (Starshova 2011a, 2011b, 2011c).[1]

There are two Karelias – Finnish and Russian. The eastern part, Russian Karelia, has always been a part of the Russian Empire/Soviet Union/Russian Federation, and consists of a large and very sparsely populated area stretching from the western shores of the White Sea in the north down to the western shores of Lake Onega in the south. Finnish Karelia consists of the western shores of Lake Ladoga and then south to the Gulf of Finland, but the border between Russian and Finnish Karelia has varied in the course of the history of Finland and Russia/the Soviet Union. In this paper we deal with the eastern part of Karelia that has always belonged to Russia/the Soviet Union, and translations into Finnish in Russian Karelia.

3 Languages and translation in Soviet Karelia

As Venuti (1998: 135) notes, translating into a minority language is always a special case and takes distinctive forms when it is done by the minorities. Translating into Finnish in Soviet/Russian Karelia is certainly a case where the political context played an exceptionally decisive and even harsh role. Soviet Karelia was a new kind

---

[1] Robert Kolomainen (2006, 2010) has drawn the basic outlines of the history of translating from and into Finnish in Russia, and the role of Karelian translators is essential in it.

of social formation, also from the point of view of linguistic policy and translation. Our presentation is based on chronology, following turning points in the history of Soviet/Russian Karelia.

3.1 Finnish in Soviet Karelia during the post-revolution years – the 1920's and 1930's

The languages traditionally spoken in Russian Karelia were Russian and Karelian. The Karelian language is a Baltic-Finnic language with three main dialects. Karelian people living in the northern parts of Karelia stretching from the shores of the White Sea to the western shores of Lake Onega spoke the North Karelian dialect, linguistically rather closely related to the Finnish language. The southern Karelian dialects Livvi and Vepsian are more remote from Finnish.[2] There has not been a written Karelian language, although since the 13th century several attempts were made using the Cyrillic alphabet. Attempts to create a written Karelian language using the Latin alphabet were undertaken in the 19th century along with the growth of nationalistic ideas, but they did not have lasting results.[3]

Finnish became the written language in Karelia after the Bolshevik revolution and the civil war that followed Finland's independence in 1917. As a result of the devastating civil war in Finland in 1918, thousands[4] of Finns who had supported the defeated "red" Socialist movement fled to Soviet Russia, mainly to Karelia and the Petrograd (later Leningrad) region. The so-called "red" Finns played a significant role in shaping the linguistic situation in Soviet Karelia. "Red" Finnish immigrants supported the new socialist rule, whereas in most cases Karelian peasants were reluctant to accept it, and Finnish immigrants gained power and ruling positions in the new form of regional government, called the Karelian Labour Commune, established in 1920. Those in power could dictate linguistic

---

2   For a detailed discussion of the differences of Karelian languages, see e.g. Austin 2009: 78–81.
3   See Austin 2009: 23–28; Ylikangas 2004: 95–98.
4   According to some sources there were 6000, to others 10 000 (Kangaspuro 2000:174). Emigration of Finnish political refugees continued in the 1920's and early 1930's. In the early 1930's, almost 5000 Finns, mostly skilled workers who had earlier emigrated to North America, were recruited to Soviet Karelia "to build socialism" (See e.g. Kruhse / Uitto 2008: 35).

policy as well. Furthermore, Karelia was considered a suitable base for spreading socialist revolutionary ideas to Finland and other Nordic countries (Kangaspuro 2000: 139). Since there was no common written language, and three dialects existed with almost equal numbers of speakers, the three dialects were pronounced dialects of the Finnish language, and Finnish became the written official language. The idea of giving the right of self-rule to minorities was in accordance with the national policy of the socialist regime, which was called *korenization* ("giving roots", indigenization).[5] Favoring Finnish, the language of the neighboring country, was unusual in the language policy of Soviet Russia, where the spoken language of the minority was usually chosen to be the basis for the creation of the official written language.[6] With the support of the revolutionary local and central leaders, Finnish immigrants regarded bringing their language to the Karelian people and to administration and education as a civilizing mission (Zakharova 2009: 301). Along with Finnish, Karelian was also given an official status, and Karelian dialects could be used in oral communication within the administration. Finnish and Russian were proclaimed the official languages in the Karelian Socialist Republic in 1924. Moreover, the Karelian population could not freely choose between the two – in those regions where the Karelian population formed the majority, Finnish was obligatory in schools and in Soviet and Party organs (*ibid.:* 303). We can call it *territorial monolingualism*, following Meylaerts (2007: 303). Hence Finnish, which was a minority language in respect to Russian, became a majority language in relation to the Karelian dialects – although the number of Finns was about 1 % of the population, whereas representatives of Karelian ethnic groups formed 41.2 % of the population (Zakharova 2009: 301).

Politics also determined the next turn of events when the national policy practiced in the Soviet Union was changed. During the repressions of the 1930's, those in charge of language decisions were accused of Finnish nationalism, which resulted in their execution. The Finnish language was forbidden in Soviet Karelia in the late

---

5 Takala (2009: 127) calls this special case of *korenization* in Soviet linguistic policy *karelianization*, derived from the name of the republic and its people.
6 The politics of the Soviet regime in linguistic matters in Karelia is discussed e.g. in Austin 2009, Kangaspuro 2000, Kilin 2002, Klementyev 2009 and Suutari / Shikalov 2010.

1930's, and literature published in Finnish was destroyed.[7] Finnish was vaguely reintroduced only during the war between Finland and the Soviet Union, when there was a need for knowing the language of the enemy.

3.2 Translating into Finnish in the 1920's, 1930's, and early 1940's

When finding answers to the question what can/cannot or must be translated, how and by whom (Meylarts 2007: 298), we will start with the question **what** was translated into Finnish in the Karelian Workers' Commune, and later in the Karelian Socialist Republic. A bibliography of Finnish literature published in Soviet Karelia in 1918–1944 (Kruhse / Uitto 2008) is a valuable source for quantitative and qualitative data.[8] In the bibliography, all published literature is divided into five main groups: (1) newspapers and magazines; (2) meeting reports; (3) society; (4) education and school books; (5) fiction, including children's literature. Within all this material, translations are not classified as a separate group, but they are marked *suom. (transl.)*. In order to obtain a rough picture of the relationship between translated and untranslated books published in Finnish in Soviet Karelia, we have counted the number of publications that are listed in all categories, except (1) newspapers and magazines. Translations published in newspapers and magazines are not included because the material published there is not listed in the bibliography, but it is worth mentioning that translations of contemporary literary works of Soviet authors and Russian classics as well as political writings were regularly published in such Finnish language magazines as *Soihtu* 'Torch' (published in 1927–1930), *Puna-kantele* 'Red kantele' (1928–1931), and *Rintama* 'Front' (1932– 1937).[9] Moreover, we cannot be sure that all translated texts are marked as such in the bibliography mentioned above. Hence the exact numbers are not given, and the

---

[7] Kolomainen (2006: 178) describes how the Finnish language was declared a fascist language, Finnish language schools were closed, newspapers and magazines banned and the stores of the publishing house were burned. See also Kruhse / Uitto 2008: 8.

[8] According to the authors, it is based on what could be found in Finnish libraries and antiquarian bookshops as well as on publications collected by the Finnish military in 1941– 1943 in Soviet Karelia.

[9] Data about the translations published in these magazines is given in Alto 1989: 31, 80. For instance, the relationship between texts originally written in Finnish and translated texts in the first numbers of *Soihtu* in 1927 was 27:3 in poetry and 15:10 in prose. See also Starshova 2011a.

results of the calculations are presented in columns, which indicate the relationship between translations and texts originally written in Finnish (see Figure 1).

Figure 1. Finnish language publications in Soviet Karelia in 1918–1944

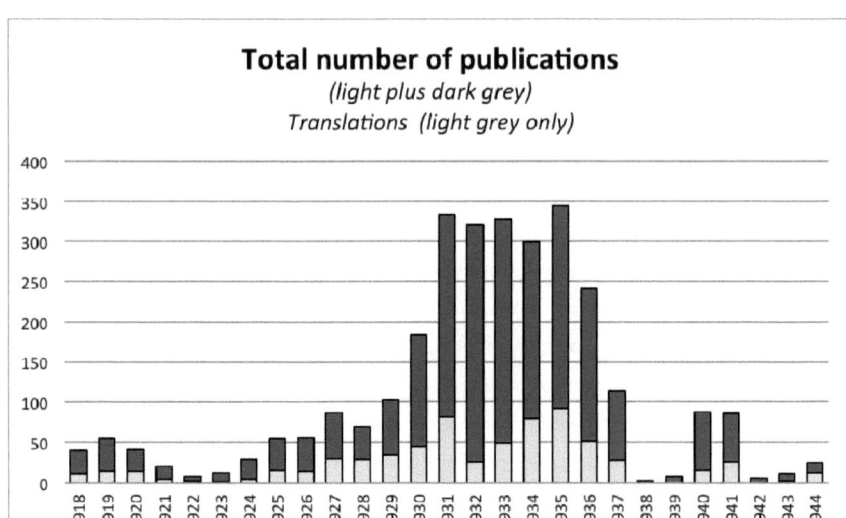

This figure shows how publishing in Finnish grew steadily in the late 1920's and remained at a high level during the first half of the 1930's. The number of translations did not, however, increase along with the number of publications originally written in Finnish in those years when publishing in Finnish grew considerably. This seems to indicate that when the position of the minority language is stable, the amount of literature originally written in that language grows, but translating into the minority language does not grow accordingly.

An analysis of the titles of the translations in the early years of the Karelian Labour Commune shows that translations were mostly those of political texts, articles by Lenin and other revolutionary leaders.[10] The civil war and unrest in the early 1920's meant an almost total stop in publishing and translating, as we can see in Figure 1. In 1923, the Karelian Labour Commune was transformed into the Karelian Autonomous Republic. In 1923, a Finnish publishing cooperative called *Kirja*

---

10 Titles of the first translations into Finnish are described in detail in Starshova 2011a.

'Book' was founded in Leningrad.[11] This establishment in Leningrad is understandable because the number of Finnish-speaking people in the city and the surrounding region exceeded that of Soviet Karelia: in addition to Finnish immigrants, Ingrians – indigenous Finnish-speaking people – lived in Ingrian areas around Leningrad.[12] However, the position of the Finnish language was stronger in Karelia, since Finns held many leading positions in the administrative and party elite in the Karelian Socialist Republic and Finnish was an official language along with Russian. Later the activities of the publishing house *Kirja* were moved to Petrozavodsk.

The early 1930's is regarded as the heyday of Finnish literature, which can be seen in the growing amounts of Finnish language publications in Figure 1. What was published in the original language and what was published in translation in those years? When analyzing the number of different categories of publications, the greatest increase was in category (3) 'society', both originals and translations. According to the titles of the translations, they dealt with education, public health, child-rearing, economics, practical agriculture etc. In category (5) 'fiction', drama played a significant role, since a professional Finnish theatre was established in Petrozavodsk in 1928.[13] This is even more significant, since most translated plays were not published.[14]

Answering the question about **how** books were translated into Finnish requires consideration of several factors: the diversity of the linguistic background of the translators, the linguistic and political context, and the lack of training and a coherent idea of what translating is and should be. The lack of dictionaries was due to the fact that the border between Finnish and Soviet Karelia was tightly closed. Discussions about the quality of Finnish translations were heated, and translations were criticized for their poor quality, such as mistakes in spelling and syntax (Jufa

---

11 For a detailed description of the history of the publishing house, see Kruhse / Uitto 2008: 26–36.

12 For more information about the Ingrian people, see Suni 2000, in English in Räsänen 1999.

13 For information about the history of the Finnish theatre, see Nikitin 1989, also Zakharova 2009: 318–321.

14 The repertoire of the early years of the theatre consisted almost totally of Finnish translations of Russian plays by contemporary Soviet authors, as can be seen in Nikitin 1989: 21–22.

1992: 144; Kolomainen 2006: 177, Starshova 2011a). The transliteration of Russian names was inconsistent: *Gorky* could be rendered as *Gorkij, Gorjkij, Gorjki, Gorki*. How to render words denoting Soviet political *realia* in Finnish was a widely discussed issue, and translators disagreed whether to use the existing Finnish and Ingrian words or to transcribe Russian words. For instance, two prominent translators, Jalmari Virtanen and Tobias Guttari (literary pseudonym Lea Helo), both descendents of Finnish families in the Petrograd region, favored using existing Finnish words. Other active translators V. Salo and Leo Letonmäki suggested transcribing Russian words and also did so, whether writing in Finnish or translating.[15] Jufa (1991: 144) concludes that using Finnish literary language was proposed as the norm, but sovietisms were approved for expressing "the spirit of the time" and the new phenomena. The following examples, taken from the names of translated publications in the category 'society' in 1930 (Kruhse / Uitto 2008: 190-192), illustrate these different ways. Some are word for word translations of Russian words, some are semicalques: *puolustuskuntoisuus* 'ability to defend', *suursuunnitelmahypoteesi* 'major hypothesis for planning', *maaseudun kesäseimet* 'rural summer camps for small children', *makarovkalaiset* 'followers of Makharov', *tuotannollis-elinkeinollinen kalastusartteli* 'fishing union for production and livelihood'. These neologisms denoting Soviet *realia* were formed according to Finnish language word formation rules. The idea of using the resources of the minority language to name new phenomena of the new surrounding social and political context can be seen as significant, as it implies "...the desired presence of the minority language in all areas of life...", which Michael Cronin (1998: 150) considers essential from the point of view of developing minority language use. It can be called a kind of *domestication* in the sense that it aimed at transparency and comprehensibility in naming such phenomena that existed in the surrounding environment, but had no Finnish name.[16] This was, however, a short episode in the history of naming Soviet *realia* in Finnish.

By **whom** were the translations undertaken? The early translators into Finnish were both Finnish political emigrants and local Finns. Few of the representatives of the

---

15 For the biographies and bibliography of Karelian translators, see Starshova 2011b.
16 Päivi Pasanen (2012) discusses the applicability of the concepts of foreignization and domestication in terminology work, and her ideas have inspired our reflections.

first generation of Karelian translators had received higher education or any training in translating (Starshova 2011b).

The political situation in the Soviet Union changed in 1933 when the Communist Party began "cleaning out" "foreign elements" among its members. In Soviet Karelia, the fact of having the Finnish bourgeois republic beyond the state border and growing hostility between Finland and the Soviet Union had fatal consequences on the development of the Finnish language and culture on the Soviet side of the border.

Along with the repressions of the Finnish cultural elite of Soviet Karelia, the influence of the Russian language grew considerably. In 1936, even if publications were not translations, Russian transcriptions of Soviet concepts were widely introduced into writings. For instance, the Finnish equivalent for the word *Soviet* had been *neuvosto*, but now it became *sovjetti*. Alto (1989: 81) gives a list of "sovietized" words used in periodicals, such as *loosunki* 'slogan', *okruga* (okrug 'district'), *susetti* (sjužet 'plot'). This new way of naming Soviet concepts was justified by forming a scientific commission that gave recommendations about the new naming system.[17] Such replacement of existing minority language words with transcribed majority language words can be described as *foreignization*, and it meant exercising the majority position to suppress the minority language use. This is in accordance with Venuti's observation (1998: 140): "Translating major into minor languages, even with the most revisionary strategies of domestication, doesn't entail a stable regime of cultural dominion or homogenizing process of identity formation."

In 1937, all the previous Finnish leaders of Soviet Karelia were dismissed and many were executed. The publishing house *Kirja* survived until 1937. In 1938 the publishing house's stores of Finnish language publications were destroyed, and only a few items of scientific literature were saved (Kruhse / Uitto 2008: 54; Starshova 2011a).

Paradoxically the loss of power by Finns meant more power in linguistic matters to the Karelian population. The Karelian language written in the Cyrillic alphabet, so-

---

17   The history of the committee is described in Belikova 2009.

called Bubrich[18] Karelian, was implemented in the late 1930's. Bubrich Karelian was used in translations; schoolbooks, for example, were mostly translated from Russian. Russian fiction was also translated into Karelian, along with some foreign fiction, such as H. C. Andersen's fairy tales, stories by Victor Hugo, Jonathan Swift and Rudyard Kipling. This episode was short lived, since publishing in the Karelian language in the Cyrillic alphabet ended in 1940.

The outbreak of the war between Finland and the Soviet Union was significant to the amount of Finnish language publications, which increased in 1940–1944, (see Figure 1). Very few of them were translations – or mentioned as such.

3.3 Finnish language and translating during the post war years – the 1940's and 1950's

After the war and annexation of parts of eastern Finland to the Soviet Union, Karelia was given the status of a Soviet republic, bearing the name Finnish-Karelian Soviet Socialist Republic. "Finnish" was preserved in the name of the republic up to 1957.[19] The name was significant in the sense that in order to legitimate it, the Finnish language had to be promoted. However, the Finnish population had almost totally fled to Finland, and the previous Finnish Karelian regions near the border were inhabited by people from other parts of the Soviet Union. A lively injection to the cultural development was the immigration of approx. 20 000 Ingrians to Karelia. Before and during the Second World War, Ingrians were forced to leave their homes around Leningrad. After many dramatic turns, Ingrians living in *diaspora* in different parts of the Soviet Union were allowed to settle in the Finnish-Karelian Soviet Republic in 1949, and immigration continued in the next decade.[20] The immigration caused the amount of Finnish-speaking people in the republic to

---

18   Professor Dmitry Bubrich had tried to develop a written Karelian using the Latin alphabet in the early 1930's, and later using the Cyrillic alphabet. For further details, see Belikova 2009: 168–172.
19   Stalin's policy in reintroducing Finnish into the name of the republic is discussed e.g. in Kangaspuro 2002: 128-129. The history of the Finnish Karelian Soviet Socialist Republic is described in Laine 2000: 251–282.
20   For more details about this phase in the history of the Ingrians, see e.g. Laine 2000: 276–277; Sihvo 2000: 174–180; Suni 2000: 92–93.

increase significantly: in 1926 it was 1 %, in 1939 1.8 %, and in 1959 4.3 % (Zakharova 2009: 303).

The revival of the Finnish language and culture in Soviet Karelia in the 1940's faced many problems, mostly due to the repressions of the 1930's. There were not enough teachers to educate a new generation of Finnish-speaking Karelians, and Finnish – not Karelian – was considered the second language of education and culture in the republic. According to Zakharova (2009: 315) the practical work for creating the written culture of Karelia was considered the task of linguists and translators. She calls the situation when the oral literary heritage was translated into literary Finnish the *folklorization* of national culture. Zakharova calls the whole process of creating a Finnish language Karelian culture *mimetic*. The result was a hybrid: linguistic mimesis was followed by *hybridization* in forming the image of the national culture by defining the "correct" proportion of texts, e.g. in school curricula, representing Russian, Soviet, and Finnish Communist literature as well as Karelian folklore (*ibid.*: 316).

As a result of Stalin's purges, only very few of the productive pre-war generation of translators into Finnish had survived. Translation nevertheless flourished: in 1945– 1957, 923 translations of works of Soviet authors were translated from Russian into Finnish (Zakharova 2009: 317). Translations were meant for Finnish readers in Karelia, and translators – who were often journalists, writers or academics – did not specialize in any particular field, and translated both fiction and non-fiction. Translations of schoolbooks were naturally in great demand (Starshova 2011a).

The publishing of Finnish-language newspapers and magazines was revived. In 1940 the first issues of the monthly *Punalippu* 'Red flag' appeared, and this magazine followed the traditions of those Finnish literary magazines that had ceased to exist in the late 1930's. It published a large number of translations of contemporary Soviet literature and Russian classics (Alto 1989: 109; Kolomainen 2006: 178). The newspaper *Totuus* ('Truth' – a direct translation of the name of the Soviet party organ *Pravda*) appeared in 1940, after the Winter War. An interesting episode in its history was its renaming as *Leniniläinen totuus* ('Leninist Truth' – a direct translation of *Leninskaya Pravda*) in 1955. The contents of the newspaper were direct translations of the Russian-language newspaper for almost two years in 1956–1957. The newspaper was renamed *Neuvosto-Karjala* 'Soviet Karelia' in 1957, publishing articles originally written in Finnish along with translated articles (Starshova 2011a).

In the mid 1950's the situation regarding the use of the Finnish language changed. The parallel system of Russian and "national" schools had not been very successful, and parents were reluctant to send their children to schools with Finnish language instruction, since it complicated their further education (Klementyev / Kozhanov 2009: 339). In 1954, the Soviet Union started introducing an eight-year education system with Russian as the medium of instruction and Russian became the language of instruction in all Karelian schools. The title "Finnish" in the name of the republic was removed in 1957, when the Karelian Autonomous Republic was formed. The Department of Finnish and Karelian Languages and Cultures at Petrozavodsk University was closed in 1958, since Finnish teachers were no longer needed.[21] On the other hand, Finnish was mentioned as an official language in the constitution of the Karelian Autonomous Republic. Accordingly, Finnish and Karelian inhabitants of the republic had the right to have legal interpreting services in their own language (Klementyev / Kozhanov 2009: 340).

3.4 New target audiences for Finnish translations by Karelian translators

The changes in the international politics of the Soviet Union, starting after Stalin's death, had consequences on translating policies. The Soviet Union wanted to spread its influence around the world. This affected translation and publishing policy in Soviet Karelia as well. Acquiring new readers for Finnish language publications and translations was considered essential, and the Karelian Finnish language newspaper *Neuvosto-Karjala*, the monthly *Punalippu* and Finnish translations of Russian fiction and non-fiction were distributed to readers outside the Soviet Union. In 1963, more than 6000 copies of the literary and political monthly *Punalippu* in Finnish were subscribed by readers in Finland, and also in Sweden, Canada and Hungary. The Finnish Department at Petrozavodsk University was

---

21 The status of the Finnish language at Petrozavodsk University is analyzed in detail in Starshova 2002.

reopened in 1963. Cultural exchange, tourism and economic cooperation with Finland grew considerably.[22]

A new publishing house, *Edistys*, which was part of the Moscow-based publishing house *Progress*, was opened in Petrozavodsk in 1961. Its publications were distributed in Finland by the Finnish left-wing publishing house *Kansankulttuuri*. In the first four years it published 105 Finnish translations of works by Soviet authors, mostly political and social literature, but also fiction. Emerging Karelian writers were among the translators. Many of them were from northern Karelia, where the local dialect was close to Finnish, and they used the Finnish language in their original writing.[23] A section of translators was formed in the Soviet Writers' Association in Karelia and it organized discussions and seminars. Frequent themes discussed at the seminars were rendering of grammatical and discursive *lacunae*, idioms, proverbs and word play. Special attention was paid to strategies that aimed at preserving national-specific features in literary works written by authors, representing various nationalities and ethnic groups of the Soviet Union.[24]

In this period, when contacts between Finnish and Karelian writers and translators were more frequent than before, Karelian Finnish translators could read more contemporary Finnish literature, which was important for the development of translating. However, as translator Raija-Liisa Pöllä (Kaunokirjallisuuden kääntäminen on taidetta 1985: 140) mentions, the Soviet literary tradition restricted the ways of rendering colloquial or vulgar language in translations – and Soviet Finnish translators had to consider the opinions of the domestic readers along of those of the foreign. Translation theory was taught to Finnish language students at the Petrozavodsk University.[25]

Translating for readers abroad meant a new challenge for the translators: should and could they really consider Finnish readers abroad their main target audience? In any case, the large number of Finnish language publications distributed abroad gives the impression of a very active Finnish language cultural life in Soviet Karelia

---

22   The growth of the cooperation is documented in Vavulinskaya 2009.
23   Works of Soviet Karelian Finnish language writers are analyzed in Jalava 1990.
24   For further details about the discussions, see Starshova 2011c.
25   Journalist and translator Robert Kolomainen makes critical comments about the teaching in Kolomainen 2010: 143.

in the 1970's and 1980's. In Finland, Finnish translations of Russian fiction made by Soviet Karelian translators were criticized for the "use of old-fashioned language." The norms of translating Russian literature into Finnish had long traditions (see Jänis, Pesonen 2007). Literary scholar and critic Pekka Pesonen (2003: 96) claims that the language in translations by Karelian translators was not the language Finnish readers were used to, and often caused an unintended comic effect. Soviet Karelian translators themselves admitted their problems in translating for foreign readers (Pakkanen 1987; Pronina 1986). Karelian translators knew about the pejorative name "Petrozavodsk Finnish language", and Robert Kolomainen, one of the active translators, remembers how his colleagues discussed "unjustified use of neologisms, the effect of bilingualism on sentence construction, and the old and 'non-Finnish' traits in the translations" (Kolomainen 2010: 144).

4 Post-Soviet years: the decline of translating into Finnish in Russian Karelia

Great changes following *Perestroika* and the eventual collapse of the Soviet Union mark a clear turning point in the position of the Finnish language in Soviet/Russian Karelia. In 1990, Finland's president Mauno Koivisto declared Ingrians to be ethnically Finnish, which gave them the right to emigrate to Finland, and this led to a large emigration from Russian Karelia. For Russian Karelia it meant a great loss. Many representatives of the cultural elite left for Finland, and the continuation of Karelian Finnish culture was threatened. At the same time, those who had remained took great pains to preserve the Finnish and Karelian languages and cultures in the republic.[26]

The Moscow-based publishing house *Progress* shut down its office in Petrozavodsk in 1988 without significant resistance from the political leaders of the Karelian Autonomous Republic. According to Pekka Mutanen, who at that time was the chairperson of the Karelian Writers' Union, it was a fatal blow to the development of Finnish and Karelian culture (Laine 1990). The publication of Finnish translations of Russian literature and non-fiction ceased by the beginning of the 1990's, and nowadays translations appear only in a few Finnish language

---

26 The fight to preserve Karelian languages and culture is described in Austin 2009: 61-103.

newspapers and the magazine *Carelia*. The Finnish language also lost its position as an official language of the Karelian Republic.

5 Conclusions

As Venuti (1998: 135) reminds us, translating into a minority language is always a special case. Translating into Finnish in Soviet/Russian Karelia is certainly a case where the political context played an exceptionally decisive and even harsh role, particularly during the Stalin era and Second World War. Translating into Finnish resumed during those periods when the Soviet Union took efforts to find political allies and influence leftist movements abroad. The fact that Finnish was used for original writing and translating suggests that it was a living minority language in Soviet Karelia in the 1960's, 1970's, and 1980's. However, the position of the Finnish language relied on a very small stratum of literary elite and was affected by its emigration. Although Finnish is still used by some literary people, translating into Finnish has practically ended in Russian Karelia. There is obviously no need for translations – first, because interest in translations of Russian literature has decreased rapidly in Finland since the 1990's,[27] and, secondly, since Russian Karelian readers read Russian.

6 Discussion

The special case of translating into Finnish in Soviet/Russian Karelia can be placed into a larger framework of questions related to translation and minority, such as the role of politics in all fields of language use, majority interference in translating into a minority language, and the relativity of the concept of a minority language.

Politics are always involved in translation and minority. As Venuti (1998: 138) writes: "The mere use of a minor language to communicate can be a political act, a protest against its minority, even a criminal offence against the majority." The ways of rendering words denoting new political and social phenomena in Finnish

---

[27] Publishing translations of Russian fiction was reduced remarkably in 1990's (Jänis / Pesonen 2006: 204–205).

translation in Karelia is a good example. At first they were rendered using Finnish language resources, a kind of domestication. Foreignization in the form of transcribing Russian words became prevalent when translating into Finnish was under political pressure, and later even banned.

Negative comments on the part of Finnish critics of "Petrozavodsk translations" can also be considered a political act and interference in translating into a minority language. The underlying message is that the minority Finnish is considered inappropriate by the majority.

Karelian Finnish is a variation of the Finnish language which is written and spoken as the majority language beyond the border. It is also a minority language in relation to the prevailing Russian language – and influenced by it in discursive practices and the naming of new concepts and items. The instability of Finnish language use indicates a dilemma in deciding which of the two "majors" Karelian Finns should turn to in search of stability in language use in different times.

It is also worth remembering that Finnish was a major language in relation to the Karelian language and its dialects in Soviet Karelia. Written Finnish, including translations, was an enunciation of this position.

The rapid disappearance of the Finnish language and especially translating into Finnish may also be explained by the fact that it was not the language spoken by all Karelian minorities. It was mainly used and developed as a literary and spoken language by immigrants – first political refugees from Finland, later by Ingrian settlers. A Finnish-language newspaper and magazine are still published in Russian Karelia, but the reason for their survival is the position of Finnish as a majority language in neighboring Finland. It seems necessary to distinguish between translating into minority languages that are not in a majority position anywhere and those that have a majority position in some cultural and territorial entities. Karelian Finnish represents the latter case.

References

Alto, E. L. (1989): *Sovetskie finnojazyčnye žurnaly 1920–1980*. Petrozavodsk: Karelija.

Anttikoski, Esa (2000): "Karjalan kielisuunnittelun strategiat 1920- ja 1930-luvulla." In: Vihavainen, Timo / Takala, Irina, [eds.] (2000): *Yhtä suurta perhettä*. Helsinki: Kikimora Publications. 233–250. (= Kikimora Publications Series B. 12).

Austin, Paul (2009): *The Karelian Phoenix*. Joensuu: Faculty of Humanities, University of Joensuu. (= Studies in Languages. 45).

Belikova, Aleksandra (2009): "Finskij jazyk v Karelii v 20–30-e gody XX veka: popytki jazykogo modelirovanija." In: Iljuha, O. P. [ed.] (2009): *Finskij faktor v jazyke i kul'ture Karelii XX veka*. Petrozavodsk: Karel'skij naučnyj centr RAN. 164–183.

Cronin, Michel (1998): "The Cracked Looking Glass of Servants. Translation and Minority Languages in a Global Age." In: *The Translator* 4 (2), 145–162.

Jalava, Aulikki (1990): *Kansallisuus kadoksissa. Neuvosto-Karjalan suomenkielisen epiikan kehitys*. Helsinki: Suomalaisen Kirjallisuuden Seura.

Jufa, Olga (1992): "Kielikysymys Neuvosto-Karjalan kirjallisuusarvostelussa 1920–1930-luvuilla." In: *Carelia* 1, 142–147.

Jänis, Marja / Pesonen, Pekka (2007): "Venäläinen kirjallisuus." In: Riikonen, H. K. / Kovala, Urpo / Kujamäki, Pekka / Paloposki, Outi [eds.] (2007): *Suomennos-kirjallisuuden historia II*. Helsinki: Suomalaisen Kirjallisuuden Seura. 189–205.

Kangaspuro, Markku (2000): *Neuvosto-Karjalan taistelu itsehallinnosta: nationalismi ja suomalaiset punaiset Neuvostoliiton vallankäytössä vuosina 1920–1939*. Helsinki: Suomalaisen Kirjallisuuden Seura.

―― (2002): "The National and International in the Republic of Karelia." In: Flink, Toivo / Hirvasaho, Katja [eds.] (2002): *Predely zemli i soznanija*. Boundaries of Earth and Consciousness. Ingrian Finns, Karelians, Estonians, and St. Petersburg's Germans in an Age of Social Transformation. Proceedings of the Sixth *ICCEES World Congress*, Tampere, 2000. Helsinki. 118–139. (= Studia Slavica Finlandensia. XIX).

"Kaunokirjallisuuden kääntäminen on taidetta." In: *Punalippu* 1, 135–141.

Kilin, Juri (2002): "Roždenie karel'skoj avtonomii." In: Flink, Toivo / Hirvasaho, Katja [eds.] (2002): *Predely zemli i soznanija*. Boundaries of Earth and Consciousness. Ingrian Finns, Karelians, Estonians, and St. Petersburg's Germans in an Age of Social Transformation. Proceedings of the Sixth *ICCEES World Congress*, Tampere, 2000. Helsinki. 88–117. (= Studia Slavica Finlandensia. XIX).

Klementyev (2009) = Klement'ev, Evgenij (2009): "Ideologija i praktika jazykovoj politiki v Karelii v 1920–1930-e gody." In: Iljuha, O. P. [ed.] (2009): *Finskij faktor v jazyke i kul'ture Karelii XX veka*. Petrozavodsk: Karel'skij naučnyj centr RAN. 149–163.

Klementyev / Kozhanov (2009) = Klement'ev, Evgenij / Kožanov, Aleksandr (2009): "Finskij jazyk v Karelii v novejšij period." In: Iljuha, O. P. [ed.] (2009): *Finskij faktor v jazyke i kul'ture Karelii XX veka*. Petrozavodsk: Karel'skij naučnyj centr RAN. 338–350.

Kolomainen, Robert (2006): "Käännöstoiminnan vaiheet Venäjällä ja Venäjän Karjalassa." In: Jänis, Marja (2006): *Venäjästä suomeksi ja suomesta venäjäksi*. Helsinki: Aleksanteri Institute. 175–184. (= Aleksanteri-sarja. 1).

—— (2010): "Käännöstoiminnan vaiheet Venäjällä ja Venäjän Karjalassa." In: Marja Jänis: *Venäjästä suomeksi ja suomesta venäjäksi* (Toinen uudistettu laitos). Helsinki: Aleksanteri Institute. 137–146. (= Aleksanteri-sarja. 4).

Kruhse, Pauli / Uitto, Antero (2008): *Suomea rajan takana 1918-1944. Suomenkielisen neuvostokirjallisuuden historia ja bibliografia*. Jyväskylä: Kansalliskirjasto.

Laine, Gladys (1990): "Kirjailija ja aika. Piirtoja Karjalan kirjailijaliiton edustajakokouksesta." In: *Carelia* 2, 126–130.

Laine, Antti (2000): "Karjalais-suomalainen neuvostotasavalta." In: Vihavainen, Timo / Takala, Irina, [eds.] (2000): *Yhtä suurta perhettä*. Helsinki: Kikimora Publications. 251–282. (= Kikimora Publications Series B. 12).

Meylarts, Reine (2007): "La Belgique vivra-t-elle? Language and Translation Ideological Debates in Belgium (1919–1940)." In: *The Translator* 13 (2), 297–319.

Nikitin, Pekka (1989): *Vallankumouksen synnyttämä teatteri*. Petroskoi: Karjala-kustantamo.

Pakkanen, Santeri (1987): "Petroskoin suomi, elävää kieltä vai?" *Punalippu* 2, 159–162.

Pasanen, Päivi (2012): "Kotouttaminen ja vieraannuttaminen sanastotyössä." In: Kemppanen, Hannu / Mäkisalo, Jukka / Belikova, Alexandra [eds.] (2012): *Kotoista ja vierasta mediassa. Svoë i čužoe v SMI*. Joensuu. 69–75. (= Publications of the University of Eastern Finland. Reports and Studies in Education, Humanities, and Theology. 4).

Pesonen, Pekka (2003): "Lähellä ja kaukana. Venäläisen kaunokirjallisuuden suomennosten vaiheista." In: Lilius, Pirkko / Makkonen-Craig, Henna [eds.] (2003): *Nerontuotteita maailmalta. Näkökulmia suomennosten historiaan*. Helsinki. 70–98. (= Helsingin yliopiston käännöstieteellisiä julkaisuja. 4).

Pronina, Galina (1986): "Karjalassa puhutaan monenlaista suomea." In: *Punalippu* 7, 187–190.

Räsänen, Matti (1999): "Background and anatomy of the project." In: Teinonen, Markku / Virtanen, Timo J. [eds.] (1999): *Ingrians and Neighbours. Focus on the eastern Baltic Sea region*. Helsinki: Finnish Literature Society. 9–17.

Sihvo, Jouko (2000): *Inkerin kansan 60 kohtalon vuotta*. Helsinki: Tammi.

Starshova (2002) = Staršova, Tamara: "Finskij jazyk v Petrozavodskom gosudarstvennom universitete." In: Zaikov, P. M. / Starshova, T. I. [eds.] (2002): *Bubrihovskie čtenija: Problemy pribaltijsko-finskoj filologii i kul'tury*. Petrozavodsk: Izdatel'stvo PetrGU. 5–11.

—— (2011a): "Istorija perevodov s russkogo jazyka na finskij v kontekste jazykovoj situacii v Respublike Karelija v XX veke." Available at: http://petrsu.karelia.ru/Faculties/Balfin/translation.html.

—— (2011b): "Perevodčiki Respubliki Karelii s russkogo na finskij." Available at: http://petrsu.karelia.ru/Faculties/Balfin/translation.html.

—— (2011c): "O perevodčeskih strategijah po sohraneniju nacional'noj specifiki proizvedenij (iz opyta raboty karel'skih perevodčikov)." Available at: http://petrsu.karelia.ru/ Faculties/Balfin/translation.html.

Suni, Leo (2000): "Inkerinsuomalaiset." In: Vihavainen, Timo / Takala, Irina, [eds.] (2000): *Yhtä suurta perhettä*. Helsinki: Kikimora Publications. 75–93. (= Kikimora Publications Series B. 12).

Suutari, Pekka / Shikalov, Yuri [eds.] (2010): *Karelia Written and Sung. Representations of Locality in Soviet and Russian Contexts*. Helsinki: Kikimora Publications. (= Aleksanteri Series. 3).

Takala, Irina (2009): "Finny sovetskoj Karelii i ih vklad v razvitie respubliki (1920-e – pervaja polovina 1930-h godov." In: Iljuha, O. P. [ed.] (2009): *Finskij faktor v jazyke i kul'ture Karelii XX veka*. Petrozavodsk: Karel'skij naučnyj centr RAN. 107–148.

Vavulinskaja, Ljudmila (2009): "Kul'turnye svjazi meždu Kareliej i Finljandiej v 1950–1970-e gody." In: Iljuha, O. P. [ed.] (2009): *Finskij faktor v jazyke i kul'ture Karelii XX veka*. Petrozavodsk: Karel'skij naučnyj centr RAN. 322–337.

Venuti, Lawrence (1998): "Introduction." In: *The Translator. Translation and Minority*. (Special Issue), 4 (2), 135–144.

Ylikangas, Mikko (2004): *Rivit suoriksi! Kaunokirjallisuuden poliittinen valvonta Neuvosto-Karjalassa 1917–1940*. Helsinki: Kikimora Publications.

Zaharova, Larisa (2009): "Sootnošenie finskogo i russkogo faktorov v processe nacional'nogo stroitel'stva v Karelii v pervye poslevoennye desjatiletija: cikly korenizacii i osobennosti kommunikacii i reprezentacii." In: Iljuha, O. P. [ed.] (2009): *Finskij faktor v jazyke i kul'ture Karelii XX veka*. Petrozavodsk: Karel'skij naučnyj centr RAN. 299–321.

Domestication and *Foreignization* in Hong Kong Translation of Western Theatre

Chapman Chen
University of Eastern Finland, Joensuu

Abstract

Venuti (1995) advocates the foreignizing translation approach, claiming that it can register the linguistic and cultural difference of the foreign text and challenge the dominant culture and language. He praises the foreignizing strategy of early Republican Chinese translators for subverting traditional Chinese culture and founding the modern national language of China. The objective of this article is to test the applicability of Venuti's theory to Western theatre in Hong Kong (later in this article HK). The hypothesis is that an internal colony may domesticate theatrical works of other countries in order to challenge the culture and the language of the colonizer. Theories employed in this article include Wan Chin's (2011) "colonialism without a home base", Itamar Even-Zohar's (1990) polysystem theory, Gideon Toury's norm theory, Theo Hermans' (1985) conception of translation as manipulation, as well as Sirkku Aaltonen's (1996) notions of acculturation and localization. The findings are that Western theatre in HK Cantonese translation is especially subversive towards Peking when the translation strategy is domestication, and that domesticated foreign works can also be self-critical rather than self-aggrandizing as claimed by Venuti.

1 Introduction

Venuti (1995) advocates the foreignizing translation approach on the ground that it can retain the linguistic and cultural dissimilarities of foreign texts and challenge the dominant culture and language. He (1998: 183–189) eulogizes the foreignizing strategy of early Republican Chinese translators, such as Lu Xun (1881–1936) and Zhou Zouren (1885–1967), for querying and subverting traditional Chinese culture and classical Chinese, eventually leading to the birth of the modern national language of China. The objective of this article is to test the applicability of Venuti's theory to theatrical translation in HK. The hypothesis is that an internal colony may in translation domesticate theatres of other countries to interrogate the culture and the language of the internal colonizer. For instance, by way of localization[1] and the Cantonese language (sometimes combined with classical Chinese), Wai-kin Szeto's (2003) translation of Neil Simon's *God's Favorite* and Brecht's *Caucasian Chalk Circle* as translated by Kwok-kui Wong (2010a) and directed by Chu-hei Chan (2010) challenge the Communist Chinese language[2] and the Chinese Communist party's "colonialism without a home base" in Wan Chin's (2011) sense (see section 2 below). Towards the end of this article there will be theoretical discussions about Venuti's theory. Theories employed by the author of this article include Rey Chow's (1998) conception of HK as a hybrid third space between two aggressors, Even-Zohar's (1995) polysystem theory, the Manipulation School's conception of translation as rewriting, and Aaltonen's (1996) notions of acculturation and localization.

2 Internal colonialism

Michael Hechter (1999: 16) defines internal colonialism as follows: "The periphery exists within an unequal and dependent economic and political relationship with

---

1 Sirkku Aaltonen (1996) uses the term in the sense of "setting a play in another spatio-temporal environment" or changing its milieu, which "introduces other changes as well" (Aaltonen 1996: 71). This term is also often used by HK theatrical practitioners and scholars, e.g. Gilbert Fong (2000), Thomas Luk (2007) and Si-wai Shing (1996) to refer to relocating the setting of a Western play to HK and making other changes regarding culture-specific items as necessitated by the new setting. A synonym of localization is probably adaptation, which, according to Shuttleworth and Cowie (1997: 3–4), by tradition denotes any target text in which an especially free translation tactic has been employed. The term by and large suggests that a considerable amount of alterations have been made so as to render the text more appropriate for a particular group of receivers or for the specific aim at the back of the rendition. Nonetheless, from a prescriptive perspective, adaptation is often something negative. For example, Nida and Taber (1982) consider it unfaithful (see Shuttleworth and Cowie 1997: 3). Another term related to localization is acculturation. As defined by Aaltonen (1996), "Acculturation is the process which is employed to tone down the Foreign and to help identification with unfamiliar "reality". It makes understanding and, in consequence, integration possible" (*ibid*.: 19). Aaltonen divides acculturation of culture-specific items of Irish realist drama in Finnish translation into geographical location, political concepts, belief systems, art worlds, contemporary life, and language. So in theatre translation studies, acculturation and localization appear to be variants of domestication.

2 Written vernacular Chinese and oral Putonghua used on the Chinese Mainland.

the metropolitan core. There is also a basic cultural conflict, usually over language and religion, between the core and the periphery." New coercive policies attempt to "increase the individual's dependence upon and loyalty to the government". According to Sonny Lo (2007: 222), recolonization is a process in which "a powerful metropole is exerting influence on its colonial enclave politically, economically, socially and culturally", and recolonization takes place in HK in the form of mainlandization, i.e. policies to render HK more and more reliant on the Chinese Mainland (*ibid.*: 179). As pointed out by Wan Chin (2011), Communist China recolonizes HK through appropriating the residual power of the Basic Law, interpreting the Basic Law arbitrarily again and again, forcing HK to depend on the Chinese Mainland by way of economic monotonization of HK (with the aid of finance and real estate tycoons), diluting the local population of HK with colonizing settlers from Mainland China, suppressing dissident opinions in the name of maintaining public order, replacing Cantonese with Putonghua as the medium of instruction of Chinese as a subject, and allowing property tycoons to damage the economic vitality and rural environment of HK.

HK has thus become an internal colony of Communist China since the handover of its sovereignty from the UK to China in 1997. According to Chin's (2011) conception of "colonialism without a home base", the Chinese Communist Party was a puppet agent sent by Soviet Russia to colonize China. Then, finding even its master to be too principled, it severed itself from Russia and became a beheaded and rootless colonizer bent on destroying Chinese culture and ecology. So HK wants to challenge neither British nor Chinese culture. On the contrary, HK wants to defend Chinese culture as preserved in the rational system left over by the British colonizer, against the colonizing hegemony of Communist China. In addition, Rey Chow (1998) shows HK to be carving a third hybrid space between its two aggressors (London and Peking).

3 Venuti on foreignization and domestication

According to Venuti (1995: 20), the foreignizing approach involves the choice of a non-fluent style and the inclusion of source language *realia* or target language archaisms. Its effect is to produce an "alien reading experience" on the part of target readers, and its merits are to subvert cultural hegemony, cultural narcissism and ethnocentrism. Venuti (1998: 183–189) eulogizes Lu Xun and Zou Zuoren for their translations that contain ample Westernized syntaxes and phrases, which "interrogated traditional Chinese culture", eventually giving birth to modern written Chinese as the new national language of China.[3]

Contrastively, domestication is a term employed by Venuti (1995) to refer to the translation tactic in which a transparent, fluent style is employed so as to reduce to a minimum the "otherness" of the foreign text for the target reader. However, for Venuti the term has undesirable connotations as it is equated with a policy widely carried out in dominant cultures which are "aggressively monolingual, unreceptive to the foreign", and which he represents as being "accustomed to fluent translations that invisibly inscribe foreign texts with [target language] values and provide readers with the narcissistic experience of recognizing their own culture in a cultural order" (*ibid.*: 15).

---

3   In 1909, near the end of the Ching Dynasty, Lu Xun (1881-1936) and his brother cum collaborator Zhou Zuoren (1885–1967) "published a pioneering anthology of [literary] translations that sought to register rather than remove the linguistic and cultural differences of foreign fiction" (Venuti 1998: 184). Their renditions were put in classical Chinese "combined with Europeanized lexical and syntactical features, transliterations of Western names, and Japanese loan words" (*ibid.*). They believed that in order to save China, the Chinese must learn from the West, and that "making foreign works resemble the Chinese" will not achieve this aim (*ibid.*). Their foreignizing strategy was meant to challenge and displace "traditional Chinese culture… to build a vernacular literature that was modern, not simply Westernized" (*ibid.*), and to confront Chinese readers with the discomforting and "unsettling strangeness of modern ideas and forms" (*ibid.*). By the time when the second edition of their anthology appeared in 1920, after the establishment of Republic of China (1911) and immediately ensuing the beginning of the May Fourth Movement (1919), Lu Xun and his brother's foreignizing practice had shifted from the periphery to the core of Chinese culture, exerting a powerful influence on young authors of the movement, who then linked up Europeanized vernacular (not classical Chinese) with "liberation of the individual from all sorts of institutions and conventions" (Venuti 1998: 186). These efforts together cultivated the evolvement of a literary discourse in vernacular, eventually giving rise to the national language of China (*ibid.*).

4 Some background information about Cantonese and Mandarin

Throughout the history of China, there has always been distance between spoken Chinese and written Chinese. China has always had dozens of major regional oral languages and thousands of minor oral dialects. Up till the Chinese Communist Party took control of China, Chinese intellectuals had always been educated in their oral regional mother tongue. In traditional China, the common language of communication or *interlingua* for Chinese from different provinces was not any oral language, but classical Chinese, a refined and concise written language that has changed very little over thousands of years. Side by side with classical Chinese literature, a traditional written vernacular literature pertaining to the Sung (960–1279), Ming (1368–1644) and Ching (1644–1911) Dynasties has existed. This vernacular written literature combines a few regional languages of China but is ultimately based on classical Chinese, too. Both Mandarin (Putonghua) and Cantonese are different from written Chinese. Cantonese is nonetheless much closer than Mandarin to classical Chinese and classical vernacular literature (see Chin 2008: 236).

Cantonese, both oral and written, can be traced back to the Qin Dynasty (221–206 B.C.) and maybe even earlier (Li 1994: 34–35). As agreed by almost all linguists, e.g. Hin-chi Tsim (1995), Chi-ming Pang (2007), Wing-keung Poon (2005), Cantonese is a living linguistic fossil that has preserved an enormous amount of ancient Han-Chinese pronunciations, phrases and syntaxes. It is much more time-honored than Mandarin, which only has a history of around three hundred years. Cantonese, still spoken by 0.1 billion people all over the world, was recognized by the United Nations as a language rather than a dialect in 2006 (see Chin 2010: 238). However, the original characters of many Cantonese words are forgotten so that the language is often mistaken by most Mainland Chinese and by some Hongkongers to be a colloquial dialect. On the other hand, Mandarin (Putonghua) is based on the Peking dialect, which had been strongly inflected by the Manchurian language since the Manchurians colonized China in 1644. In fact, "Mandarin" originally means Manchurian lords.

When the famous Chinese scholars Hu Shi and Chen Duxiu initiated the modern written Vernacular Movement as part of the May Fourth Movement in 1919, they advocated that this modern written vernacular, as the modern national written language of China, be based on the Peking oral dialect, be somehow Westernized, and be seen as a continuation of the traditional written vernacular language (see Yok Yung 1999: 35). No doubt, the introduction of Western features could have enriched the national language. However, Chinese intellectuals in those days probably suffered from an inferiority complex. Blaming the cultural heritage of China for all its misfortunes and humiliations ever since the late Ching Dynasty, they took to complete foreignization of the Chinese language. They thought that just as the political and military power of China lagged behind the West, the expressive power of the Chinese language lagged behind Western languages. Consequently, they began to ruthlessly sever the Chinese language from its cultural tradition and design a highly Europeanized written vernacular based on the Peking spoken dialect, thereby self-inducing cultural colonization by the West (Chin 2008: 61).

Under Communist rule, the modern Chinese language has become ever more foreignized, because the Chinese Communist Party (CCP) forces everybody on the Chinese Mainland to memorize in their childhood poor Chinese translations of German canons of Karl Marx and Russian classics of Lenin (Chin 2010: 225). Furthermore, it has made Putonghua, i.e. Mandarin or the Peking dialect, the medium of instruction in all schools on the Chinese Mainland. The ultimate aim of the CCP is to exterminate all Chinese "dialects" so that Putonghua will remain the only authoritative and prestigious language in China (Li 1994: 69).

In contrast, thanks to the protection of British colonial rule, HK was able to preserve and develop Cantonese language and culture, classical Chinese, and traditional Chinese culture (Chin 2011: 88), Cantonese being the mother tongue of most HK people. Since the 1950's, Cantonese has become the official spoken Chinese language (side by side with English) used on radio and television, on the stage, in schools and on other public occasions in HK. It has also evolved an informal written form used widely in newspapers, magazines, advertisements, court records, etc. (see Bauer 1998, 2000).

Since the 1999 handover, however, under pressure and encouragement from Peking, some schools in HK have replaced Cantonese with Putonghua as the medium of instruction, particularly of Chinese as a subject. (According to the Basic Law, Chinese and English are the two official languages of HK, but it is not specified whether the Chinese language referred to therein is Cantonese or

Putonghua.) Robert Bauer (2000) predicts that if this trend continues, the tradition of HK students reading written Chinese in Cantonese will vanish within a couple of decades; the publication of Cantonese works will shrink; educated and/or young Hongkongers will feel ashamed of speaking Cantonese in public. Cantonese will then become a sub-class and sub-culture language. And with the continuous influx of Putonghua-speaking immigrants from Communist China, HK Cantonese may even become extinct. Thus, it is very important for Hongkongers to preserve Cantonese by writing and translating in this language.

5 The "centre" writing back to the "periphery"[4]

Although HK is now an internal colony of Communist China, thanks to liberal and enlightened British rule it has, as argued by Wei-ming Tu (2005), Koon-chung Chan (2007) and Wan Chin (2011), preserved Han pronunciations (Cantonese[5] rather than Putonghua), Han characters (traditional rather than simplified characters), and Han culture (ethics, customs, traditional vernacular Chinese and classical Chinese), all of which have more or less disappeared in Communist China. HK is thus the centre rather than the periphery of Chinese culture.

It is against this background that Chow (1998) and Chin (2010) think that HK must write back to its aggressive and monolingual second colonizer – Peking – assert its autonomy, and mould itself in its own language – not the foreignized Putonghua, but Cantonese organically combined with classical Chinese, traditional vernacular, fluent and succinct modern Chinese, and a moderate amount of English words and

---

4 As pointed out by Annedith Schneider (2001: 85), the binary of center/periphery is a fundamental concept of colonial discourse, which Edward Said (1978) explains as a system that has organized the colonial and postcolonial world. According to this neat division, the colonizing center is home to science, order, and modernity, while the colonized periphery harbors superstition, chaos, and backwardness. Following this logic, the colonizer center must control these negative aspects of the periphery in order to protect both the center and the periphery from itself.
According to Ashcroft, Griffiths and Tiffin (1989: 33), "in Salman Rushdie's phrase, the 'Empire writes back' to the imperial 'centre'" by way of "proclaiming itself central and self-determining…challenging the world-view that can polarize centre and periphery", and subverting imperial language and literature.

5 Cantonese is the oldest living Han-Chinese language.

syntaxes (Chow 1998: 54, 55, 58; Chin 2010: 249, 258). As linguistic foreignization has already become the norm in Communist China, linguistic domestication (translation into fluent and refined Cantonese-Chinese with cultural heritage) on the part of Western theatre in HK Cantonese translation is more subversive than foreignization with regard to the hegemony of Putonghua.

Similarly, according to Selby Lai-yan Chan (2007), as Cantonese is the mother tongue of most Hongkongers, translating classical Western plays into Cantonese for performance is a means of establishing HK Cantonese as HK's own voice, and to raise it to the status of a legitimate standard language.

In fact, over 98 percent of translated plays performed in HK are performed and written in Cantonese. Those published before the 1980's are mostly written in modern written Chinese while starting from the 1980's, because of the rise of the local identity (Luk 2007: 32), almost all of them are principally written in Cantonese. Some of them combine Cantonese with classical Chinese and/or fluent modern Chinese, as opposed to the highly Europeanized modern Chinese written language prevalent on the Chinese Mainland. For example, Jane Lai translates Shakespeare's *King Lear* into Cantonese combined with a modern Chinese language close to classical Chinese, and the rhythm is inspired by HK Cantonese opera. Rupert Chan (1990) relocates the 17th century French background of Edmund Rostand's *Cyrano de Bergerac* to the Tang Dynasty of China and translates the play mostly into simple classical Chinese combined with Cantonese, replacing the poems in the original with Chinese poems of a style typical of Tang poetry.[6] Yat Yau (2010) relocates the main text of Brecht's *Caucasian Chalk Circle* from Georgia to ancient China 3000 years ago, and translates the lines into Cantonese and the lyrics sung by the chorus and the protagonists into a succinct vernacular close to classical Chinese. Part of the lyrics are sung in a Cantonese opera style.

6 Subversive domestication

Venuti, as mentioned above, accuses domestication of serving cultures which are "aggressively monolingual, unreceptive to the foreign" (1995: 15), and of "pursuing

---

6   With a strict tonal pattern and rhyme scheme and five or seven characters each line.

a cultural narcissism that is imperialistic abroad and conservative, even reactionary, in maintaining cultural hierarchies in the receiving situation" (2008 [2005]: 266).

Domestication in HK theatrical translatio[7] is, however, not infrequently subversive. To borrow a Chinese idiom, it often "abuses the locust while pointing at the mulberry". In other words, by mimicking Western culture, it often aims at questioning not the particular Western culture being mimicked, but the political, cultural and linguistic hegemony of HK's second colonizer, Peking (Chen 2011a). For instance, as an immediate response to Sino-British negotiations about the future of HK in the early 1980's, Chiu-yu Mok's *1984/1997* relocates George Orwell's *1984* to HK (in the future, after the 1997 handover) and Communist China. The original Big Brother becomes the Chinese Communist Party, which, having turned to state capitalism after the Cultural Revolution ended in 1976, ruthlessly exploits Chinese workers for their labour (represented by actors moving boxes incessantly on the stage), and atrociously tortures and executes dissidents and homosexuals.

Another example is Ping-chiu Chan's (2003) version of Kafka's *Metamorphosis*, as a response to the Tiananmen Square Massacre (1989) and to the imminent 1997 handover of HK to Communist China. Chan resets *Metamorphosis* in contemporary HK and, among other acts of acculturation, provides the performance with the sad song "Home Disaster" – sung by Ro-man (1950–2002), a prestigious HK artist – as accompanying music. The resulting atmosphere is dark and bizarre, but the symbolic significance is obvious. The hero Samsa and his kin bear a heavy post-Tiananmen Square complex, e.g. Samsa twice recites long passages from the "Declaration of Fasting" originally made by the protesting students in the Tiananmen Square in 1989. They are also deeply suspicious about the handover of HK to China in 1997: for example at the beginning of the play, Samsa's father says "Fuck his mother!" when he reads news about the handover in the papers. The

---

7   In accordance with Lefevere's (1992) notion of translation as rewriting, not only "faithful" theatre translations but also adaptations are regarded as translation in this article. In the West, the domesticating solution is often created for the audience familiar with the original. In HK, this is sometimes the case, e.g. Ping-chiu Chan's (1995) localization of Kafka's *Metamorphosis*, the plot of which is known to many HK spectators; and sometimes not the case, e.g. Rupert Chan's (2003) adaptation of Ayckbourn's *A Small Family Business*, which is not known to most HK people.

major theme is Samsa's being forced by his three cousins to become part of the corrupt and cannibalistic economic system of Communist China (cf. Fat-lam 2003: xviii). The cousins are a substitute for the lodgers in the original and they are proxies of Communist China, who kowtow to Peking and betray HK.

Another example is Szeto's (2003) translation of Neil Simon's *God's Favorite*, which is in turn based on the Biblical story of Job. This HK version is a response to the governing crisis of HK Chief Executive C. H. Tung around 2003. In Szeto's subversive domestication, God becomes Chairman Jiang Zemin of Communist China, Satan becomes Chris Pattern (last governor of HK), and Job becomes a rich HK businessman pathetically loyal to the Communist Party of China and ironically subjected to unspeakable ordeals by Chairman Jiang in order to test his loyalty to the Chinese Communist Party (Chen 2011b). This HK Job reminds the local audience of C. H. Hung, who was good-willed but incompetent and submissive to the CCP.

Yet another example is Kwok-Kui Wong's (2010a) *Winds of Change*, a rewriting of Brecht's *Caucasian Chalk Circle* as a response to the rise of sundry local consciousness movements in HK since 2007. In Wong's subversive domestication, the bad biological mother in the original becomes a good real mother persecuted by a totalitarian State strongly suggestive of Communist China (see Shek 2010); the good foster mother becomes an evil fake mother sent by the State; the child represents the future[8] of HK; and the Judge a wavering or potentially treacherous HK politician.[9] The message appears to be that as the city of HK, founded in 1841, is already aged 170, much more senior than the 60-year-old People's Republic of China, the citizens of HK must stop acting like children. They must stand on their own feet and fight for their future like the people who start a revolution at the end of the translated play. Otherwise, they will be betrayed by local politicians who kidnap public opinion, and they will get trampled upon by Communist China just like the child in the play concerned.

No doubt, Venuti's main point is that foreignization gives the reader a chance to get acquainted with the foreign culture, while domestication leaves the reader inside their own culture. But around half of the theatrical translations done in HK still

---

8 As disclosed by the director of the play, Chu-hei Chan (see Duksit Cinhei 2010).
9 As confirmed by Kwok-kui Wong (2010b).

adopt the foreignizing approach. And in many domesticated Western plays performed in HK, only the setting and related culture-specific items are localized while the original plot and characterization remain unchanged. Further, even strongly domesticated Western plays may still manage to introduce the audience to the foreign: for example Chu-hei Chan, in directing *Winds of Change* mentioned above employs the Brechtian technique of alienation (e.g. two "stage managers" giving cues on the stage) and a chorus reminding one of the Greek tragedy.

7 Code-switching/swapping

Somewhere between linguistic domestication (the use of Cantonese sometimes combined with classical Chinese as the language of translation) and domestication of contents (localization/adaptation) is code-switching/swapping. Since, as aforementioned, most translated plays in HK are performed in Cantonese, the mother tongue of HK people, whenever the language is switched in the middle of a Cantonese-speaking play to Mandarin, the HK audience is bound to think immediately that it refers to the colonizer Communist China, and to expect the reference to be somewhat critical.

According to Lefevere (1992: 58), "Dialects and idiolects tend to reveal the translators' ideological stance toward certain groups thought of as 'inferior' or ridiculous', both inside their culture and outside." For instance, in *Animal Farm* as directed by William Yip (2010), the character Napoleon, like all the other characters, usually utters his lines in Cantonese, but from time to time he bursts into Putonghua. For example, when he visits the stallion in hospital, he says in Putonghua, "Sorry, comrades, I came late", reminiscent of Premier Wen Jiaobao, who said the same words in Putonghua when he visited the earthquake-stricken area of Sichuan in 2008. The political significance of this use of the Mandarin language is confirmed by the audience's nervous laughing immediately afterwards in at least one of the performances of the translated play, as observed by me on 21 November 2011. Another example is Hardy Tsoi's (2008) direction of Bolt's *A Man for All Seasons*. No sooner had the archbishop begun to interrogate Thomas Moore in Mandarin than "the audience found themselves between tears and laughter" (Fat-lam 2008). In my interpretation (Chen 2011a: 50), the switch to

Mandarin reminds the HK audience of Peking's twice ruling out universal suffrage for HK and condemnations in Mandarin of pro-democracy HK politicians.

Yet another instance is Danny Yung's (2000) domesticating direction of Shakespeare's *King Lear*, in which a dictatorial King-father strongly suggestive of the Chinese Communist Party (e.g. his eldest daughter Goneril mentions "revolutionary martyrs" in her dialogue with him) repeatedly asks his youngest daughter Cordelia whether she loves him or not (questioning the ex-British colony HK's loyalty to Peking). This straightforward allegory is however made more complex by Lear speaking Cantonese and Cordelia singing Peking opera in Mandarin. When the two parties swap languages, the resulting defamiliarization and oddity forcefully highlight the identity and power differences between them. In addition, the male's Cantonese vocal sound increasingly overrides the female's singing, in that way hinting at HK's resolve to maintain an autonomous position vis-à-vis Communist China (see Ferrari 2008).

8 Theoretical discussions about Venuti's foreignization theory

8.1 Moralizing

Venuti's foreignization theory is moralistically prescriptive (cf. Tymoczko 2010) despite the fact that the source-text oriented prescriptive approach has long been undermined by descriptive theorists like Lefevere and Hermans (see below). Bassnett and Lefevere (1992: xi) maintain that all translations are rewriting undertaken in service of power; Hermans (1985: 11) argues that all translations are to a certain extent manipulation for a certain purpose. And the theatre translation theoretician, Sirkku Aaltonen (2000), observes that translated plays invariably reflect the ideology of the target culture more than that of the source culture. Theatre translation characteristically engages adaptation of a text from abroad. Faithfulness to the letter is thus by no means a norm. In the theatre, the translator is a writer who authors the text from within his or her own community, civilization and theatre (Aaltonen 2000: 98). Similarly, Annie Brisset (1996: 196) concluded, after scrutinizing the relationship between the rewriting tactics used in the rendition of theatrical works from abroad and the societal discourse in Quebec, that naturalization or domestication was an essential requirement for the admittance of the Foreign into the literary institution. The translator's job was not so much as to present the receptor with what was strange or innovative in the foreign play, but rather to transform the foreign play into a tool for portraying the Quebec *realia*. Moreover, Venuti (2008: 19) asserted that "the terms 'domestication' and 'foreignization' indicate fundamentally ethical attitudes towards a foreign text and culture", thereby prescriptively implying that the domestication approach is unethical and immoral. Surprisingly, Venuti (1998: 11) himself admits that translation is fundamentally ethnocentric and its very function is assimilation.

8.2 Relative and time-bound

Tymoczko, in summing up a dozen articles written by translation scholars from different culture on activist translation and edited by herself, states that though the foreignizing approach as advocated by Venuti may often be a suitable resistant strategy in hegemonic and self-centred cultures like North America, it is not apt for oppressed or marginalized cultures that are "already flooded with foreign materials and foreign linguistic impositions" and that are attempting to set up or uphold "their own discourses and cultural forms" (Tymoczko 2010: 109) .In criticizing Venuti, Robinson (1997: 111) says: "What seems 'familiar' or 'ordinary' or 'fluent' is never intrinsic…it too can and will change with time…in other cases it is purely situational". According to Venuti (2008: 19) himself, "what constitutes fluent translating changes from one historical moment to another and from one cultural constituency to another". To Lu Xun and his revolutionary contemporaries, the classical Chinese language of the Ching Dynasty was a hegemonic and reactionary language to be dismantled by way of Westernization. However, as mentioned before, what was foreign in early Republican China has already become domestic as far as the Communist Chinese language is concerned. Now oral Putonghua and rigidly and extensively Europeanized written Chinese constitute the hegemonic language of Communist China, while HK as a minority ethnic group oppressed by Peking has to protect and shore up its local culture by writing in, and translating (e.g. plays) into, the HK language combining Cantonese with classical Chinese and succinct and fluent modern Chinese. This kind of language is domestic for HK but maybe archaic and alien for Communist China.

8.3 Subversive function

Venuti argues that the major purpose of foreignization is to subvert the dominant language and culture. However, as mentioned before, since linguistic foreignization has already become the norm in Communist China, linguistic domestication on the part of Western drama in HK Cantonese translation is more subversive than foreignization with regard to the hegemony of Putonghua. Similarly, content domestication or localization of Western plays in HK can be as subversive as or even more so than foreignization. According to Ying-fung Ho (2000: 2), until the early 1980's, most dramatic performances in HK had been direct importation/imitation/foreignizing translation of Western works without any profound reflection or local consciousness. It was not until the signing of the Sino-British Joint Declaration in 1984 that HK theatres began to read, reflect upon and interpret foreign plays more seriously. Especially after the Tiananmen Square Massacre in 1989, the social relevance and local significance of drama (original as well as translated plays) have been emphasized, meaning more manipulation and domestication of foreign plays.

No doubt, Venuti would retort that "…no culture should be considered immune to self-criticism, whether hegemonic or subordinate, colonizer or colonized. And without such practices as foreignizing translation to test its limits a culture can lapse into… narcissistic complacency…nationalism and fundamentalism" (Venuti 2008: 19–20).

In reality, however, domesticated foreign works can also serve the function of self-criticism. For example, Rupert Chan (2003) relocates Alan Ayckbourn's *A Small Family Business* to Shenzhen, China, and criticizes many a HK businessman for their joining in the evildoings of commercial circles in Communist China. Moreover, Kwok-kui Wong's (2010a) domestication of Brecht's *Caucasian Chalk Circle*, as aforementioned, criticizes the majority of HK citizens for their selfishness, stupidity and cowardice in failing to fight against the colonizing tyranny of Communist China and in entrusting wavering politicians with the task of protecting their interests.

8.4 Vague, ambiguous and self-contradictory

Venuti's definition of foreignization and domestication is misty, elusive and inconsistent. While he denounces domestication, he also says, "domestication need not mean assimilation, that is, a conservative reduction of the foreign text to dominant values. It can also mean resistance, through a recovery of the residual or an affiliation with the emergent or the dominated" (Venuti 2008 [1995]: 125). While Venuti endorses Lu Xun's foreignizing translations, he also concedes that in their domesticating translations, late Ching translators like Lin Shu (1852–1924) and Yan Fu (1853–1921) aptly make use of classical Chinese, and revise, expurgate, and annotate foreign texts in order that Western values and their own (Lin's and Yan's) nationalist agenda may be accepted by their countrymen (Venuti 1998: 178–189).

Moreover, many HK translations of Western theatre encode Western subversive ideologies by way of local settings and a local language which, to repeat, may sound archaic or alien to Communist China but is homely and familiar to the local people. So these translations can be at the same time foreignizing and domesticating according to Venuti's own discourse on foreignization and domestication.[10]

8.5 Other more explanatory theories

Although the following theories emerged earlier than Venuti's foreignizing theory, they can already explain Western theatre in HK translation more clearly and powerfully than Venuti.

8.5.1 The Descriptive Approach

For centuries until the first half of the last century, academic discussions about translations, in both the East and the West, had focussed upon the original. This kind of understanding about translation may be called "source-text oriented". It is mainly prescriptive rather than descriptive. As put by Wang-chi Wong (1999: 10), it

---

10 These translations, according to Venuti's own definition of foreignization and domestication, are foreignizing from the perspective of Communist China but domesticating from the perspective of HK people.

views translation as a reproduction of the source text. And whether a piece of translated work is good or bad depends on how much it resembles the source text.

Since James Holmes put forth the idea of "Descriptive Translation Studies" at a conference held in Copenhagen in 1972, the descriptive approach has gained more and more currency in translation studies. It is now the mainstream school in the field. Theo Hermans (1985) summarizes the characteristics of this school of scholars as follows: Basically, they believed that the direction of literary translation studies should be descriptive, target-text oriented, functional and systematic; they were interested in studying the norms and restrictions of the production and reception of translation, the relationship between translation and the processing of other texts, and the role and position of translation in a specific literature as well as in the interaction between different literatures (Hermans 1985: 10–11). Representative scholars of the descriptive approach include Itamar Even-Zohar, Gideon Toury, Theo Hermans, Andre Lefevere, etc.

8.5.2 Even-Zohar's polysystem theory

According to the polysystem theory of Itamar Even-Zohar (1990), in the course of translation, if the indigenous literature is in a weak position, then translated works will tend to differ significantly from the local literature, in order to introduce new forms of expression and thoughts for changing and reforming the local literature; on the other hand, if the indigenous literature is in a powerful position, then translations of foreign works will have to defer to and align themselves with the indigenous literature. Following this scenario, Gilbert Fong (2000: 130–131) argues that when HK drama was still in its developmental stage in the 60's and 70's, it capitalized on the achievements of Western drama and most theatrical translations adopted the foreignization approach. Since the mid 80's, when HK drama more or less matured, and with the local consciousness growing increasingly strong, domestication has been more and more popular in HK translation of Western theatre.

8.5.3 Toury's norm theory

Even-Zohar's polysystem theory has influenced Gideon Toury (1978) to put forth a target-text oriented translation theory – the concept of "translation" should be broadened. What is most important is whether the target language reader regards a certain text as a translation, rather than how the translation is done. This is very different from the source-text oriented concept of translation. From this new perspective, literal translation, semantic translation, free translation, adaptation, recreation, and even pseudo-translation may all be regarded as translation and consequently studied. Toury (1978) advocates that a large amount of translated texts be empirically scrutinized (just like Even-Zohar) in order to find out certain norms of the target culture. This concept of norm had been put forth by Even-Zohar, but it was Toury who seriously looked into the relationship between translation and norm and formally put forth the concept of translational norms.

According to Gideon Toury's norm theory (1978), translation is a compromise (an encounter and clash) of the linguistic and socio-cultural norms of two different systems. To follow this scenario, placed in this context, domestication should mean an attempt to break certain norms of the SL, such as poetics, in order to break certain norms of the TL, such as ideology (see Wong 1999: 40). For instance, in their domesticating version of Brecht's *Caucasian Chalk Circle*, the translator Kwok-kui Wong (2010a) and the director Chu-hei Chan (2010) render the everyday German-speaking scene, in which the indifferent aristocratic mother and the loving maid strive for the child Michael within the chalk circle, into a scene with a classical Cantonese opera feel in order to challenge the hegemony of Peking and bring forth the local cultural consciousness. Another example is Chapman Chen's (2005) translation of Alexis Kivi's *Kullervo*, where the old Karelian setting of the original is sacrificed and turned into a classical *kungfu* world of China, in order to introduce the independent and indignant spirit of the Finnish hero Kullervo for the purpose of challenging the collective ideology of Communist China (cf. Chen 2006; Chen 2010).

On the other hand, foreignization means an attempt to comply with and introduce the linguistic and cultural norms of the SL. King-fai Chung's (1979) literal translation of Peter Shaffer's *Equus,* typical of theatrical translations done before the 1980's in HK, may serve as an example.

8.5.4 Manipulation school

"Translation as rewriting of the original" is a very important concept. The Manipulation School, a branch of the Descriptive Approach, originated from the idea proposed by Theo Hermans (1985: 11) that all translations are to a certain extent manipulation of the source text for a certain purpose. This concept is a most radical challenge of the source-text oriented theory, for it argues that in the process of translation, the translator will certainly deliberately (for a certain purpose) rewrite the source text. So there is no reason why the translation has to be compared with the original and, to borrow Venuti's (1995: 20) words, "register the linguistic and cultural difference of the foreign text". Similarly, Andre Lefevere (1992) points out that translation is bound to be governed by the ideology and poetics of the translator and/or patronage, that it can never truthfully reflect the original outlook of the source text. He thus calls translation, editing, compilation of collected works, literary history writing and dictionary compilation alike "rewriting". And rewriting is manipulation, a kind of effective means to serve power (Lefevere 1992: 4–9). It follows that we may regard foreignization and domestication as just manipulation of the foreign in different ways.

9 Conclusions

In conclusion, Venuti's conception of foreignization and domestication has a lot of room for improvement. It is self-contradictory, for while Venuti denounces domestication as intolerant and narcissistic, he also says that "domestication can also mean resistance". Venuti's concepts are never intrinsic. For example, what was foreignizing about Europeanized features in the modern Chinese language in the early 20th Century has now become the domestic norm in Communist China. Furthermore, it is unscholarly to suggest that one translation approach (foreignization) is "ethical" while another one (domestication) is not. This kind of prescriptive approach to translation studies has long been undermined by the descriptive theorists. Venuti claims that foreignization is much more subversive than domestication. However, domestication could be as effective in interrogating hegemonic cultures as, or even more so than, foreignization, as illustrated by HK theatrical translation. Domestication in Western theatre in HK translation, which may take the form of linguistic domestication (the use in performances of spoken

Cantonese rather than Mandarin, and the use in script-writing of written Cantonese combined with classical written Chinese and/or fluent written modern Chinese as opposed to Europeanized modern written Chinese prevalent in China), or domestication of contents (localization/adaptation), or code-switching/swapping (between Cantonese and Mandarin), or all of the above, powerfully fulfils the function of challenging the hegemony of the colonizer's language and world-view. In reality, all theatrical translations have to more or less acculturate or domesticate the foreign in order to communicate with the target audience and address the concerns of their society. No doubt, descriptive translation theories emerged earlier than Venuti's theory. But still, Venuti's foreignization translation theory ought to be supplemented, if not replaced, with well-defined and useful ones like Even-Zohar's, Toury's, Aaltonen's, and Brisset's, which more readily explain the development of Western theatre in HK translation and the use of translation strategies therein.

References

Aaltonen, Sirkku (1996): *Acculturation of the Other – Irish Milieux in Finnish Drama Translation*. Joensuu: Joensuu University Press.

Aaltonen, Sirkku (2000): *Time-sharing on Stage*. Clevedon/Buffalo/Toronto/Sydney: Multilingual Matters.

Ashcroft, Bill / Griffiths, Gareth / Tiffin, Helen [eds.] (1989): *The Empire Writes Back*. London/New York: Routledge.

Bassnett, Susan (1993): *Comparative Literature: A Critical Introduction*. Oxford: Blackwell Publisher.

Bauer, Robert (1998): "Written Cantonese of Hong Kong." In: *Cahiers de Linguistique Asie Orientale*, XVII (2), 245–293.

––––– (2000): "Hong Kong Cantonese and the Road Ahead." In: Li, David C. S. / Lin, Angel / Tsang, Wai-king [eds.] (2000): *Language and Education in Postcolonial Hong Kong*. HK: Linguistic Society of HK. 35–38.

Brisset, Annie (1996): *A Sociocritique of Translation: Theatre and Alterity in Quebec, 1968–1988*. Translated by Gill, R. and Gannon, R. Toronto: Toronto UP.

Chan, Chu-hei (2010): *Bin-tin* [Winds of Change]. [Bertolt Brecht. Caucasian Chalk Circle]. Translated by Wong, Kwok-kui. (Directed by Chu-hei Chan; acted by Emotion Cheung). Performed by Theatrehorizon, HK. 30–31 July.

Chan, Koon-chung (2007): "Hong Kong Viscera." In: *Postcolonial Studies* 10 (4), 379–389.

Chan, Lai-yan Selby (2007): "Bunngo dik Syu-sei jyu Taacefaa [Local Writing and Otherization]." *HK Drama Review* 6, 1–14.

Chan, Ping-chiu (2003): "Gaabin Gaung [Home Disaster 95]" [Franz Kafka, Metamorphosis]. Translated by Chan, Ping-chiu In: Fat-lam [ed.] (2003): *All the Rainbow: HK Plays from the 1990's* (in Chinese). HK: International Association of Theatre Critics (HK).

Chan, Rupert (1990): *Meijan yu Juk Kim yu Hung* [The Belle is like Jade and the Sword is like Rainbow] [Edmond Rostand: Cyrano de Beregerac]. (Directed by James Mak; acted by Adam Cheng). Performed by Chung Tin Production Ltd. 22-29 October.

—— (1997): *Miutiu Sukneoi* [Bernard Shaw. *Pygmalion*]. Translated by Rupert Chan. (Directed by Tin-lung Ko; produced by Clifton Ko; acted by. King-fai Chung and Dominic Cheung). Performed by Spring Time Group Production, HK. 31 October – 30 November.

—— (2003): *Gaating Zokjip* [Alan Ayckbourn. *A Small Family Business*]. Translated by Rupert Chan. (Directed by Fred Mao and Wai-cheuk Szeto; acted by Chau-sang Wong). Performed by HK Repertoire, HK. 3 March – 4 April.

Chen, Chapman (2005): *Wuhoi Yansau Luk* [Aleksis Kivi, Kullervo]. Translated by Chapman Chen. HK: International Association of Theatre Critics (HK).

—— (2006): "Finnish Kullervo and Chinese Kungfu." In: *Polissema* (Portugal) 6, 73–86.

—— (2010): "Länsimaista draamaa Hongkongissa [Western Drama in HK]." In: Aaltonen, Sirkku [ed.] (2010): *Matkalippu maailmalle* [A Travel Ticket to the World]. Helsinki: Like. 168–189.

—— (2011a): "Postcolonial HK Drama Translation." In: Kujamäki, Pekka / Kolehmainen, Leena / Penttilä, Esa / Kemppanen, Hannu [eds.] (2011): *Beyond Borders – Translations Moving Languages, Literatures and Cultures*. Berlin: Frank & Timme Verlag für wissenschaftliche Literatur. 39–57.

—— (2011b): "Rethinking Postcolonial Theories – Two Western Plays in HK Translation." In: Chalvin, Antoine/Lange, Anne et al. [eds.] (2011): *Between Cultures and Texts. Itineraries in Translation History*. Hamburg: Peter Lang. 307–317.

Chin, Wan (2008): *Zungman Gaaiduk* [Detoxifying the Chinese Language]. HK: Enrich Publishing Ltd.

—— (2010): *Zungman Heiji* [Uprising of the Chinese Language]. HK: Enrich Publishing Ltd.

—— (2011): *Hoenggong Singbong Leon* [On HK as a City-State]. HK: Enrich Publishing Ltd.

Chow, Rey (1998): "Between Colonizers: HK's Postcolonial Self-Writing in the 1990's." In: *Ethics after Idealism: Theory, Culture, Ethnicity, Reading*. Bloomington; Indiapolis; Indiana University Press. 149–167.

Chung, King-fai (1979): *Maa* [Horse] [Peter Shaffer. *Equus*]. Translated by King-fai Chung. HK: Lyun Siu Ltd.

Duksit Cinhei (2010): *Stage TV Duksit Cinhei* [Foreplay of Poisonous Tongue]." I (Full Edition). Available at: http://www.youtube.com/watch?v=yzPjpJtlYhE. Visited November 2011.

Even-Zohar, Itamar (1990): *Polysystem Studies*. Durham: Duke University Press. A special issue of Poetics Today, 11 (1). Available at: http://www.tau.ac.il/~itamarez/works/books/ez-pss1990.pdf.

Fat-lam (2003): "Dou-jin [Introduction]." In: Fat-lam [ed.] (2003): *All the Rainbow: HK Plays from the 1990's* (in Chinese). HK: International Association of Theatre Critics (HK). ix–xxiii.

—— (2008): "Jatjyut Zingzung dik Seigwai Jan [The Faithful Man for All Seasons]." In: *Takungpao*. HK, 23 December. Available at: http://dagong.iflove.com/news/08/12/23/MFTX-1008509.htm. Visited 3 July 2009.

Ferrari, Rosella (2008): "Transnation/transmedia/transtext: Border Crossing from Screen to Stage in Greater China." In: *Journal of Chinese Cinemas* 2 (1), 53–65.

Fong, Gilbert (2000): "Gan Jisap Nin Hoenggong Waakek dik Fatzin (1977–1997) [Development of HK Drama in the Last Twenty Years (1977–1997)]." In: Fong, Gilbert [ed.] (2000): *San Geijyun dik Waaman Heikek* [Chinese-speaking Drama in the New Age]. HK: HK Drama Association and Drama Project, CUHK. 121–140.

Hechter, Michael (1999): *Internal Colonialism: the Celtic Fringe in British National Development*. New Brunswick, NJ and London: Transaction Publishers.

Hermans, Theo (1985): *The Manipulation of Literature: Studies in Literary Translation*. London and Sidney: Croom Helm.

Ho, Ying-fung (2000). "Zeoi: Wuigu Hoenggong Moutoi Citgaai Jisap Nin [Preface: A Review of Twenty Years' Stage Design in HK]." In: Lo, Tak-yi [ed.] (2000): *Hoenggong Moutoi Citgaai Jisap Nin* [Twenty Years of Stage Design]. HK: Yat Yuet. 2–4.

Lefevere, Andre (1992): *Translation, Rewriting and the Manipulation of Literary Fame*. London and New York: Routledge.

Lai, Jane (2005 [1983]): *Lei-ji Wong* [William Shakespeare: King Lear]. Translated by Jane Lai. HK: International Association of Theatre Critics (HK).

Li, Xin-hui (1994): *Gwongdung dik Fongjin* [The Dialects of Canton]. Canton: Guangdong People's Publishing Co.

Lo, Sonny (2007): "The Mainlandization and Recolonization of HK: A Triumph of Convergence over Divergence with Mainland China." In: Cheng, Joseph [ed.] (2007): *The Hong Kong Special Administrative Region in its First Decade*. HK: HKCityU Press. 179–223.

Luk, Thomas Y. T. (2007): *Translation and Adaptation of Western Drama in HK* (in Chinese). HK: Chinese University Press.

Pang, Chi-ming (2007): *Zingzi Zikok* [Correct Cantonese Characters]. HK: Sub-culture.

Poon, Wing-keung (2005): *Kwongdung Zukju Tamkei* [Exploration of Cantonese]. HK: Chung Wah Bookstore.

Robinson, Douglas (1997): *Translation and Empire – Postcolonial Theories Explained*. Brooklands: St. Jerome.

Said, Edward (1978): *Orientalism*. New York: Vintage Books.

Schneider, Annedith M. (2001): "Center/Periphery". In: Hawley, John C. [ed.] (2001): *Encyclopedia of Postcolonial Studies*. Westport, Connecticut/London: Greenwood Press. 85–89.

Shek, Kei (2010): "Zingzi Beikek: Bintin [A Political Tragedy – Winds of Change]." In: *Mingpao* 3 August.

Shing, Si-wai (1996): *Hoenggong Faanjik Kek dik Buntoufaa jinzoeng* [The Localization Phenomenon of Translated Plays in HK]. M. Phil. thesis. Chinese University of HK.

Shuttleworth, Mark and Cowie, Moira (1997): *Dictionary of Translation Studies*. Brooklands: St. Jerome.

Szeto, Wai-kin (2003): *Ngo loudau hai dongfui* [My Father is Ash of the Party]. [Neil Simon: God's Favorite]. Translated by Wai-kin Szeto. (Directed by Chun-tung Sin; acted by Ka-sheung Ting). Performed by One/eight Theatre. 21–23 February.

Toury, Gideon (1978): "The Nature and Roles of Norms in Literary Translation." In: Holmes, James / Lambert, Jose / Broeck, Raymond Van den [eds.] (1978): *Literature and Translation: New Perspectives in Literary Studies*. Leuven: Academic Publishing Company. 83–100.

Tsim, Hin-chi (1995): *Kwongzau Ju Bunzi* [Original Characters of Cantonese]. HK: Chinese University Press.

Tsoi, Hardy (2008): *Seigwaijan* [A Man for All Seasons]. [Robert Bolt. A Man for All Seasons]. Translated and directed by Hardy Tsoi. Performed at Tu, Mac. TNT Theatre, HK. 5–7 December.

Tu, Wei-ming (2005): "Cultural China: The Periphery as the Center." In: *Daedalus* 134 (5), 145–167.

Tymoczko, Maria (2010): "Translation, resistance, activism: an overview." In: Tymoczko, Maria [ed.] (2010): *Translation, Resistance, Activism*. Massachusetts: U. of Massachusetts Press. 1–22.

Yat-yau (2010): *Fuilaan* [Chalk Circle] [Bertolt Brecht. *Caucasian Chalk Circle*]. Translated and directed by Yat-yau. (Acted by Elton Lau). Performed by Class 7A Drama Group, HK. 29–31 January.

Yip, William (2010): *Dungmat Nungzong* [Animal Farm] [George. Orwell. *Animal Farm*]. Translated by Frankie Ho. (Directed by William Yip; acted by Pichead Amornsomboon). Performed by Theatre Noir, HK. 20–21 November.

Venuti, Lawrence (1995): *The Translator's Invisibility*. London and New York: Routledge.

—— (1998): *The Scandals of Translation*. London and New York: Routledge.

—— (2008 [1995]): *The Translator's Invisibility*. London and New York: Routledge.

Wong, Kwok-kui (2010a): *Bintin* [Winds of Change] [Bertolt Brecht. *Caucasian Chalk Circle*]. Translated by Kwok-kui Wong. (Directed by Chu-hei Chan; acted by Emotion Cheung). Performed at Cheung, Emotion. Theatrehorizon, HK. 30–31 July.

—— (2010b): "Zinggoi zihau Hosi Bintin? [After the Constitutional Reform, When will the Governing Heaven be Changed?]." In: *Mingpao* 25 July.

Wong, Wang-chi (1999b): *Cungsik Seon Tat Ngaa* [Reinterpreting 'Fidelity, Communicativeness and Elegance']. Shanghai: Dongfang Press.

Yung, Danny (2000): *Experimental Shakespeare: King Lear* [William Shakespeare. *King Lear*]. Translated and directed by Danny Yung. Performed by Zuni Icosahedron, HK. 16–19 March.

Yung, Yok (1999): *Manhok Geibun Gung* [The Basics of Literature]. HK: Lau Shing and Co.

Author index

Per AMBROSIANI, Professor of Russian, Umeå University (Sweden). E-mail: per.ambrosiani@ryska.umu.se

Alexandra BELIKOVA, PhD Student in Translation Studies, University of Eastern Finland. E-mail: alex.belikova@gmail.com

Alexandra BORISENKO, Lomonosov Moscow State University (Russia). E-mail: alexandra.borisenko@gmail.com

Chapman CHEN, PhD Student in Translation Studies, University of Eastern Finland. E-mail: kivilonnrot@yahoo.com

Marja JÄNIS, Docent in Translation Studies, University of Eastern Finland. E-mail: marja.janis@kolumbus.fi

Hannu KEMPPANEN, Professor of Russian Language and Translation, University of Eastern Finland. E-mail: hannu.kemppanen@uef.fi

Kinga KLAUDY, Professor, Head of Department of Translation and Interpretation, Eötvös Loránd University (Hungary). E-mail: kklaudy@ludens.elte.hu

Kaisa KOSKINEN, Professor of Translation Studies, University of Eastern Finland. E-mail: kaisa.koskinen@uef.fi

Jukka MÄKISALO, Senior Lecturer in Methodology of Language Studies, University of Eastern Finland. E-mail: jukka.makisalo@uef.fi

Pirkko MUIKKU-WERNER, Professor of Finnish Language, University of Eastern Finland. pirkko.muikku-werner@uef.fi

Esa PENTTILÄ, Professor of Translation Studies in English, University of Tampere (Finland). E-mail: esa.penttila@uta.fi

Piet Van POUCKE, Lecturer in Russian Language and Culture, University College Ghent & Ghent University (Belgium). E-mail: piet.vanpoucke@hogent.be

Elena RASSOKHINA, PhD Student in Russian, Umeå University (Sweden). E-mail: elena.rassokhina@ryska.umu.se

Tamara STARSHOVA, Associate Professor, Dean of the Faculty of Baltic and Finnish Language and Culture, Petrozavodsk State University (Russia). E-mail: starshova@psu.karelia.ru

TRANSÜD. ARBEITEN ZUR THEORIE UND PRAXIS DES ÜBERSETZENS UND DOLMETSCHENS

Die Bände 1 bis 5 sind bei der Peter Lang GmbH erschienen und dort zu beziehen.

Band 6   Przemysław Chojnowski: Zur Strategie und Poetik des Übersetzens. Eine Untersuchung der Anthologien zur polnischen Lyrik von Karl Dedecius. 300 Seiten. ISBN 978-3-86596-013-9

Band 7   Belén Santana López: Wie wird *das Komische* übersetzt? *Das Komische* als Kulturspezifikum bei der Übersetzung spanischer Gegenwartsliteratur. 456 Seiten. ISBN 978-3-86596-006-1

Band 8   Larisa Schippel (Hg.): Übersetzungsqualität: Kritik – Kriterien – Bewertungshandeln. 194 Seiten. ISBN 978-3-86596-075-7

Band 9   Anne-Kathrin D. Ende: Dolmetschen im Kommunikationsmarkt. Gezeigt am Beispiel Sachsen. 228 Seiten. ISBN 978-3-86596-073-3

Band 10   Sigrun Döring: Kulturspezifika im Film: Probleme ihrer Translation. 156 Seiten. ISBN 978-3-86596-100-6

Band 11   Hartwig Kalverkämper: „Textqualität". Die Evaluation von Kommunikationsprozessen seit der antiken Rhetorik bis zur Translationswissenschaft. ISBN 978-3-86596-110-5

Band 12   Yvonne Griesel: Die Inszenierung als Translat. Möglichkeiten und Grenzen der Theaterübertitelung. 362 Seiten. ISBN 978-3-86596-119-8

Band 13   Hans J. Vermeer: Ausgewählte Vorträge zur Translation und anderen Themen. Selected Papers on Translation and other Subjects. 286 Seiten. ISBN 978-3-86596-145-7

Band 14   Erich Prunč: Entwicklungslinien der Translationswissenschaft. Von den Asymmetrien der Sprachen zu den Asymmetrien der Macht. 442 Seiten. ISBN 978-3-86596-146-4 (vergriffen, siehe Band 43 der Reihe)

Band 15   Valentyna Ostapenko: Vernetzung von Fachtextsorten. Textsorten der Normung in der technischen Harmonisierung. 128 Seiten. ISBN 978-3-86596-155-6

TRANSÜD. ARBEITEN ZUR THEORIE UND PRAXIS DES ÜBERSETZENS UND DOLMETSCHENS

Band 16　Larisa Schippel (Hg.): TRANSLATIONSKULTUR – ein innovatives und produktives Konzept. 340 Seiten. ISBN 978-3-86596-158-7

Band 17　Hartwig Kalverkämper/Larisa Schippel (Hg.): Simultandolmetschen in Erstbewährung: Der Nürnberger Prozess 1945. Mit einer orientierenden Einführung von Klaus Kastner und einer kommentierten fotografischen Dokumentation von Theodoros Radisoglou sowie mit einer dolmetschwissenschaftlichen Analyse von Katrin Rumprecht. 344 Seiten. ISBN 978-3-86596-161-7

Band 18　Regina Bouchehri: Filmtitel im interkulturellen Transfer. 174 Seiten. ISBN 978-3-86596-180-8

Band 19　Michael Krenz/Markus Ramlow: Maschinelle Übersetzung und XML im Übersetzungsprozess. Prozesse der Translation und Lokalisierung im Wandel. Zwei Beiträge, hg. von Uta Seewald-Heeg. 368 Seiten. ISBN 978-3-86596-184-6

Band 20　Hartwig Kalverkämper/Larisa Schippel (Hg.): Translation zwischen Text und Welt – Translationswissenschaft als historische Disziplin zwischen Moderne und Zukunft. 700 Seiten. ISBN 978-3-86596-202-7

Band 21　Nadja Grbić/Sonja Pöllabauer: Kommunaldolmetschen/Community Interpreting. Probleme – Perspektiven – Potenziale. Forschungsbeiträge aus Österreich. 380 Seiten. ISBN 978-3-86596-194-5

Band 22　Agnès Welu: Neuübersetzungen ins Französische – eine kulturhistorische Übersetzungskritik. Eichendorffs *Aus dem Leben eines Taugenichts*. 506 Seiten. ISBN 978-3-86596-193-8

Band 23　Martin Slawek: Interkulturell kompetente Geschäftskorrespondenz als Garant für den Geschäftserfolg. Linguistische Analysen und fachkommunikative Ratschläge für die Geschäftsbeziehungen nach Lateinamerika (Kolumbien). 206 Seiten. ISBN 978-3-86596-206-5

F Frank & Timme

TRANSÜD. ARBEITEN ZUR THEORIE UND PRAXIS DES ÜBERSETZENS UND DOLMETSCHENS

Band 24 Julia Richter: Kohärenz und Übersetzungskritik. Lucian Boias Analyse des rumänischen Geschichtsdiskurses in deutscher Übersetzung. 142 Seiten. ISBN 978-3-86596-221-8

Band 25 Anna Kucharska: Simultandolmetschen in defizitären Situationen. Strategien der translatorischen Optimierung. 170 Seiten. ISBN 978-3-86596-244-7

Band 26 Katarzyna Lukas: Das Weltbild und die literarische Konvention als Übersetzungsdeterminanten. Adam Mickiewicz in deutschsprachigen Übertragungen. 402 Seiten. ISBN 978-3-86596-238-6

Band 27 Markus Ramlow: Die maschinelle Simulierbarkeit des Humanübersetzens. Evaluation von Mensch-Maschine-Interaktion und der Translatqualität der Technik. 364 Seiten. ISBN 978-3-86596-260-7

Band 28 Ruth Levin: Der Beitrag des Prager Strukturalismus zur Translationswissenschaft. Linguistik und Semiotik der literarischen Übersetzung. 154 Seiten. ISBN 978-3-86596-262-1

Band 29 Iris Holl: Textología contrastiva, derecho comparado y traducción jurídica. Las sentencias de divorcio alemanas y españolas. 526 Seiten. ISBN 978-3-86596-324-6

Band 30 Christina Korak: Remote Interpreting via Skype. Anwendungsmöglichkeiten von VoIP-Software im Bereich Community Interpreting – Communicate everywhere? 202 Seiten. ISBN 978-3-86596-318-5

Band 31 Gemma Andújar / Jenny Brumme (eds.): Construir, deconstruir y reconstruir. Mímesis y traducción de la oralidad y la afectividad. 224 Seiten. ISBN 978-3-86596-234-8

Band 32 Christiane Nord: Funktionsgerechtigkeit und Loyalität. Theorie, Methode und Didaktik des funktionalen Übersetzens. 338 Seiten. ISBN 978-3-86596-330-7

Band 33 Christiane Nord: Funktionsgerechtigkeit und Loyalität. Die Übersetzung literarischer und religiöser Texte aus funktionaler Sicht. 304 Seiten. ISBN 978-3-86596-331-4

Frank & Timme

TRANSÜD. ARBEITEN ZUR THEORIE UND PRAXIS DES ÜBERSETZENS UND DOLMETSCHENS

Band 34 Małgorzata Stanek: Dolmetschen bei der Polizei. Zur Problematik des Einsatzes unqualifizierter Dolmetscher. 262 Seiten. ISBN 978-3-86596-332-1

Band 35 Dorota Karolina Bereza: Die Neuübersetzung. Eine Hinführung zur Dynamik literarischer Translationskultur. 108 Seiten. ISBN 978-3-86596-255-3

Band 36 Montserrat Cunillera/Hildegard Resinger (eds.): Implicación emocional y oralidad en la traducción literaria. 230 Seiten. ISBN 978-3-86596-339-0

Band 37 Ewa Krauss: Roman Ingardens „Schematisierte Ansichten" und das Problem der Übersetzung. 226 Seiten. ISBN 978-3-86596-315-4

Band 38 Miriam Leibbrand: Grundlagen einer hermeneutischen Dolmetschforschung. 324 Seiten. ISBN 978-3-86596-343-7

Band 39 Pekka Kujamäki/Leena Kolehmainen/Esa Penttilä/Hannu Kemppanen (eds.): Beyond Borders – Translations Moving Languages, Literatures and Cultures. 272 Seiten. ISBN 978-3-86596-356-7

Band 40 Gisela Thome: Übersetzen als interlinguales und interkulturelles Sprachhandeln. Theorien – Methodologie – Ausbildung. 622 Seiten. ISBN 978-3-86596-352-9

Band 41 Radegundis Stolze: The Translator's Approach – Introduction to Translational Hermeneutics. Theory and Examples from Practice. 304 Seiten. ISBN 978-3-86596-373-4

Band 42 Silvia Roiss/Carlos Fortea Gil/María Ángeles Recio Ariza/Belén Santana López/Petra Zimmermann González/Iris Holl (eds.): En las vertientes de la traducción e interpretación del/al alemán. 582 Seiten. ISBN 978-3-86596-326-0

Band 43 Erich Prunč: Entwicklungslinien der Translationswissenschaft. 3., erweiterte und verbesserte Auflage (1. Aufl. 2007. ISBN 978-3-86596-146-4). 528 Seiten. ISBN 978-3-86596-422-9

TRANSÜD. ARBEITEN ZUR THEORIE UND PRAXIS DES ÜBERSETZENS UND DOLMETSCHENS

Band 44 Mehmet Tahir Öncü: Die Rechtsübersetzung im Spannungsfeld von Rechtsvergleich und Rechtssprachvergleich. Zur deutschen und türkischen Strafgesetzgebung. 380 Seiten. ISBN 978-3-86596-424-3

Band 45 Hartwig Kalverkämper/Larisa Schippel (Hg.): „Vom Altern der Texte". Bausteine für eine Geschichte des interkulturellen Wissenstransfers. 456 Seiten. ISBN 978-3-86596-251-5

Band 46 Hannu Kemppanen/Marja Jänis/Alexandra Belikova (eds.): Domestication and Foreignization in Translation Studies. 240 Seiten. 978-3-86596-470-0

Band 47 Sergey Tyulenev: Translation and the Westernization of Eighteenth-Century Russia. A Social-Systemic Perspective. 272 Seiten. ISBN 978-3-86596-472-4

Band 48 Martin B. Fischer/Maria Wirf Naro (eds.): Translating Fictional Dialogue for Children and Young People. 422 Seiten. ISBN 978-3-86596-467-0

Band 49 Martina Behr: Evaluation und Stimmung. Ein neuer Blick auf Qualität im (Simultan-)Dolmetschen. 356 Seiten. ISBN 978-3-86596-485-4

Band 50 Anna Gopenko: Traduire le sublime. Les débats de l'Église orthodoxe russe sur la langue liturgique. 228 Seiten. ISBN 978-3-86596-486-1

Band 51 Lavinia Heller: Translationswissenschaftliche Begriffsbildung und das Problem der performativen Unauffälligkeit von Translation. 332 Seiten. ISBN 978-3-86596-470-0

Band 52 Claudia Dathe/Renata Makarska/Schamma Schahadat (Hg.): Zwischentexte. Literarisches Übersetzen in Theorie und Praxis. 300 Seiten. ISBN 978-3-86596-442-7

Band 53 Regina Bouchehri: Translation von Medien-Titeln. Der interkulturelle Transfer von Titeln in Literatur, Theater, Film und Bildender Kunst. 334 Seiten. ISBN 978-3-86596-400-7

TRANSÜD. ARBEITEN ZUR THEORIE UND PRAXIS DES ÜBERSETZENS UND DOLMETSCHENS

Band 54 Nilgin Tanış Polat: Raum im (Hör-)Film. Zur Wahrnehmung und Repräsentation von räumlichen Informationen in deutschen und türkischen Audiodeskriptionstexten. 138 Seiten. ISBN 978-3-86596-508-0

Band 55 Eva Parra Membrives/Ángeles García Calderón (eds.): Traducción, mediación, adaptación. Reflexiones en torno al proceso de comunicación entre culturas. 336 Seiten. ISBN 978-3-86596-499-1

Band 56 Yvonne Sanz López: Videospiele übersetzen – Probleme und Optimierung. 126 Seiten. ISBN 978-3-86596-541-7

Band 57 Irina Bondas: Theaterdolmetschen – Phänomen, Funktionen, Perspektiven. 240 Seiten. ISBN 978-3-86596-540-0

Band 58 Dinah Krenzler-Behm: Authentische Aufträge in der Übersetzerausbildung. Ein Leitfaden für die Translationsdidaktik. 480 Seiten. ISBN 978-3-86596-498-4

Band 59 Anne-Kathrin Ende/Susann Herold/Annette Weilandt (Hg.): Alles hängt mit allem zusammen. Translatologische Interdependenzen. Festschrift für Peter A. Schmitt. 544 Seiten. ISBN 978-3-86596-504-2

Band 60 Saskia Weber: Kurz- und Kosenamen in russischen Romanen und ihre deutschen Übersetzungen. 256 Seiten. ISBN 978-3-7329-0002-2

Band 61 Silke Jansen/Martina Schrader-Kniffki (eds.): La traducción a través de los tiempos, espacios y disciplinas. 366 Seiten. ISBN 978-3-86596-524-0

Band 62 Annika Schmidt-Glenewinkel: Kinder als Dolmetscher in der Arzt-Patienten-Interaktion. 130 Seiten. ISBN 978-3-7329-0010-7

Band 63 Klaus-Dieter Baumann/Hartwig Kalverkämper (Hg.): Theorie und Praxis des Dolmetschens und Übersetzens in fachlichen Kontexten. 756 Seiten. ISBN 978-3-7329-0016-9

Band 64 Silvia Ruzzenenti: «Präzise, doch ungenau» – Tradurre il saggio. Un approccio olistico al *poetischer Essay* di Durs Grünbein. 406 Seiten. ISBN 978-3-7329-0026-8

TRANSÜD. ARBEITEN ZUR THEORIE UND PRAXIS DES ÜBERSETZENS UND DOLMETSCHENS

Band 65 Margarita Zoe Giannoutsou: Kirchendolmetschen – Interpretieren oder Transformieren? 498 Seiten mit CD. ISBN 978-3-7329-0067-1

Band 66 Andreas F. Kelletat/Aleksey Tashinskiy (Hg.): Übersetzer als Entdecker. Ihr Leben und Werk als Gegenstand translationswissenschaftlicher und literaturgeschichtlicher Forschung. 376 Seiten. ISBN 978-3-7329-0060-2

Band 67 Ulrike Spieler: Übersetzer zwischen Identität, Professionalität und Kulturalität: Heinrich Enrique Beck. 340 Seiten. ISBN 978-3-7329-0107-4

Band 68 Carmen Klaus: Translationsqualität und Crowdsourced Translation. Untertitelung und ihre Bewertung – am Beispiel des audiovisuellen Mediums *TEDTalk*. 180 Seiten. ISBN 979-3-7329-0031-1

Band 69 Susanne J. Jekat/Heike Elisabeth Jüngst/Klaus Schubert/Claudia Villiger (Hg.): Sprache barrierefrei gestalten. Perspektiven aus der Angewandten Linguistik. 276 Seiten. ISBN 978-3-7329-0023-7

Band 70 Radegundis Stolze: Hermeneutische Übersetzungskompetenz. Grundlagen und Didaktik. 402 Seiten. ISBN 978-3-7329-0122-7

Band 71 María Teresa Sánchez Nieto (ed.): Corpus-based Translation and Interpreting Studies: From description to application / Estudios traductológicos basados en corpus: de la descripción a la aplicación. 268 Seiten. ISBN 978-3-7329-0084-8

Band 72 Karin Maksymski/Silke Gutermuth/Silvia Hansen-Schirra (eds.): Translation and Comprehensibility. 296 Seiten. ISBN 978-3-7329-0022-0

Band 73 Hildegard Spraul: Landeskunde Russland für Übersetzer. Sprache und Werte im Wandel. Ein Studienbuch. 360 Seiten. ISBN 978-3-7329-0109-8

Band 74 Ralph Krüger: The Interface between Scientific and Technical Translation Studies and Cognitive Linguistics. With Particular Emphasis on Explicitation and Implicitation as Indicators of Translational Text-Context Interaction. 482 Seiten. ISBN 978-3-7329-0136-4

Frank & Timme

TRANSÜD. ARBEITEN ZUR THEORIE UND PRAXIS DES ÜBERSETZENS UND DOLMETSCHENS

Band 75 Erin Boggs: Interpreting U.S. Public Diplomacy Speeches. 154 Seiten.
ISBN 978-3-7329-0150-0

Band 76 Nathalie Mälzer (Hg.): Comics – Übersetzungen und Adaptionen. 404 Seiten.
ISBN 978-3-7329-0131-9

Band 77 Sophie Beese: Das (zweite) andere Geschlecht – der Diskurs „Frau" im Wandel.
Simone de Beauvoirs *Le deuxième sexe* in deutscher Erst- und Neuübersetzung.
264 Seiten. ISBN 978-3-7329-0141-8

Band 78 Xenia Wenzel: Die Übersetzbarkeit philosophischer Diskurse. Eine Übersetzungskritik an den beiden englischen Übersetzungen von Heideggers *Sein und Zeit*.
162 Seiten. ISBN 978-3-7329-0199-9

Band 79 María-José Varela Salinas/Bernd Meyer (eds.): Translating and Interpreting
Healthcare Discourses/Traducir e interpretar en el ámbito sanitario.
266 Seiten. ISBN 978-3-86596-367-3

Band 80 Susanne Hagemann: Einführung in das translationswissenschaftliche Arbeiten.
Ein Lehr- und Übungsbuch. 360 Seiten. ISBN 978-3-7329-0125-8

Band 81 Anja Maibaum: Spielfilm-Synchronisation. Eine translationskritische Analyse
am Beispiel amerikanischer Historienfilme über den Zweiten Weltkrieg.
144 Seiten mit CD. ISBN 978-3-7329-0220-0

Band 82 Sybille Schellheimer: La función evocadora de la fraseología en la oralidad ficcional
y su traducción. 356 Seiten. ISBN 978-3-7329-0232-3

Band 83 Franziska Heidrich: Kommunikationsoptimierung im Fachübersetzungsprozess.
276 Seiten. ISBN 978-3-7329-0262-0

Band 84 Cristina Plaza Lara: Integración de la competencia instrumental-profesional
en el aula de traducción. 222 Seiten mit CD. ISBN 978-3-7329-0309-2

Band 85 Andreas F. Kelletat/Aleksey Tashinskiy/Julija Boguna (Hg.):
Übersetzerforschung. Neue Beiträge zur Literatur- und Kulturgeschichte
des Übersetzens. 366 Seiten. ISBN 978-3-7329-0234-7

TRANSÜD. ARBEITEN ZUR THEORIE UND PRAXIS DES ÜBERSETZENS UND DOLMETSCHENS

Band 86 Heidrun Witte: Blickwechsel. Interkulturelle Wahrnehmung im translatorischen Handeln. 274 Seiten. ISBN 978-3-7329-0333-7

Band 87 Susanne Hagemann/Julia Neu/Stephan Walter (Hg.): Translationslehre und Bologna-Prozess: Unterwegs zwischen Einheit und Vielfalt / Translation/Interpreting Teaching and the Bologna Process: Pathways between Unity and Diversity. 434 Seiten. ISBN 978-3-7329-0311-5

Band 88 Ursula Wienen/Laura Sergo/Tinka Reichmann/Ivonne Gutiérrez Aristizábal (Hg.): Translation und Ökonomie. 274 Seiten. ISBN 978-3-7329-0203-3

Band 89 Daniela Eichmeyer: Luftqualität in Dolmetschkabinen als Einflussfaktor auf die Dolmetschqualität. Interdisziplinäre Erkenntnisse und translationspraktische Konsequenzen. 144 Seiten. ISBN 978-3-7329-0362-7

F Frank & Timme